SCHELLING AND MODERN EUROPEAN PHILOSOPHY

SCHELLING AND MODERN EUROPEAN PHILOSOPHY

An Introduction

Andrew Bowie

London and New York

First published 1993
by Routledge
2 Park Square, Milton Park, Abingdon, Oxon, OX14 4RN

Simultaneously published in the USA and Canada
by Routledge
270 Madison Ave, New York NY 10016

Transferred to Digital Printing 2006

Typeset in Palatino by Megaron, Cardiff, Wales

British Library Cataloguing in Publication Data
A catalogue record for this book is available from the British Library.

Library of Congress Cataloging in Publication Data
Bowie, Andrew, 1952–
Schelling and modern European philosophy: an introduction/
Andrew Bowie.
p.   cm.
Includes bibliographical references and index.
1.   Schelling, Friedrich Wilhelm Joseph von, 1775–1854.
2.   Idealism, German.   I.   Title.
B2898.B68   1993   93-13079
193--dc20   CIP

ISBN 0–415–10346–0 (hbk)
ISBN 0–415–10347–9 (pbk)

Publisher's Note

For Liz

CONTENTS

CONTENTS

ACKNOWLEDGEMENTS

I should like to thank the Alexander von Humboldt Foundation for enabling me to complete my work on Schelling in the idyllic and very appropriate surroundings of Tübingen. I am very grateful indeed to Manfred Frank, whose essential work in restoring the philosophical reputation of Schelling was my main inspiration, and whose friendship, advice, support, fine wines and congenial company made the work in Tübingen all the more enjoyable. Liz Bradbury's company, forbearance during my protracted absences, persuasive defences of Hegel, and support in the midst of crises were vital. Peter Dews and I discussed many of Schelling's ideas, Furtwängler's interpretations of Beethoven, and much else late at night in Tübingen, to my great profit, and his comments on the first draft were vital. Raymond Geuss obtained the necessary guarantee of publication for my initial more modest project of a translation and introduction to Schelling's lectures *On the History of Modern Philosophy*, and made helpful suggestions when this book emerged together with that project. Anglia Polytechnic University kindly gave me leave of absence to take up the Humboldt Fellowship. The students on the European Thought and Literature degree at Anglia keep my faith in the power of great philosophy judging by their ability to come to terms with ideas that are wrongly seen as too difficult for them by many in British higher education. The Tübingen philosophy faculty offered an exemplary open-mindedness to differing approaches which is sorely absent in so many philosophy departments in Britain. Andrew Benjamin, Phil Blond, Rüdiger Bubner, Matthew Festenstein, Heidrun Hesse, Nick Jardine, Chris Lawn, Peter Middleton, Julian Roberts, Cara Ryan, Kiernan Ryan, Birgit Sandkaulen-Bock, Simon Schaffer, Gianfranco Soldati, Bob Stern, Martin Swales, Nick Walker, other members of the Philosophisches Seminar at Tübingen, and many others were invaluable interlocutors at various times. Adrian

ACKNOWLEDGEMENTS

Driscoll at Routledge was an exemplary editor. My Anglia colleague
Henry Merritt restored my faith in computer technology in a crisis.
My parents, as always, were enormously encouraging and supportive.

Andrew Bowie,
Tübingen and Cambridge

INTRODUCTION

SITUATING SCHELLING

The significance of the work of Friedrich Wilhelm Joseph von Schelling (1775–1854) in the history of modern philosophy has only recently begun to be understood. For too long the importance of Schelling's later work in particular was obscured by the demise of German Idealism, which led to him being seen as merely a precursor of Hegel. I want to argue that, in the light of the contemporary concern with the end of 'Western metaphysics' and with 'post-metaphysical thinking', Schelling's work is in need of re-assessment. Most recent work on Schelling in English has continued to regard him as an adjunct to Hegel. This has meant that he is understood either as the target of Hegel's revelation of previous philosophy's failure to overcome 'immediacy', the failure to articulate the relationship of being and thinking within philosophy, or as merely an episode in the story which sees Hegel as definitive of all that happens in philosophy until Nietzsche and Heidegger begin the real process of liberation from 'Western metaphysics'. In the following I will try to show that, rather than being merely a foil to Hegel, Schelling in fact helps define key structures in modern philosophy by revealing the flaws in Hegel in ways which help set the agenda for philosophy even today.[1] My aim here is to facilitate access to Schelling's work by a reconsideration of his philosophical project in the light both of the recent attempts to establish new conceptions of reason and of the attacks on the very notion of reason that have been associated with post-modern thinking.

Having dominated the philosophical scene until his death in 1831, Hegel's philosophy was then subject to massive attack from many directions. What is too rarely realised is how significant Schelling's contribution was to this attack. The fact is that some of the Young Hegelians heard Schelling's lectures in Berlin in 1841–2, when he took up Hegel's chair of philosophy, or were aware via others' lecture notes of some of the content of these lectures, as well as of Schelling's earlier criticisms of Hegel. Clearly Schelling was regarded, not least because of his undoubted conservatism in later life, as another enemy of the 'philosophy of the future' (Feuerbach). This was in part an apt judgement, in that Schelling remained faithful to many Idealist conceptions even as he was undermining them in other ways. In histories of philosophy in the Idealist tradition, the vital stage is the highest and final one, which has to comprehend the preceding stages within itself. The aim, the common aim of the German Idealists from Fichte onwards, is nothing less than the completion of metaphysics, the understanding of the 'Absolute' (the meaning of this notorious term will become clear later) in the light of Kant's critiques of dogmatic metaphysics. In order to achieve this understanding, the philosopher has to make sure that his own philosophy is the last possible philosophy. For the later Schelling this was to be his 'positive philosophy', which would lead beyond Hegel's Idealist system to a new historically based philosophical religion by showing the impossibility of a system of reason grounding itself. Schelling does lead beyond Hegel, but he does not achieve a higher synthesis: the ideas of the later Schelling that matter now are those that reveal the impossibility of the sort of metaphysics advocated by Hegel.

One hardly needs to suggest that the ambitions of the philosophy of the period of Schelling and Hegel belong to a bygone era. We are now more likely to ponder what comes 'after philosophy', given the failure of totalising projects like Hegel's. The situation these days, as Richard Rorty puts it, is one where we 'find Hegel, Nietzsche, Heidegger, Derrida, and pragmatical commentators on Derrida like myself jostling for the position of history's first really radical anti-Platonist' (Rorty 1991b p. 96). Rorty cites Michel Foucault's contention that the crucial danger now is that philosophers are 'doomed to find Hegel waiting patiently at the end of whatever road we travel' (ibid.), because attempts to get beyond metaphysical concepts will always at some level presuppose precisely such concepts. The very notion of overcoming metaphysics keeps revealing itself as dialectically dependent on what is to be overcome. Schelling was one of the first philosophers to try to avoid the fate of really being Hegel despite oneself. In this he was followed by the Young Hegelians, who were the first to talk of the 'end of philosophy', much in the sense that has become familiar again in recent years.

2

Jürgen Habermas has suggested the importance of this particular constellation in the history of philosophy: 'I suspect that our point of departure is not essentially different from that of the first generation of the pupils of Hegel' (Habermas 1988 p. 36); and 'There is nothing for it: we are philosophically still contemporaries of the Young Hegelians' (ibid. p. 277). Habermas sees modern metaphysical thinking, which begins with Descartes and Kant and 'remains in force until Hegel', as characterised by the 'reform, in the terms of the philosophy of consciousness, of identity thinking, the doctrine of Ideas and the strong concept of theory [in the sense of its being prior to praxis]' (ibid. p. 41). As such Habermas shares Heidegger's view that modern philosophy has been characterised by the primacy given to the subject which attempts to determine the true nature of the object world via its own activity. The move beyond the model of 'subject-philosophy' is therefore what constitutes the way into post-metaphysical thinking. In his later philosophy Schelling clearly does not adhere to the conception of modern metaphysics outlined by Habermas, and he even suggests a different perspective in aspects of his earlier philosophy. It is therefore worth asking whether the putative 'end of metaphysics', both in the older sense of the completion of metaphysics, and in the contemporary sense of the overcoming of metaphysics in the name of 'post-metaphysical thinking', may yet be better understood by looking again at Schelling.

The later Schelling's reputation in the English-speaking world would seem to make him an unlikely candidate for examination in such a context. After all, much of his later philosophy is concerned with speculations influenced by Jakob Böhme's and others' theosophy, and with the attempt to turn Christianity, Nietzsche's 'Platonism for the people', into a philosophically viable religion. Even contemporaries of the late Schelling, such as Kierkegaard and Marx's friend Arnold Ruge, who heard his lectures in Berlin in 1841–2, when he took up what had been Hegel's chair of philosophy, thought he was hopeless. Kierke-gaard: 'I have completely given up on Schelling' (quoted in Schelling 1977 p. 455); Ruge: 'To consider Schelling as still a philosopher is the most stupid thing one could do' (ibid. p. 464). If Schelling is as dead as such influential thinkers during his later life thought, why bother to resurrect him now?

Historians of science working in the climate of post-empiricist philosophy of science have no trouble in suggesting, in line with Marx's positive assessment of the young Schelling, that the Schelling of the *Naturphilosophie* is a significant figure, whose speculative

3

formulations of a theory of nature's 'productivity' and its inherent polarity were important, for example, in the discovery of ultra-violet, the formulation of the principle of the conservation of energy, and the discovery of electro-magnetism (see, e.g., Kuhn 1977 pp. 97–9; Cunningham and Jardine 1990). Even they, however, have little reason to look at the later Schelling of the Lectures or the *Philosophy of Mythology* and the *Philosophy of Revelation*, to which Schelling devoted most of his energy from the end of the 1820s onwards. By the 1840s, of course, the natural sciences were beginning to fall under the spell of materialism and positivism, which effectively killed off *Naturphilosophie* as part of the overt praxis of modern science. The later Schelling's work rarely touches on natural science, and when it does the results are often anything but impressive. The very fact of his shift of attention towards mythology and theology is often seen as yet another demonstration of Schelling's inability to formulate a coherent philosophy, a charge familiar in Schelling's lifetime from Hegel's *Lectures on the History of Philosophy*.

Schelling's later work, like his early work, *is* often unsatisfactory in many different ways. There can be no doubt, however, about its historical importance for the development of modern philosophy: thinkers like Schopenhauer, Kierkegaard, Feuerbach, Nietzsche and Heidegger owe far more to Schelling than they admit. For example, in the *Concluding Unscientific Postscript* of 1846, Kierkegaard, having heard some of Schelling's Berlin lectures in 1841–2, attacks Idealism's (Hegel's) abstract demonstration of the identity of subject and object in the following manner:

> finally, if it is possible for a human being to become anything of the sort . . . he becomes the pure abstract conscious participation in and knowledge of this pure relationship between thought and being, this pure identity; aye, this tautology, because the being which is ascribed to the thinker does not signify that he is, but only that he is engaged in thinking.
>
> (Kierkegaard 1968)

In fact Kierkegaard is here clearly echoing Schelling's proto-'Heideggerian' critique of Cartesian idealism, which also informs his critique of Hegel in the Lectures: 'The *sum* that is contained in the *cogito* is, therefore, only *sum qua cogitans*, I am as thinking, i.e. in that specific way of being which is called thinking' (I/10 p. 10). There are many such cases of disguised – in Feuerbach's case often not even disguised – borrowing in Schelling's successors.

4

However I do not, as I have suggested, just want to demonstrate Schelling's historical importance. I also want to show, particularly in the light of recent German work on Schelling's philosophy, that some of his work, early and late, still matters to contemporary theory. Sometimes this is easy to achieve, for example in relation to Schelling's reflections on identity philosophy or on self-consciousness. Clearly, though, speculations about God before the creation of the universe, of the kind that occupy much of the work of the later Schelling, do not seem to offer much to the post-Nietzschean, post-Heideggerian, post-Wittgensteinian concerns of much contemporary philosophy. Some of his work is evidently dead. How, then, can we approach his work in a fruitful manner? As we saw, post-empiricist historians of science are now better able to appreciate Schelling's importance than their empiricist predecessors. Empiricist historians of science worked on the assumption that *Naturphilosophie* had been an obstacle to hard science because of its cavalier attitude to empirical research and its tendency to work merely from analogy. Now that serious attention is being paid to the role of all aspects of language in scientific discovery this rigid division between the empirical and the speculative is breaking down.

METAPHOR AND METAPHYSICS

A key factor here is metaphor, as suggested by thinkers as diverse as Mary Hesse, Thomas Kuhn, Donald Davidson, Michel Foucault, and many others. Examination of the role of metaphor in scientific discovery clearly has consequences which reach beyond the realm of natural science. Rorty claims there are:

> three ways in which a new belief can be added to our previous beliefs – viz., perception, inference, and metaphor . . . . Both perception and inference leave our language, our way of dividing up the realm of possibility, unchanged. They alter the truth-values of sentences, but not our repertoire of sentences . . . . By contrast, to think of metaphor as a third source of beliefs, and thus a third motive for reweaving our networks of beliefs and desires, is to think of language, logical space, and the realm of possibility, as open-ended. It is to abandon the idea that the aim of thought is the attainment of a God's-eye view.
>
> (Rorty 1991b p. 12)

Now Schelling's goal evidently was something like a God's-eye view, albeit one informed by Kant's critiques of metaphysics, which is, one

5

SCHELLING AND MODERN EUROPEAN PHILOSOPHY

should always keep in mind, a very different matter from pre-Kantian attempts to reach an Absolute. The implications of the totalising aims of Idealist philosophy for the language of that philosophy are ambiguous and more complex than has generally been appreciated. The desire to grasp the identity of subject and object tends to lead, as it does in Hegel, towards a notion of language as the embodiment of *Geist*, as the sensuous reflection of the infinite. However, it also leads, particularly in Schelling's *Ages of the World*, towards a conception of language which does not regard language as simply the sensuous representation of supersensuous ideas. Whilst remaining concerned with metaphysical problems Schelling's answers can, then, often be understood in terms which are now seen as 'post-metaphysical', in that they do not always rely upon some of the central assumptions of metaphysics.

The fact is that the question of metaphor inherently complicates the question of metaphysics, as Jacques Derrida has repeatedly reminded us. Karl-Otto Apel suggests, in the light of Wittgenstein's later philosophy, that most of the big words in the history of metaphysics, such as 'being',[2] which are at the heart of Schelling's writings, give rise to 'metaphorical illusion', rather in the way that Kant saw the traditional concepts of dogmatic metaphysics as giving rise to 'transcendental illusion'. The big words create insoluble philosophical problems because they tempt us to ignore the fact that language cannot meaningfully say anything about such words as 'being'. However, Apel goes on to maintain that:

> one can ask whether it is not the case that the same metaphorical hypostasisations, which have recurrently given rise to illusory ontological problems, are not on the other hand indispensable for the progressive extension of human consciousness in the history of thought, e.g. not least for the heuristics of scientific questions and models. Were not all speculative metaphors – as Heidegger puts it – 'at the same time revealing-concealing'?
>
> (Apel 1976 pp. 326–7)

He also makes the point, which will be relevant for Schelling's critique of Hegel, that:

> all arguments which reduce the universal (be it the universal of generic concepts, of 'categories', or finally the 'transcendental' being of beings (*Sein des Seienden*)) just to factors belonging to language (concepts, meanings, semantic rules) are self-contradictory; they deny to the use of language precisely the

function of the pre-understanding of the world which they themselves still call upon in their reduction of being to language.

(ibid. p. 358)

This pre-understanding becomes most obviously visible in the working of metaphor.

Rorty, supposedly following Davidson, makes a rigid distinction between metaphor and meaning.[3] Metaphor is innovative, non-standard use of language without 'meaning', where 'meaning' is 'the property which one attributes to words by noting standard inferential connections between the sentences in which they are used and other sentences' (Rorty 1991b p. 13). Metaphorical use becomes 'meaning' when the metaphor 'dies' by becoming integrated into everyday language. The problem with Rorty's conception is that it involves retaining a firm distinction between 'problem-solving' (meaning) and 'world-disclosure' (metaphor), which he, along with Habermas, wishes to keep strictly separate. This, though, makes it hard to understand how it is that metaphors can be, as they indubitably are, heuristically effective in redefining and solving problems in virtually any domain. The 'standard inferential connections', it can be argued, are not as stable or certain as Rorty wishes. Davidson's suggestion that any use of language can make us notice more than what is asserted in a proposition can suggest why. It is therefore worth leaving open the question as to whether the world-disclosing and problem-solving aspects of language can be finally separated. By doing so we leave open interpretative space that prevents us from dismissing arguments, of the kind sometimes encountered in Schelling, whose force might seem only to lie in their metaphoricity.

In this perspective one can suggest, against Rorty's desire simply to have done with metaphysics, that in Apel's terms 'metaphysics' cannot come to an end, because its key words cannot be finally cashed in and given 'meaning': the very rules for the use of the word 'being', for instance, exclude this. The continued interest in Heidegger's struggle with the word *Sein* – which included only using it 'under erasure' – is evidence of what I mean. As such, metaphor can be said inherently to keep alive certain approaches to philosophy that analytical philosophy in particular had for a time tried to consign to oblivion. It is, therefore, significant that reflection on metaphor is very much a part of the German philosophical traditions in question here. The following remarks from a book on Ernst Bloch by H.H. Holz in 1975 make this clear. Both Bloch and Holz make Schelling central to their thinking:

7

Every philosophy, then, is basically metaphorical, because it names and opens up with the means of the known what is not yet known . . . . Everything which is not empirical (*Alles Unanschauliche*) can only be said in metaphor. By being made into an image it can be generally experienced – and this experience is always initially an understanding of the image. The concept arises from analogy, comparison, and metaphor, when the image comes to be used in a fixed and identical way and more and more loses its metaphorical character.

(Cited in Wüstehube 1989 p. 146)

This might seem a contemporary concern, having recently become a central issue in analytical philosophy, as well as being vital to psychoanalysis.

The fact is, however, that F.D.E. Schleiermacher, himself deeply influenced by Schelling, was saying almost identical things about metaphor in the early nineteenth century when analysing literary language's attempt to overcome the inherent generality of literal meanings in order to reveal something new about the world (on this, see A. Bowie 1990 pp. 146–75). The question of metaphor in philosophy is actually a key factor in Romantic philosophy. In the work of Schleiermacher, Humboldt, Novalis and Friedrich Schlegel, all of whom were acquaintances of Schelling, and in Schelling's own early work, literary and other art is seen as having a status equal or even superior to philosophy because it can show what philosophy cannot say. Our approach to Schelling can thus be helped by the idea that understanding his 'metaphors' need not only be a question of trying to judge his speculations in terms of their success in establishing a positive metaphysics. Furthermore it is also clear that Schelling himself consciously relied upon the disclosing power of metaphor, as passages throughout his philosophy make plain.

Taking account of metaphor can help to explain why key terms and conceptual structures in Schelling's work play a part in the most varied subsequent theories. The examples are legion: Schelling uses a notion of the unconscious in ways which point to Freud; his cosmological speculations lead him to notions that sound like the 'big bang'; his *Naturphilosophie* echoes contemporary ecological concerns; the way he analyses the question of being points to Heidegger and Derrida; his conception of language points to Jacques Lacan. These links are not fortuitous: one can trace historical patterns of influence in all these examples. A central interpretative problem is that many of these ideas begin as conceptions in grand Idealist philosophy, but seem most productive when they have been re-worked on the level of conceptions, such as psychoanalysis, that are concerned with the world of individual human consciousness. The key question under-lying these preoccupations, though, is precisely the question of how consciousness is conceived in relation to the rest of nature, and it is here that Schelling arrives at some of his greatest insights.

The linking of consciousness to nature leads, of course, to the complaint that Schelling relies on an anthropomorphism which invalidly projects from the human onto nature in the early work, and onto God in the later work (see, e.g., Jaspers 1955 pp. 178–84). Heidegger pointed out the problem with a hasty judgement of Schelling's anthropomorphism in his book on Schelling's *On the Essence of Human Freedom*, suggesting that just registering the existence of such metaphors does not engage with the issue they involve. The objection to anthropomorphism relies upon the 'conviction, which is not further examined, that everybody really knows in general what man is' (Heidegger 1971 p. 196). If the essence of 'man' is that he is precisely that being which 'is not only and not primarily itself' (ibid. p. 197), to whom, therefore, a determinable essence cannot be assigned, then it may well be that the anthropomorphic vocabulary of Schelling has to be interpreted more carefully. Rather than projecting an already known human essence on to the Other, the later Schelling attempts to come to terms with the realisation that, as he puts it in the 1842–3 *Introduction to the Philosophy of Revelation*:

> our self-consciousness is not at all the consciousness of that nature which has passed through everything, it is precisely just *our* consciousness . . . for the consciousness of man is not = the consciousness of nature . . . . Far from man and his activity making the world comprehensible, man himself is that which is most incomprehensible.
>
> (II/3 pp. 5–7)

The passage here is one of Schelling's most extreme statements on the matter, and he is anything but consistent throughout his career in this respect, but it does reveal that he was thoroughly aware of the problem of projecting anthropomorphic metaphors onto God and nature. This fact alone should make one careful about how one interprets passages of Schelling's philosophy that may at first sight appear indefensible because they involve either anthropomorphic or traditional theological vocabulary.

Schelling's reasons for using anthropomorphic metaphors may vary, but one source of them is plain. The fact is that Schelling spends most of his philosophical life attempting to avoid the deterministic and mechanistic implications of Spinoza's philosophy, a philosophy which still has substantial echoes in present-day thinking. Schelling's battle was to find a way of sustaining notions of freedom and reason that could account for the emergence and development of living nature and consciousness, but which also took account of the fact that the ground of nature and consciousness could not itself appear in philosophical reflection.

The reasons why his thought still matters to philosophy relate, then, to the contemporary suspicion, reflected in the growing interest in Nietzsche, Heidegger, Horkheimer and Adorno, that Western rationality has proven to be a narcissistic illusion, which is at the root of 'nihilism', the 'forgetting of being', the 'universal context of delusion', the ecological crisis: in short, of the ills of modernity. The vital question, however, is understanding *how* metaphysical thinking relates to the ills of modernity. Many of the recent ways of understanding this issue seem inadequate, and Schelling has much to offer in showing why they are inadequate. Habermas suggests that metaphysical thinking is inherently reflexive, in that it relies on reason recognising itself in the mirror of the world:

> Philosophy remains true to its metaphysical beginnings as long as it can assume that cognitive reason can recognise itself in the rationally structured world or can itself give a rational structure to nature and history – whether in the manner of a transcendental grounding or via the dialectical penetration of the world. A totality that is reasonable in itself, be it that of the world or of world-constitutive subjectivity, guarantees participation in reason to its individual members or moments.
>
> (Habermas 1988 p. 42)

Critiques of metaphysics like those of Horkheimer and Adorno regard the imposition of subjective, 'instrumental' reason on nature as a result of philosophy's striving to enforce the link of human reason to this totality. This relationship is, though, in a post-metaphysical perspective, narcissistic: reason only sees the world as a reflection of itself. The later Schelling clearly breaks with this metaphysical conception of the link of reason to the totality:

> The whole world lies, so to speak, in the nets of the understanding or of reason, but the question is how exactly it got into those nets, as there is obviously something other and

something more than mere reason in the world, indeed there is something which strives beyond these barriers.

(I/10 pp. 143–4)

He even asks the question 'why is there sense/meaning (*Sinn*) at all? Why is there not nonsense/meaninglessness (*Unsinn*)?' (Schelling 1972 p. 222). Though Schelling's theological answers may not finally satisfy us, then, his questions cannot be ignored, in that some of them have become the centre of contemporary philosophical debate over post-metaphysical thinking.

My strategy for trying to do justice to some of Schelling's work will entail a radical and deliberate exclusion of many possible approaches. I am not interested here in the man and his life, however clear it may be that moves in his philosophy are related to changes in his life – how could they not be? Schelling actually seems to me to have been quite an unpleasant individual, but I hope no one is interested in my judgement in this respect. I am less interested in what Schelling takes up from the philosophy of the past than in how he reinterprets it for the future. My concern is to suggest the interest and importance of some of the best of Schelling's work: to this end I shall cite a great deal from translated and as yet untranslated works (all translations will be my own). I am above all not unduly concerned to be critical. The reason for this perhaps surprising stance is simple: problems in Schelling's work are easier to find than in most modern philosophers, which is one reason why he disappeared from view in the English-speaking world. The zealous search for easy flaws in his arguments can, though, quickly lead to serious hermeneutic failings, as I have already tried to suggest in relation to Schelling's anthropomorphism. The ideas I wish to present in detail will leave enough space for criticism, but they are still *worth* critically appraising. Because I shall concentrate on what is still of interest, the view I present is evidently distorted: at times I will only take on board a small aspect of a larger text, and I will sometimes reconstruct arguments in ways that are not fully explicit in Schelling but follow from what he does say. It is possible to find examples of Schelling also at times saying the opposite of some of the things I show him as saying: my criterion of selection and emphasis is simply whether Schelling arrives at new insight. That he sometimes does so inconsistently is the cross Schelling interpreters have to bear. Such distortion is preferable, I would maintain, to the kind of pigeon-holing history of philosophy that would consign Schelling to the role of an eccentric precursor of Hegel.

If we are to remain concerned with the history of philosophy, one of the major tasks must be to save what is valuable from being lost in the levelling process that increasingly dominates discussions of 'Western metaphysics'. It is too often the case that versions of philosophy based on the new vogue for textuality depend for their biggest claims upon a caricature of Western philosophy, which assumes we have already finally understood Kant, Hegel and the rest, including the philosophers, such as Schelling, whom few people have even read. Many contemporary thinkers who are so willing to announce a new era of post-modern thinking are actually more violent in their understanding of philosophy than the metaphysicians they see as doing violence to 'alterity'. In this they come to share the blindness of those analytical philosophers who think, even though they have little or no idea of what was actually said in the history of philosophy, that they have finished with that history and can get on with solving real problems.

STAGES IN SCHELLING'S PHILOSOPHY

In order to make access to a difficult thinker more simple, I shall begin with a very brief outline of the stages of Schelling's philosophy, from his early to his late work. I shall then, in the chapters that follow, concentrate on key issues as they emerge in a mainly chronological selection of some of the most important texts, trying both to bring out the key insights and to relate these insights to subsequent issues.

Schelling gives an account of his own philosophy in the Lectures. Not surprisingly, he is concerned to show that his earlier work is both historically important and compatible with his later work. Not everyone would agree. Attitudes to Schelling's philosophy can usually be gauged by seeing whether the commentator or critic thinks that Schelling has a fundamental philosophical idea or that he is a Proteus capable of flashes of insight but incapable of a sustained philosophical project. The degree of admiration or hostility will depend on this judgement. Clearly Schelling did change his mind and the focus of his attention a great deal, and it would be pointless to spend one's time trying to conceal the extent to which he did so. However, there is a sense in which he can be said to pursue one fundamental project, albeit one that might initially seem so general as to be meaningless. Manfred Frank talks of the 'Schellingian fundamental thought, according to which being or absolute identity is irreducible to the happening of reflection' (Schelling 1985 p. 8). A major task will be to explicate the implications of Frank's apt, but oracular, phrase. It is the work of Frank above all that has brought Schelling back into contemporary philosophical debate.

The overlapping and interrelating stages of Schelling's philosophy begin with his enthusiasm in the mid-1790s for Fichte's attempts to revise Kant's transcendental philosophy, which gave the primary role to the activity of consciousness in the constitution of the knowable world. Along with this goes the beginning of a lifelong preoccupation with Spinoza's conviction that philosophy must begin with a self-contained Absolute. Towards the end of the century Schelling develops the *Naturphilosophie*, which extends the notion of the activity of the subject into the idea of all of nature as 'productivity', thereby refusing, in a manner characteristic of all his work, to regard even inanimate nature as rigidly opposed to living thinking. The *System of Transcendental Idealism* of 1800, which tries to square Fichte and the *Naturphilosophie*, sees art as the medium in which the activity of thought and the 'unconscious' productivity in nature can be understood as ultimately the same. The 'identity philosophy' – Schelling's attempt at a complete system which would demonstrate that 'mind' and 'matter', the 'ideal' and the 'real' (the meaning of such terms will vary greatly according to the context in which they are used) are only different degrees, or aspects, of the Same – concerns him in the early 1800s (and, it should be remembered, for the rest of his life). During this period he finally breaks with Fichte, whom he regards as failing to move beyond the sphere of self-consciousness to consciousness's ground in a being of which it is only one aspect. In the 1809 *On the Essence of Human Freedom* (the last substantial text published by Schelling in his lifetime), and more coherently in the 1811–15 *Ages of the World*, Schelling breaks up the tendency towards a static, balanced relationship of the 'ideal' (mind, subject) and the 'real' (matter, object) in much of his preceding work, where a preponderance of either meant a diminution of the other, and he becomes concerned with trying to understand the ground of which the conflicting principles which constitute the manifest world are the consequence. Here Schelling demonstrably sets the scene for the agonistic universes of Schopenhauer, Nietzsche, Freud and their epigones. The 'positive philosophy', some of which is already implicit in the *Ages of the World*, develops in the 1820s and concerns Schelling for the rest of his life. 'Positive philosophy' seeks to get beyond 'negative philosophy', which, like as Hegel's *Logic*, explicates the forms of pure thought that determine what things are, to a conception which comes to terms both with the fact that things are and with the real historical emergence and movement of consciousness: 'For it is not because there is thinking that there is being, but rather, because there is being, there is thinking' (II/3 p. 161). The 'positive philosophy' tries to derive a philosophically viable religion from a reinterpretation of the historical development of Christianity. Despite its failure to achieve this, many of the initial moves in the positive philosophy have prophetic importance for the subsequent history of philosophy.

Apart from giving some necessary points of orientation, such an outline tells one little of what is really at issue in Schelling's work, least of all for us now. It is only at the level of engaging with specific aspects of that work that Schelling's insights really become apparent. The standard work on the history of Schelling's thought is Xavier Tilliette's monumental *Schelling: une philosophie en devenir* (Tilliette 1970). Alan White has provided a highly recommendable English-language introduction to Schelling's work (White 1983a) and an important account of Schelling's philosophical relationship to Hegel (White 1983b), which takes the opposite position to the one I shall advance here. I have dealt with certain key aspects of Schelling in my *Aesthetics and Subjectivity: From Kant to Nietzsche* (A. Bowie 1990) and in other published essays. The characterisation that follows will, then, of necessity repeat some things that have already been said, but the perspective from which these points are made will, I hope, be new to most readers.

1

ABSOLUTE BEGINNINGS

FICHTE AND SPINOZISM

The importance of Kant's 'Copernican turn' has generally been acknowledged in both the analytical and the European traditions of philosophy. Until recently only some areas of the European tradition have taken the critiques of Kant in German Idealism and Romanticism seriously: analytical philosophy, with very few exceptions, has tended to ignore them, assuming, usually without any argument, that they are misguided speculations of an effectively pre-Kantian nature. It is now clear that such a view is untenable, as recent works in English have suggested. Frederick Neuhouser (1990) has, for example, given a mainly analytical account of Fichte which shows that any philosophical engagement with Kant cannot ignore Fichte's criticisms. Looking somewhat further afield, the initial thesis of Thomas Nagel's *The View from Nowhere* (Nagel 1986) is a Fichtean thesis: namely, that subjectivity cannot be understood in the same manner as the world of objects, because that which understands objects cannot have the same cognitive status as what it understands. The point is familiar from Sartre's reflections upon subjectivity and freedom, as Manfred Frank, Neuhouser and others have pointed out, and has again become a significant issue in the analytical philosophy of mind, in relation to the issue of whether self-consciousness has a propositional structure (on this, see Frank 1991).[1] Schelling takes up key aspects of the question of the subject in the light of Fichte's critique of Kant, but eventually moves in a different direction from Fichte.

From the beginning Schelling tries to reconcile fundamentally divergent philosophical worlds: on the one hand he concurs with Fichte's transcendental idealist emphasis on the primacy of the subject in the constitution of a world of objects, and on the other he is drawn to the monist, largely materialist conception of being as that which is self-caused and whose essence involves its existence, which Spinoza termed God. Schelling's constant target is any form of dualism, yet he is fully aware that Kant has made certain monist positions impossible to defend. At the same time, Kant had established a dualism, which seemed equally indefensible, between our knowledge of things and 'things in themselves'. Kant restricted the domain of knowledge to the laws governing phenomena as they are given to consciousness, which excluded knowledge of what was not given in intuition. It is only via our awareness of the moral law and in the experience of the sublime that we have a sense of that in us which is not constrained by our finite, law-determined nature. This awareness, however, does not have the same status as knowledge of the world of nature, in that it applies to ourselves as noumena, not as causally bound phenomena. The Kantian split between the phenomenal and the noumenal worlds is the primary target of German Idealism.

Because of his monism Spinoza is an obvious point of reference from the past. Seen in the light of Kant's philosophy, however, Spinoza's notion of God involves an indefensible claim to knowledge of the infinite from a finite position, as do all attempts to prove the existence of God or to describe His nature. However, despite Fichte's conviction that he is completing Kant's project, he and Spinoza do share a reliance on the *causa sui* in a manner Kant would not accept. In Fichte's case the 'I' can have no prior determining ground because if it did its freedom to step back from itself and reflect upon itself in philosophy would become incomprehensible. In Spinoza's case 'substance' must be its own ground, as otherwise the unity of the substance would be lost and there would have to be more than one substance, which would lead back to all the problems of Cartesian dualism. Fichte's importance for Schelling lies in his suggestion of how, within the subject, there is an 'infinite' aspect which philosophy can show more emphatically than Kant thought possible. Schelling adopts from Spinoza the refusal to consider the ground of thought and the ground of material existence as ultimately separable.

The problem is that the positions seem thoroughly incompatible. Fichte's notion of undetermined freedom derives from the spontaneity of the I, which he sees as absolute, in the sense that it cannot depend on anything else to be what it is; Spinoza is a determinist, in that everything follows of necessity from the absolute nature of that which is *causa sui*. Schelling is faced with trying to get beyond one conception, which sustains the absolute status of the subject, without which the world's intelligibility and the possibility of moral autonomy seem incomprehensible, and another, which seems to provide much of the conceptual apparatus necessary for articulating the intelligibility of the finite world, but which does so at the price of turning that world into the mere mechanical articulation of itself by an infinite substance. In this view of Spinoza the answer to the question why that world should be revealed to itself in our consciousness is left in the dark. Is this tension, though, just a piece of metaphysical wrangling that merely repeats the basic error of metaphysics in looking for an absolute foundation, on either the subject or the object side of philosophy, that would guarantee the rationality of the world?[2] One can acknowledge that metaphysical debates of this kind are no longer straightforwardly on the agenda of contemporary philosophy. However, it may well be that what is at issue reappears later in a different form: the conception of a pure break between metaphysical and post-metaphysical thinking creates the risk of blindness to resources from the 'metaphysical' past. We saw how Habermas suggested that we are still in the situation of the Young Hegelians. The fact is that we can go back a stage further, as I shall try to show in the course of the next section.

JACOBI, FICHTE AND THE PANTHEISM CONTROVERSY

Schelling's fears about Spinoza were shared by many philosophers at the end of the eighteenth century, as Frederick Beiser has shown in his erudite philosophical thriller *The Fate of Reason* (Beiser 1987). The vital point in the 'Pantheism controversy', which began in 1783 and exercised many of the great minds of a remarkable intellectual era, is that Spinoza is perceived as the 'prophet of modern science' (ibid. p. 83). This is most graphically expressed in the conviction that Spinozism leads to what F.H. Jacobi prophetically termed 'nihilism'. 'Nihilism', Jacobi maintains, results from thinking based solely on the principle of sufficient reason; he thinks nihilism is also the result of Kant's separation of knowledge based on the judgements of the understanding from things in themselves. Spinozism is seen as reducing our understanding of what we are to what science can tell us on the basis of causal laws. The road is therefore open to what is now familiar to us from the worst aspects of scientism and materialist reductionism, and certain aspects, as we shall see, of structuralism. One of the aims of Kant's philosophy was, of course, to find a way of taking on board natural determinism as the basis of modern science whilst sustaining the autonomy of rational beings. Kant achieves this by separating the realms of legislation of the laws of nature and the moral law, but he thereby splits the world in half. The question is how to avoid this separation.

Fichte's strategy was to suggest that these realms had a common source, which Kant himself had necessarily invoked but had not made as central as it must be if his arguments are to work. In Kant the 'transcendental unity of apperception' is the necessary condition of theoretical knowledge: 'The *I think* must be able to accompany all my representations', as 'otherwise I would have a self which is as differently multi-coloured as I have ideas of which I am conscious' (Kant 1968 B p. 132). Kant sees this condition as a 'fact', but a fact which cannot appear in empirical consciousness because it is the condition of our ability to synthesise intuitions, and thus of the very intelligibility of empirical consciousness. Fichte seizes upon this condition, which Kant leaves largely unexplicated. For Fichte it is 'the ground of explanation of all facts of empirical consciousness that before all positing in the I the I must itself previously be posited' (Fichte 1971 p. 95). Instead of this being a 'fact' (*Tatsache*), it is to be conceived of as an action (*Tathandlung*), literally a 'deed–action', which combines both practical and theoretical reason, the latter depending on the former. We cannot have theoretical access to this action because it, as the act which is the condition of possibility of objectivity, cannot itself be an object. Access to the I can only be by the I itself, in the act of reflection upon itself. What allows this access is 'that through which I know something because I do it' (ibid. p. 463), which Fichte terms 'intellectual intuition'. Neuhouser says of 'intellectual intuition':

> such awareness is nondiscursive in nature. This implies that the subject's immediate positing of its representations as its own is not to be understood as involving a synthesis of diverse, otherwise unconnected units which are given independently of the activity that brings them together. Self-positing is not to be thought of as a composite of two distinguishable elements, concept and intuition, but as a simple unitary awareness.
> (Neuhouser 1990 p. 84)

The I is therefore the condition of there *being* representations. Kant had himself already hinted at such a conception in his initial version of the *Critique of Pure Reason*, in which the imagination had played a hybrid role, by both producing and receiving intuitions.

There is in Fichte's view, then, *pace* Davidson and Rorty, no division of scheme and content, because both are simply aspects of the primary spontaneity of the I. If there were such a division, I would have no way of being able to account for how the content of my experience is *my* experience, because the relationship of scheme and content always already separates concept and intuition, leaving the insoluble problem of reuniting them. This thoroughgoing Idealism is a result of Fichte's opposition to 'dogmatism': Spinozism as he (and others, like Jacobi) understood it. As Neuhouser puts it, Spinozism

> takes the thing in itself – or 'substance' – as its point of departure and from there attempts to give an account of all of reality, including subjectivity. Such a system, on Fichte's view, is obligated to understand all of the features of consciousness as effects of the action of external things upon the subject.
>
> (ibid. pp. 55–6)

For Fichte the difficulty in all this lies in explaining our encounter with an external world of brute sensation and resistance. If the I is unlimited, why should it feel limited by the world? Fichte's answer is that this limitation is the reflection back into the subject of its *own* unlimited activity by what he terms the *Anstoss* (usually translated as the 'check'), which takes the place of Kant's 'thing in itself'. This makes sense in as much as a feeling of compulsion has as its *prior* condition that which can feel compelled, which must therefore be aware of its freedom. The I thus depends upon a not-I to reflect its activity back into itself. This dependence, though, contradicts the essence of the I, its spontaneity and independence of external causality. The ultimate goal of the 'striving' of the I is, then, to overcome this resistance. Our awareness of the striving derives for Fichte from our sense of Kant's moral law, which demands that the object world be brought into conformity with practical reason. The unity of subject and object would be a result of the completion of the process, which in these terms depends on the I. Importantly, Fichte has to argue in terms that require a relative I and not-I within an Absolute which is still conceived of as I. None of this, of course, explains why Fichte's I should split itself in this way to begin with.

Schelling later becomes prophetically aware of the dangers that ensue from accepting Fichte's version of overcoming the Kantian divisions.[3] He also realises, however, that one cannot so easily dismiss certain aspects of what Fichte proposes, without falling prey to the problems inherent in Spinozism. Two texts of 1795 are informative in this respect. The very title of *On the I as Principle of Philosophy, or On the Absolute (das Unbedingte) in Human Knowledge* has a Fichtean ring;

Philosophical Letters on Dogmatism and Criticism is more circumspect. *On the I as Principle of Philosophy* begins with the demand for an absolute ground: 'The last ground of all reality is namely a something which is only thinkable via itself, i.e. thinkable via its being, which is only thought insofar as it is, *in short, in which the principle of being and of thinking coincide*' (I/1 p. 163). This formulation could be either Spinozist or Fichtean. Schelling goes on to insist against Spinoza, though, that the ground cannot be an object, for, in line with Kant, an object can only be such for a prior subject. At the same time, however, at this level, the subject is only determinable by the fact of its not being the object.

Schelling is therefore led to the demand for an 'Absolute' that would encompass the relationship of the two. By using the word *unbedingt* (understood as 'un**thing**ed', rather than just 'absolute'), he is able to play on the etymology, which suggests 'nothing (*nichts*) can be posited by itself as a thing, i.e. an absolute thing (*unbedingtes Ding*) is a contradiction' (ibid. p. 166). The consequence is a Fichtean move, which demands an absolute I, as that which could never finally become an object. As is the case for Fichte, there can be no objective proof of this I, because this would mean the I was conditioned (*bedingt*) by our objective knowledge of it, and thus not absolute. Schelling exclaims, echoing the Fichtean inversion of Descartes: *'I am!* My I contains a being which precedes all thinking and representing. It is by being thought and it is thought because it is; the reason for this is that it only is and is only thought to the extent to which it thinks *itself*' (ibid. p. 167). The overall argument here depends, however, on the Spinozist thought, which recurs in various ways in all of German Idealism, that the determination of something is the determination of what it is not. Each object is part of a chain of ob-jects (*Gegen-stände*), which 'stand against' each other. Objects, then, are not absolutely real because they only become themselves by not being other objects. In this sense objects are 'negative' in a specific sense that will become vital later: both Schelling and Hegel understand that which depends on its relation to an other for it to be itself as 'negative'. German Idealism demands an account of what makes these interrelated moments intelligible as objects, which cannot therefore itself be an object. They therefore term it the 'Absolute', because it cannot be understood in terms of its relation to something else. The 'Absolute', which will concern us constantly from now on, should not, then, be thought of in mystical terms: it is initially just the result of the realisation of the relative status of anything that can be explained causally. A vital factor in the development of this notion of the Absolute was Jacobi's understanding of Spinozism.

Jacobi's argument is that a complete system of reason that purports to explain the world, of the kind present in the notion of determination by negation in the *Ethics*, has a fatal lack. Birgit Sandkaulen-Bock explains, citing Jacobi's *On the Doctrine of Spinoza in Letters to Herr Moses Mendelssohn* of 1789:

> Reason is a mechanism '. . . all philosophical cognition, as it is effected in accordance with the principle of sufficient reason, i.e. by *mediation*' can therefore 'necessarily always only be a mediated cognition'. If rational comprehension consists in nothing other than the logical *'mediation'* of ground and consequence in the 'dissection, linking, judging, concluding and grasping again' then it obviously always only moves in a connection which it has constructed itself.
>
> (Sandkaulen-Bock 1990 p. 15)

Explaining the world is based on finding its 'condition' (*Bedingung*). Finding the condition of something is the basis of all explanation, but 'to the extent to which something can only be considered to be grasped whose condition is discovered, it is itself conditioned' (ibid.). The problem is that the conditions in a system of reason are those posited by thought itself, and are thus conditioned by thought. Jacobi maintains: 'we remain, as long as we grasp things conceptually (*begreifen*), in a chain of *conditioned conditions*' (quoted ibid. p. 15). In this way there is no way of arriving at what is not conditioned, the *Unbedingte*, the Absolute, the ground of the real existence of what we try to understand within reason. There can be no further condition of this ground, which Jacobi terms (dubiously equating it with Spinoza's substance) *Seyn*, 'being'. 'Being' cannot be an object of knowledge, as that would make it relative to a condition: it is 'that which cannot be explained: the indissoluble, immediate, the simple' (quoted ibid. p. 17). As such 'being' cannot be finally understood in terms of 'reflection', of its relation to anything else. Jacobi uses this notion of the inarticulable ground to suggest that the only possible course for philosophy is to realise that it must transcend itself into revelation and belief in a personal God who is this Absolute. He thereby separates philosophy from theology, which becomes the realm of what cannot be explained but only revealed.

The later Schelling will be very concerned not to accept this final consequence:[4] he wishes to understand the Absolute philosophically, in order to arrive at a philosophically viable theology – hence, for example, the notion in the later work of the *'Philosophy of Revelation'*. If one ignores Jacobi's final consequence, it is evident, though, that he has made a vital point in relation to Spinozism, considered as a system of necessity. The significance of the conception of the 'chain of conditioned conditions', and of Jacobi's response to it, can be understood without having to consider it as the basis for a leap of faith beyond reason. The fact is that the basic structure of this problem is evident in other areas of modern thinking. Consider the following example: a great deal of recent philosophy has taken Saussurean linguistics as its point of departure. In Saussure the sign is dependent for its identity upon its not being other signs: 'cat' is not 'bat' is not 'hat', etc. There are therefore no positive terms in language for Saussure, in the same way as there are no positive 'conditions' for Jacobi. In Saussure this is a way of beginning to understand how, in the absence of any representational relationship of the sign to the object or to the mental representation of the object it designates, we are yet able to articulate worlds of identifiable – and thus different – things in language. What is missing in this conception of the sign, as Saussure himself, unlike his structuralist successors, was well aware, is that for which these signs have meaning. In themselves they are not even determinate as different, in that they require that for which they are different, which must itself remain identical, for them to be *known* as different. Furthermore there is in a merely differential model no way of understanding how it is that signs are bearers of meanings, because mere difference leaves an endless series of interdependent negative terms and no way of making sense of how they can be linked to constitute iterable meanings.

What applies to the sign conceived of merely as a diacritical mark applies to the world of objects in Jacobi's understanding of the Spinozist conception: nothing within the chain of difference tells us how it is that we can be *aware* of the chain of difference. This awareness must be of a different order from the chain of difference because it entails a prior identity that is the condition of difference (in the Christian tradition God is, of course, the basis of this identity). One might say, in this respect, that structuralists are the new representatives of Spinozism after the linguistic turn: Althusser, after all, was a noted expert on Spinoza. Seen in this light, Schelling's concern to avoid the consequences of Spinozism gains a new relevance, as I shall show in later chapters.

22

The power of Fichte's conception for Schelling lies precisely in the fact that it tries to escape the consequences suggested by a differential system of necessity. 'Dogmatism' has, Schelling claims:

> never proved that a Not-I can give itself reality, and mean anything at all, except just in its being opposed to an absolute I. Spinoza as well has nowhere proved that the absolute (*das Unbedingte*) could lie and would have to lie in the Not-I; rather he posits the Absolute (*das Absolute*), led only by his concept of it, directly in an absolute object, as if he presupposed that everyone who had once allowed him the concept of the unconditioned (*des Unbedingten*) would automatically follow his assumption that it necessarily would have to be posited in a Not-I.
>
> (I/1 p. 171)

There would, however, be no possibility of a not-I becoming aware of itself unless it already had within it what could result in the I, which means in these terms that it must already in some way *be* an I. Otherwise the transition from thing in itself to I would be inexplicable. What is able to know itself must be more than *what* it knows. Schelling insists, against Kant, that the empirical I is not the principle with which he is concerned. He cites Kant's fundamental question: 'how are synthetic a priori judgements possible?' (ibid. p. 175), which Kant had answered in terms of the necessary syntheses of empirical data from which he deduces the nature of the transcendental subject. Schelling responds to Kant's question with a Fichtean re-formulation of it: 'this question, thought of in its highest abstraction, is none other than the following: how is it that the absolute I goes out of itself and opposes a Not-I to itself?' (ibid.), i.e. why is there an appearing world at all? There would be no need for the syntheses of theoretical knowledge if they were not preceded by a One which had become split, which the striving for knowledge wishes to reunite. As such: 'The completed system of science begins with (*geht aus vom*) the absolute I, which excludes everything opposed to it' (ibid. p. 176). Without this prior 'absolute identity' the capacity for establishing relative identity between differing things in the synthetic judgements of the subject is devoid of a basis. Knowledge in this view would have no foundation. If this were so, the Kantian project, and German Idealism, would necessarily fail.

Schelling's argument depends on making Spinoza's substance into the absolute I, a move he will come to suspect soon afterwards, not least because of Jacobi. Access to this principle is only possible in 'intellectual intuition', which, as we saw, must be non-conceptual. Concepts unite multiplicity into unity: what is demanded here must always already be One and cannot be made such by something else, as the something else would then be the Absolute. Schelling insists that it is only via our freedom, in the sense of that which allows us to transcend our status as determined natural objects, that we approach what is meant by the absolute I:

> Do you ask to be conscious of this freedom? But do you also consider that all your consciousness is only possible via your freedom and the condition cannot be contained in what is conditioned? Do you consider at all that the [absolute] I, to the extent to which it is present in consciousness, is no longer pure absolute I, that there can be no object anywhere for the absolute I, and that it therefore can even less become an object itself? *Self-consciousness* [i.e. your or my individual I] presupposes the danger of losing the [absolute] I.
>
> (ibid. p. 180)

By striving to sustain our personal conscious identity in the 'torrent of change' (ibid.) we become determined by the Other, our experiences of the object world opposed to us, thus surrendering our absolute status as I. The empirical I 'is determined by something posited outside itself, by objects, its being is not given to it absolutely, but via objective forms – as an existence (*Daseyn*)' (ibid.). *Daseyn*, being-there, ex-sisting, poses a problem with regard to its relationship to its Other. If the relationship is merely reflexive, whereby the object world reflects myself back to me, it becomes impossible to understand how it is that I know myself: how would I know it was *my* reflection, unless I already knew in another way? The vital fact about the subject, which Fichte had identified, is lost if it is merely such a reflection. Alternatively, without the object world, do I not become enclosed in a merely narcissistic relationship with myself, whereby I am not real at all? What would make me be more than just a thought? Schelling's attention to Spinoza and his awareness of Jacobi already tend to push him beyond the Fichtean conception in ways that will be vital in the future.

In Fichte intellectual intuition is what makes my experiences into my experiences, and is therefore present as the condition of the empirical subject's ability to reflect upon himself or herself. In *On the I* Schelling extends the conception of intellectual intuition in such a way that it cannot be 'present' in individual consciousness, and actually requires the surrender of that consciousness if it is to play the grounding role it must for this conception of the absolute I to work. By trying to hang on to the identity of my individual consciousness, which is constituted by its experiences, I turn it into an object for itself and thus lose what is most fundamental about it, its freedom from being determined as a knowable identity, as an object. The problem is much the same as Sartre suggested in *Being and Nothingness*, where the attempt to make *pour soi* and *en soi* coincide leads to the 'bad faith' of trying reflexively to know what one is. This tension in Schelling's conception of the subject recurs throughout his work.

THE GROUND OF JUDGEMENT

The tension which Schelling tries to overcome between Spinoza and Fichte can suggest how he is already moving towards a position which will be seen as one of the achievements of Heidegger for twentieth-century philosophy. My repeated attention in what follows to the links of Schelling to Heidegger is intended to suggest that Heidegger's making the history of metaphysics into something which only he can overcome ignores the fact that key aspects of Heidegger's argument are already part of the history of philosophy. Ernst Tugendhat claims of Heidegger, in relation to Kant and German Idealism:

> Even if Kant and German Idealism considered the condition of possibility of the thinking (*des Vorstellens*) of an objective world, they presupposed thinking as such and considered regressively or constructively the possibility of a thinking which was objectively determined in such and such a way, not the conditions of disclosure (*Erschlossenheit*) as such.
>
> (Tugendhat 1970 p. 271)

Now consider Schelling in the *Philosophical Letters*, where he makes an interesting shift, altering the question he had asked in relation to Kant in an ontological direction. The Kantian question gains a genetic aspect: 'How is it that we come to make synthetic judgements at all?' (I/1 p. 294): the primary concern is not, therefore 'thinking that was objectively determined in such and such a way', but the fact that there is thinking at all. Schelling's re-formulation is now also significantly different: 'How is it that I step at all out of the Absolute and move towards something opposed (*auf ein Entgegengesetztes*)?' (ibid.). The absolute I has disappeared; the beginning now is the Absolute, not characterised as an I. Schelling has moved away from Fichte (on this, see also White 1983a pp. 28–37). Manfred Frank has pointed out

(Frank 1985; see also, for a more detailed account than I can give here, A. Bowie 1990 pp. 67–72) that it was probably Friedrich Hölderlin, Schelling's and Hegel's friend at the Tübingen seminary, who made Schelling move away from the Fichtean point of view. The other main influence was Jacobi.

Hölderlin realises in 1794–5, when he was in contact with Schelling, that Fichte's notion of the absolute I that is grounded in intellectual intuition is deficient. In a letter to Hegel he claims Fichte's

> absolute I . . . contains all reality; it is everything, and outside of it there is nothing; there is therefore no object for this absolute I, for otherwise the whole of reality would not be in it; but a consciousness without an object is unthinkable, and if I am this object myself, then as such I am necessarily limited, even if it may only be in time, thus not absolute; thus there is no consciousness thinkable in the absolute I; as absolute I (*Ich*), I (*ich*) have no consciousness, and to the extent to which I have no consciousness I am (for myself) nothing, therefore the absolute I is (for me) nothing.
>
> (Cited in A. Bowie 1990a p. 68)

Schelling concludes from this argument that the fact that there is a world of knowledge depends upon the *loss* of the Absolute: 'Synthesis namely only ever arises via the conflict (*Widerstreit*) of multiplicity against the original unity' (I/1 p. 294). The question is now 'where the principle of that unity expressed in synthetic judgement lies' (ibid. p. 295). This question is, as we have seen, subsequent to the prior fact of 'world-disclosure'.[5]

The essential point is that there cannot, as Jacobi suggested, be any knowledge of the Absolute, because knowledge has a subject–object, propositional structure, which implies a prior separation of what is joined in the judgement. In another piece of this period, 'Judgement and being', Hölderlin saw the split of subject and object as presupposing a 'whole of which subject and object are the parts' (cited in A. Bowie 1990 p. 68), which he termed 'being', as opposed to the *Urteil*, the judgement, which splits this whole and tries to reunite it. 'Criticism', Kant's critical philosophy (and, albeit not explicitly, some aspects of Fichte), suggests Schelling, may be valid as an account of empirical knowledge: it 'can prove the necessity of synthetic propositions for the realm of experience' (I/1 p. 310). Experience is not merely inchoate. The real issue, though, is the move out of the prior unity of the Absolute: 'why is there a realm of experience at all? Every answer I give to this question already presupposes the existence of a world of experience' (ibid.). The question cannot be answered as a 'theoretical' question about knowledge, and thus demands the move into the practical realm which is not subject to the determinism of the theoretical realm. Only by achieving the unity of subject and object, Schelling claims, would we finally understand the division that leads to a realm of experience.

This position again leads to the renunciation of self-consciousness:

> *Where there is absolute freedom there is absolute bliss*, and vice-versa. But with *absolute* freedom no self-consciousness can be thought any more. An activity for which there is no *object*, no resistance any more, never returns back into itself. Only by return to oneself does *consciousness* arise. Only *limited* reality (*Realität*) is *effective reality* (*Wirklichkeit*) for us.
>
> (ibid. p. 324)

Schelling, though, still wants to insist against Spinoza that the substance cannot be an absolute object. Spinoza, he claims, sees all finite existents, above all ourselves, as

> modifications of the same infinity; thus there should be no transition, no conflict, only the demand that the finite should strive to become identical with the infinite, and to be lost (*untergehen*) in the infinity of the absolute object.
>
> (ibid. p. 315)

Spinozism would thus lead to the demand that one destroy oneself as a subject capable of the autonomy of practical action by realising that one's own causality was just a derived version of the causality of the Absolute. The demand to lose yourself is, however, contradictory: what does the losing is what must be lost, but in the act of losing itself it affirms its own existence: the *Letters* begin, significantly, with reflections on tragedy and on why it is sublime to lose a fight against an absolute power. Schelling will repeatedly use analogous arguments to defend the subject against conceptions that wish to reduce it to what can be objectively determined. Spinoza can only think in terms of dissolving oneself into objectivity, Schelling claims, because he, as the determinist that made everyone worried in the Pantheism controversy, has already denied any autonomy to the subject.

Dogmatism for Schelling thus becomes linked to mysticism, and indeed leads to nothingness: Fichte's subject which cannot become an object must be regarded as 'nothing' in relation to the absolute objectivity of Spinoza's system. The consequences of this are significant in ways that have already been indicated. If one understands Spinoza as the 'prophet of modern science', his system becomes the correlate of materialist views of self-consciousness, which regard self-consciousness as merely the result of the interaction of matter in the brain. The differential structure that is the core of Spinoza's conception has, of course, become the basis of the attempt to replicate what the brain does with digital computers. A belief in this view of science can lead to a desire for mystical self-annihilation on the basis of the futility of self-consciousness, which is seen as only isolating us in epiphenomenal torment from the rest of the universe. Schopenhauer, for whom Buddhist conceptions of the annihilation of the Will go along with a strict adherence to the demands of modern science, clearly points in this direction. The basis of Schopenhauer's conception was, of course, itself derived from aspects of Schelling's philosophy (see A. Bowie 1990 chapter 8). In a related manner, the structuralist and post-structuralist announcement of the death of the subject, based on the notion of the subject's dependence for its identity on the 'other' of differentially constituted language, can be understood as a result of the same false objectification as Schelling fought against in Spinozism – I shall return in more detail to this particular parallel with contemporary thought in later chapters.

Schelling is not least important, then, for the ways he fought both against the kind of objectifying thinking suggested here, *and* against the 'Fichtean' attempt to subdue nature in the name of the subject. He claims the 'critical philosophy' – Fichte's attempt to complete Kant's project – can only demand, in opposition to the dogmatic view, that I try to 'realise the Absolute *in myself* via an endless striving' (I/1 p. 335). The realisation cannot, however, be thought of as really possible, as this would lead again, but via the opposite route, to mysticism: instead of the object swallowing the subject, the subject would swallow the object. Schelling at this point is suspended between Spinoza and Fichte: he wishes to sustain the autonomy and life of the subject, but the demand, which Hölderlin perhaps best understood at this time, is to encompass the relationship of the subject to the object world in the Absolute. This dilemma is, as should now be apparent, not just a distant episode in the history of metaphysics. The same issues in somewhat different guises are at the root of the recent debates concerning artificial intelligence, physicalism and the post-structuralist attempt to deconstruct metaphysics.

Unsurprisingly Schelling does not simply find a way beyond the positions outlined here: in the years following 1795 he moves between the positions, sometimes making progress, sometimes slipping back via hasty attempts to move forward. Despite its evident failings, the next aspect of his philosophy to emerge, the *Naturphilosophie*, raises issues in ways which are definitive of Schelling's own particular philosophical project.

2

THE HERMENEUTICS OF NATURE

MATTER AND LIFE

Schelling's early writings on *Naturphilosophie*, unlike his later philosophical writings, have recently received a good deal of attention in
both English and German.[1] The aspect of the *Naturphilosophie* that I
wish to examine is not, however, its now acknowledged contributions
to the 'advance of science' in the late eighteenth and early nineteenth
centuries, but rather its possible philosophical contribution to the kind
of hermeneutic approach to the natural sciences that has become
influential in recent years in the post-empiricist history and philosophy
of science. Clearly, *Naturphilosophie* generally ceased to be regarded as
a tool for scientific discovery by the second half of the nineteenth
century, and in certain versions was a positive hindrance to
warrantable science.[2] The important point here, though, is that
Schelling's *Naturphilosophie* has not necessarily outlived its significance
for trying to understand what science is. Now that the realist
conceptions, based on the notion of a world of absolute objects 'out
there', that have dominated much Anglo-American philosophy are
coming to be seen as relying on indefensible, pre-Kantian metaphysical
premises,[3] a philosophical view of natural science need no longer be
bound to the probably futile task of explaining how it is that science
'works' (whatever that exactly may mean). One can accept the fact of
the problem-solving success of modern science without thinking that
there is no reason to ask whether some kinds of modern science might
not be leading to problems which could turn out to be more serious
than the problems solved by that science. The fact is that the questions
posed by Schelling have gained a new actuality because they offer
conceptual tools that enable one to gain a philosophical understanding
of contemporary doubts about the dangers of a scientistic approach to
nature. How is it, though, that an evidently metaphysical conception

30

like Schelling's, which relies above all on the idea of the whole of nature as an organism, now seems relevant to a 'post-metaphysical' anti-foundationalist understanding of science that has broken with the realist notion of the true representation of objects? As in so many questions regarding contemporary conceptions of science, one is led back to issues first raised by Kant.

The vital factor which has sustained the actuality of Schelling's *Naturphilosophie* is its refusal to see the thinking subject as simply opposed to nature as a world of objects, because the subject is itself part of nature. The *Naturphilosophie* is another product of Schelling's dissatisfaction with Kantian dualism; it will also lead by 1801 to his prophetic rejection of Fichte's manner of overcoming that dualism. The dissatisfaction with dualism came in certain ways to be shared by Kant himself, a fact which had considerable consequences in Idealist and Romantic philosophy. The point of Kant's theoretical philosophy, prompted by Hume's arguments on causality, was not to make claims about nature in itself, and to concentrate on what could be said with certainty about the subject's knowledge of nature. Nature was therefore considered as that which can be subsumed under laws of the understanding. *Naturphilosophie*, though, does make claims about nature in itself, albeit whilst acknowledging certain of Kant's strictures. In doing so it touches on vital issues that repeatedly troubled Kant.

In the *Metaphysical Foundations of Natural Science* of 1786 Kant had warned against 'hylozoism', the idea that life is inherent in matter. The second law of mechanics, the law of inertia, 'All change in matter has an external cause', made it clear that matter 'has no absolutely inner determinations and grounds of determination' (Kant 1977b p. A 120). Matter is lifeless, whereas '*Life* is the capacity of a substance to determine itself via an *inner principle* to act, of a *finite substance* to determine itself to change, and of a *material substance* to determine itself for movement or rest, as a change of its state ' (ibid. pp. A 120–1). All such self-determined change must be conceived of by us in terms of thought and will, which are not appearing phenomena, and thus do not belong to matter *qua* appearing object. Kant maintains that the very possibility of natural science depends on the law of inertia:

The opposite [of the law of inertia] and thus also the death of all natural philosophy [in a Newtonian sense, not in the sense we shall come across in Schelling's *Naturphilosophie*] would be *hylozoism* . . . . Precisely from the same concept of inertia as mere

31

lifelessness, it follows of its own accord that inertia does not mean a *positive striving* to preserve its state.

(ibid. p. A 121)

The claim that inertia is a positive force would entail access to nature in itself, because nature would in some way have to be like the intelligible subject, by not being subject to the iron law of natural determinism. Such a claim would introduce again precisely those kinds of inherent metaphysical forces with which Kant's critique of dogmatic meta-physics had dispensed.

A central aim of the *Critique of Pure Reason* is to provide an account of how the understanding synthesises empirical data into general laws governing phenomena, without entailing claims about nature in itself. Once such laws existed they could be applied to other empirical cases, in what Kant in the 1790 *Critique of Judgement* called 'determinant judgement'. Even here, however, there is no automatic relationship between general law and particular case. Laws do not apply themselves to what they subsume: they depend upon the faculty of judgement for their application (on this, see Bell 1987). Kant also realised that we cannot give an account of how these differing laws relate to each other: that would require a higher principle, which would be beyond the bounds of legislation of the understanding. In the *Critique of Judgement* Kant therefore introduces a further kind of judgement: 'reflective judgement'.

In order to be able to make the move from the particular phenomenon to general judgements about the interrelations of natural laws one must assume that nature really is articulated in a system in which the laws all share the same status as parts of a whole. Nature is, then, looked at as if it had *in itself* the kind of principle of coherence provided for the subject by the understanding. The need for 'reflective judgement' is most evident in trying to explain the apparent purposiveness of natural organisms, the combination of particular physical and chemical processes into more than the sum of their parts: 'It is namely quite certain that we cannot adequately get to know, let alone explain, organic bodies and their inner possibility according to merely mechanical principles of nature' (Kant 1977a p. B 338, A 334). A Newton who could explain the production of even a blade of grass solely by mechanical laws, without invoking purposiveness, is unthinkable, Kant claims. One cannot prove the objective reality of purposiveness, but nor can one disprove it, and it at least gives an explanation of the coherence and development of organisms, a fact of which we are aware by experience. Instead, then, of the mechanical nature which was required by his earlier work, Kant moves towards a relationship between the intelligible subject and nature in itself. It is the attempt to articulate this relationship that Schelling undertakes in the *Naturphilosophie*.

Schelling thinks, as we saw, that the Kantian questions need a deeper foundation: the question of the possibility of synthetic a priori judgements became, for instance, a question about the fact of there being experience at all. Schelling is now led to a new version of ideas encountered in Leibniz, one of the key representatives of the metaphysics which Kant had rejected. The crucial task for Schelling is to overcome the separation of mind and nature. Leibniz suggests, thereby pointing the way to Schelling's identity philosophy: 'For because the nature of things is uniform our own substance cannot be infinitely different from the other simple substances of which the whole universe consists' (letter to de Volder 30.6.1704; cited in Heidegger 1978 p. 90). This evidently offends the Kantian limitations upon the scope of the knowledge provided by the understanding because it tries to understand nature 'in itself'. Schelling, though, wants to know how it is that anything can get into the understanding at all, which cannot be explained in Kantian theoretical terms. He is therefore forced to seek ways of achieving what dogmatic metaphysics had failed to achieve.

Schelling reformulates the problem suggested by Leibniz, in the *Introduction to: Ideas for a Philosophy of Nature*:

> The question is not whether and how that connection of appearances and the sequence of causes and effects which we call the course of nature has become real *outside ourselves*, but how it has become real *for us*, how that system and that connection of appearances found the way to our mind, and how they gained that certainty in our thinking with which we are absolutely compelled to think of them?
>
> (I/2 p. 30)

This can only be possible if one accepts the necessity of monism:

> one can push as many transitory materials as one wants, which become finer and finer, between mind and matter, but some time the point must come where mind and matter are One, or where the great leap that we so long wished to avoid becomes inevitable.
>
> (I/2 p. 53)

Reinhard Löw summarises Schelling's basic question as follows: 'How must nature be thought, such that its appearing in products and processes can become comprehensible?' (Löw 1990 p. 57). The answer to this question opens up the way for a genetic theory of subjectivity. In this theory subjectivity emerges from nature and develops to the point where it has the ability to grasp nature theoretically. The attempt to develop such a theory will form the basis of much of Schelling's philosophy, early and late. The theory, as Fichte had shown, depends upon more than theoretical knowledge: the ability, let alone the need or desire, to formulate mechanical natural laws cannot itself be known to be the result of such laws.

Schelling does not simply ignore Kant's strictures on the limits of theoretical explanation, as is sometimes assumed: the very fact that the attempt to overcome the problem of Kantian dualism gives rise to a theory of the genesis of *subjectivity*, rather than dogmatic assertions about nature in itself, is proof of this. Given the dominant assumptions about the two thinkers, it is surprising to find that it is Kant rather than Schelling who opens the space for the kind of vitalism that takes on such questionable forms in Schopenhauer, in Bergson, in some of the work of Nietzsche, and in the serious irrationalists like Ludwig Klages. Kant's problem is the gap between matter and thinking life. Why do some forms of matter become organisms, let alone think about the fact that they have? Recent biology has shown that even the problem of the self-reproduction of the organism can be explained mechanically, in terms of genetics, which brings it within the realm of jurisdiction of the understanding. But this does nothing to answer the more fundamental problem that goes to the heart of the Kantian project: how does one explain the genesis of transcendental subjectivity itself? Because it has in the last analysis to presuppose the transcendental subject as the condition of possibility of anything that we can know, Kant's theoretical philosophy has no way of explaining this genesis. For the Kant of the theoretical philosophy, answers to such questions of genesis depend upon the cognitive functioning of the already constituted subject, which means that one has no right to ask how such a subject itself becomes constituted. Schelling justifiably thinks that this is insufficient to account for our ability to understand the nature of which we are a part.

THE PRODUCTIVITY OF NATURE

In her account of Schelling's *Naturphilosophie*, Marie-Luise Heuser-Kessler makes an important distinction between 'self-organisation' and 'self-reproduction': the latter may be explicable in the terms of Kant's First Critique, the former is not. She gives the following apt example: 'The emergence of inheritance millions of years ago was not itself inherited' (Heuser-Kessler 1986 p. 32). Kant himself insists in the *Critique of Judgement* that Blumenbach is right when he claims the idea

> that raw matter should have originally formed itself according to mechanical laws, that life should have been able to emerge from the nature of what is lifeless, and that matter should have been able to constitute itself of its own accord into the form of a purposiveness which sustains itself
>
> (Kant 1977a p. B 379, p. A 374)

is 'against reason', but he does not confront the consequences that ensue if one is to understand this emergence of life from matter. If one accepts Kant's dualism or his conviction in the Third Critique that the principle of the emergence of organisms is not scientifically explicable, there is a temptation to assume some kind of 'life force' which is of a different order from the mechanically explicable universe of matter. It is, then, precisely those people most attached to a rigidly mechanistic view of the functioning of nature as seen by natural science who will add the life force in order to explain what is inexplicable in mechanistic terms. Schopenhauer, for instance, follows the First Critique as far as the world of appearance is concerned, but turns the thing in itself into the irrational Will which is the ground of these appearances (see A. Bowie 1990 pp. 206–14).

Schelling, although he is not always consistent, does not become a vitalist, and certainly does not descend into irrationalism. The key question here is the status of matter, which Kant metaphysically determined in terms of the law of inertia – though by the time of the Third Critique he is hedging his bets. The fact is that as long as the rigid distinction between matter and life of the *Metaphysical Grounds of Natural Science* is held to, transcendental philosophy is unable to explain its own emergence. Schelling's basic strategy is therefore to cut the Gordian knot by insisting that all of nature be thought of in inherently dynamic terms, as a 'productivity'.[4] What we encounter in empirical nature are 'products'. The particular sciences deal with these 'products', which appear fixed and can be subsumed under rules. *Naturphilosophie*, which cannot, therefore, be subsumed into the sciences, deals with the ground of appearances, which does not appear as itself because it is not a fixed object determined by a reflexive relationship to its other, the subject: 'As the object is never absolute (*unbedingt*) then something per se non-objective must be posited in nature; this absolutely non-objective postulate is precisely the original productivity of nature' (I/2 p. 284). The primary concern is, therefore, not the mechanical laws of nature and nature as object. This is why it is a mistake to write off *Naturphilosophie* because of its empirical failings: whilst *Naturphilosophie* does attempt to give empirical results, that is not its primary aim. The 'productivity' is not, then, a separate, inaccessible thing in itself (even though it is not an object of knowledge), because it is also at work in the subject, as that which moves the subject beyond itself.

From this perspective the problem becomes how it is that nature does appear in determinate processes and products, including ourselves. As simple productivity it would never become determinate, it would dissipate itself at infinite speed. There must, then, be a conflict of forces within nature, in which the 'inhibiting' of the productivity by itself leads to products:

> Think of a river, which is *pure identity*; where it meets a resistance an eddy is formed, this eddy is nothing fixed, but disappears at every moment and reappears at every moment. In nature nothing can originally be distinguished; all products are still, as it were, dissolved and invisible in the universal productivity.
>
> (I/3 p. 289)

What constitutes the eddy – Schelling's metaphor for nature at any one moment in time – are molecules of water which are continually being displaced by the flow of the stream, even though the shape may remain relatively stable for a long time. Something similar applies also to the human body over time. The articulated moving and living world of nature is not, Schelling claims, in itself something random for living beings: it only becomes random to a certain kind of scientific gaze, which sees it as a separate, dead object. If nature is turned merely into an object of analysis, which splits it into an infinity of particularity, it becomes incomprehensible unless the investigation of nature seeks to move beyond the contingency of causal laws to the question of why those laws hold at all. This was what forced Kant to introduce reflective judgement to account for nature's empirically evident interrelatedness and thus made him reject mechanistic explanations of the emergence of life.

Schelling explicitly denies that his is a vitalist argument, which means it does not offend Kant's critique of dogmatic metaphysics by making claims about an inherent force in things in themselves. In the same way as it is nonsense to talk of the dormitive force of opium, so it is nonsense to say that because things are alive they must be driven by a life-force. He explains his position as follows: in living processes chemical processes are demonstrably overridden, which requires a principle that transcends the laws of chemistry:

> and if this process is now called *life-force*, then I would assert against this that life-force (however familiar this expression might be) is a completely contradictory expression if it is taken in this sense. For we can only think of a force as something finite. But no force is finite in terms of its *nature* unless it is limited by an opposed force. Hence, when we think of a force (as we do in matter), we must also think of an *opposed* force.
>
> (I/2 pp. 49–50)

The essence of a thing is the concatenation of forces *which it is*, not something else beyond this concatenation. The opposing forces in nature which are observable via their effects when they encounter each other require that within which they relate to each other, which cannot be a force and which is, in consequence, 'absolutely outside the limits of empirical research into nature' (ibid.). The play of forces at this level makes life possible, which is therefore not something added externally, but is the *immanent* movement of this play, upon which there can be no external perspective.

In *On the World-Soul* Schelling distinguishes between 'formative force' (*Bildungskraft*) and 'formative drive' (*Bildungstrieb*). The former is inherent in matter as the basis of it taking on forms at all, and, as such, is the basis of inorganic nature. It is, though, as Löw points out, 'our interpretative concept, not an objective observable quantity' (Löw 1990 p. 60); Schelling insists: 'force only announces itself to your *feeling*. But feeling alone does not give you any objective concepts' (I/2 p. 23). Beyond this a further account of what makes matter form itself into organisms is required:

> the *essence of life* does not consist at all in a force, but rather in a *free play of forces* which is continually sustained by some external influence. What is *necessary* in life are the universal forces of nature that are in play; what is contingent, which sustains this play by its influence, must be something *particular*, i.e. in other words a *material principle*.
>
> *Organisation and life* do not express anything at all which exists *in itself*, but only a specific *form* of being, *something which is common to them, consisting of several causes which interact*. The

principle of life is therefore only the cause of a certain *form* of being, not the cause of being itself (for such a cause cannot be thought).

(ibid. p. 566)

Put in this way, the idea of nature as a 'universal organism' ceases to be a mere projection or poetic metaphor: Schelling is concerned to understand how life emerges without relying on the dualism of matter and life, which creates the gulf between them that Kant could not cross. He is also concerned not just to fall back into the metaphysics which Kant had destroyed.

Heuser-Kessler has made the implications of these thoughts particularly clear in relation to Prigogine's controversial ideas about non-linear dynamics, which suggest, against the assumptions of most modern science, that processes of energy dissipation can also be constructive, despite the inevitable increase in entropy. She suggests that Schelling at this point in his career was able to discover something that the mechanistic science which led to the death of *Naturphilosophie* obscured. Rather than the principle of entropy, which moves towards a static balance of all forces, being the primary process, the primary process must actually be self-constitution, otherwise the emergence of life and thinking become inexplicable:

> The process of self-constitution is . . . not just an ephemeral marginal phenomenon in a course of nature which is otherwise determined, but contains the 'primal ground of all reality', for mechanisms [such as that of genetic inheritance] can be created by organising processes, whilst organising processes, on the other hand, cannot arise mechanically. Self-organisation must be the primary process not only of mind but of *all* of nature.
>
> (Heuser-Kessler 1986 p. 98)

This is not just a version of philosophical idealism, because it relies upon the interaction of self-organising process, which cannot be merely material process, with matter, which cannot organise itself.[5] Much of Schelling's subsequent work will be an attempt to work out this relationship of material and mental process.

NATURE AS VISIBLE MIND

Schelling's fundamental idea in the *Naturphilosophie* is that the organised character of mind (*Geist*) and the organised character of nature cannot be absolutely separate. As he puts it in famous formulations, which may now appear less implausible than his critics would suggest:

> Nature is to be visible mind (*Geist*), mind invisible nature. *Here*, therefore, in the absolute identity of the mind *in* us and the nature *outside* us, the problem of how a nature outside ourselves is possible must dissolve.
>
> (I/2 p. 56)

> Philosophy is, then, nothing but a *doctrine of the nature of our mind* (*Naturlehre unseres Geistes*) . . . the system of nature is at the same time the system of our mind.
>
> (I/2 p. 39)

> there is nothing impossible in the thought that the same activity via which nature reproduces itself at every moment anew is reproductive in thought but via the medium of the organism.
>
> (I/3 p. 274)

In the same way as new thoughts spontaneously organise themselves in our mind from past thoughts, nature continually reforms itself from its elements. The difference between the two kinds of process is only relative: their relationship will concern us later.

Perhaps surprisingly for those who think of Schelling as a naive identity thinker who works via suspect analogies between thinking and natural process,[6] he moves, on the basis of these arguments, towards a hermeneutic conception of natural science of the kind which will play a significant role in aspects of the work of the early Marx, Heidegger and the first-generation Frankfurt School. Schelling sees scientific experiments as follows:

> Every experiment is a question addressed to nature that nature is forced to answer. But every question contains a hidden a priori judgement; every experiment which is an experiment is prophecy; experimentation is itself a production of the phenomena.
>
> (ibid. p. 276)

Heidegger will claim in the *Letter on Humanism*: 'It could be that nature precisely hides its essence in the side which it turns towards technical control by man' (Heidegger 1978 p. 322).[7] Neither Schelling nor Heidegger sees scientific investigation in terms of a representation of the objective truth about nature. Schelling's 'production of phenomena' is not a creation of the very existence of what appears, but is what enables it to appear as something determinate. Without the activity of investigation there would be no possibility of producing a world of law-governed phenomena: even mechanisms, as Kant had shown, require the judgement of self-conscious beings to be differentiated mechanisms. A world of pure objectivity is and will remain inconceivable for Schelling, not least because it could never lead to that which can *think* of nature in even purely mechanistic terms. If all is mechanism, nothing is mechanism. This means that no final objectivity can be arrived at by experiment:

> The fact that experiment never leads to such [absolute] knowledge is evident in the fact that it *can never get beyond the natural forces which it itself uses as its means* [my emphasis] ... the last *causes* of the phenomena of nature no longer appear themselves.
>
> (I/3 pp. 276–7)

We can only have empirical access to products. What we encounter in a product is a limitation of the productivity by itself: anything determinate that we know in nature is therefore not finally fixed. It has its place in an overall process which cannot be thought of in objective terms: the very condition of objectivity is reflexive division within the whole, that includes ourselves as one part of the organism which is the totality of nature. The implication for empirical science is the following:

> as every new discovery throws us back into a new ignorance, and as one knot is untied, another is tied, then it is conceivable that the complete discovery of all connections in nature, that therefore our science itself, is also an endless task.
>
> (ibid. p. 279)

As such, any realist conception of the approach to the absolute truth about nature is revealed as doomed to failure by our inextricable role as part of what is to be investigated.

The *Naturphilosophie* articulates the system of nature on the basis of a fundamental principle of difference within identity:

> If we assume, e.g., which must be assumed, that the essence (*Inbegriff*) of the appearances is not just a world, but necessarily a nature, i.e. that this whole is not just product but is at the same time productive, then it follows that it can never come to absolute identity within this whole, because this would lead to an absolute transition of nature, to the extent that it is

40

productive, into nature as product, i.e. an absolute stasis (*Ruhe*); that hovering (*Schweben*) of nature between productivity and product must therefore appear as a universal duplicity of the principles, by which nature is sustained in continual activity and is prevented from exhausting itself in its product; universal duality as the principle of all explanation of nature will be as necessary as the concept of nature itself.

(ibid. p. 277)

Without reflexive differences nature would not appear: if it were to become only product, as entropy suggests, it would cease to exist as something that could be known.[8] The differences are seen as an ascending series of 'potentials' in nature, which entail a polar opposition within themselves. The model is the magnet, whose opposite poles are inseparable from each other: 'sensibility is only the higher potential of magnetism, irritability only the higher potential of electricity, the drive for constitution only the higher potential of the chemical process' (ibid. p. 325). Inorganic nature can reach 'indifference', a state where no further internal change will result, where only external mechanical changes are possible. If all of nature were like this, the consequence would be the absolute product. The higher potential of life, though, 'consists precisely in continuously *preventing the point of indifference being reached*' (ibid. p. 323). In nature, 'The opposites must eternally flee each other, in order eternally to seek each other, and seek each other eternally, in order never to find each other; only in *this* contradiction does the ground of all activity of nature lie' (ibid. p. 325). These potentials are all ultimately contained within the universal organism. The differentiated moments of nature are grounded in an absolute identity which transcends cognition because one cannot say *what* this identity is.[9] Its necessity can, though, be shown in philosophy by the theory of the 'productivity' that cannot be fixed in a final product. The description of the actual articulated system of nature, which Schelling carried out in varying ways at various times, cannot concern us here. The system does not now stand up to scientific scrutiny and many elements are merely bizarre to the modern scientific mind (though others have come to seem less bizarre as science has become more concerned with processes than with objects). The influence of the *Naturphilosophie* on the history of science is, though, beyond dispute and the specifically philosophical premises it is founded on are, as I hope to have shown, worth serious scrutiny.

41

THE FACTICITY OF NATURE

The next specifically philosophical question Schelling confronts is how to move from the development of organic nature to self-consciousness. However, before considering this move it is important to make a final point that will make understanding some aspects of the later Schelling easier, as well as being relevant to assessing Schelling's contemporary significance. Löw rightly remarks that, although the treatment of nature in German Idealism is remarkably successful at showing ways of grasping the unity in opposition of nature and mind, and thus of escaping Kantian dualism, it failed to deal with nature's facticity. Because reason and nature are conceived of as in some way identical, the tendency is to try to suggest that nature is therefore inherently reasonable. Given the fact of thought and the fact that there is nature, it is possible for Schelling and Hegel to show how thought can produce accounts of the nature of which it is an aspect that are often plausible at the theoretical level. Löw maintains, though, that Hegel, whose thinking coincides in certain ways with that of the Schelling of the *Naturphilosophie*, fails to take any serious account of the actual facticity that science has to deal with, as in his wrong deduction of the number of the planets. Schelling is guilty of very many similar failures as a result of his using the endless capacity for analogy generated by the principle of polarity. These failures obviously relate to the ultimate demise of systematic *Naturphilosophie* in the light of the attacks by Helmholtz and others, who wish to avoid metaphysical principles in scientific explanation. The simple fact is that the praxis of scientific research not based on a single philosophical system produces more usable results in the real history of modern science *because* it does not work from one grounding principle.

Does this, then, mean that the very attempt at a *Naturphilosophie* is an essentially pointless exercise? Clearly one cannot legitimate Schelling's *Naturphilosophie* at the level of the usable scientific results which it produced.[10] Why not, then, simply regard nature materialistically and see our cognitive access to it in essentially pragmatic terms? The problem is, as Löw argues, that this has led to the 'scientistic nihilism' (Löw 1990 p. 68) of contemporary 'evolutionary epistemology', which explains cognitive achievements in materialist fashion as merely the forms of human adaptation to a nature conceived of in realist terms as a fixed set of ultimate objects. Reason, in this view, is the capacity for discovering pre-existing truths as part of the process of adaptation. The objection to this result of transporting concepts from empirical science into philosophy is not merely sentimental.

Theories of evolutionary epistemology are open to precisely the arguments against explaining the emergence of life and intelligibility by mechanical processes that we have already considered in both Kant and Schelling. These theories also ignore the implications of Schelling's notion of experiment as 'prophecy', which reminds us of the inherently hermeneutic aspect of all scientific investigation. Hilary Putnam suggests against evolutionary epistemology:

> Truth in the only sense in which we have a vital and working notion of it, is rational acceptability (or, rather, rational acceptability under sufficiently good epistemic conditions; and which conditions are epistemically better or worse is relative to the type of discourse in just the way rational acceptability itself is). But to substitute this characterisation . . . into the formula 'reason is a capacity for discovering truths' is to see the emptiness of that formula at once: 'reason is a capacity for discovering what is (or would be) rationally acceptable' is *not* the most informative statement a philosopher might utter. The evolutionary epistemologist must either presuppose a 'realist' (i.e. a metaphysical) notion of truth or see his formula collapse into vacuity.
>
> (Putnam 1983 p. 231)

The evolutionary epistemologist returns us to a pre-Kantian conception of theory–neutral objects, of the kind that no serious philosophical reflection on the nature of scientific investigation can countenance, and which Schelling's theory reveals as wholly untenable.

The contemporary correlate of evolutionary epistemology is the contrary tendency, which turns nature in itself into something mystical and incomprehensible. Löw regards the avoidance of these bad alternatives as crucial to a 'hermeneutics of nature'. Such a hermeneutics does not work with an objectifying pre-understanding of what nature or science is, and thereby keeps open our relationship to the nature of which we are a part and which we therefore understand. What Löw does not mention is the fact that the later Schelling is concerned exactly with the facticity, the 'thatness' of nature, as opposed to its 'whatness'. The later Schelling is clear that an understanding of the fact of this actual world cannot be arrived at from the premises of transcendental philosophy, and this forms the basis of his critique of Hegel, and thus of his move towards a conception of reason which has so many echoes today. He also wishes to avoid the mystical option, as is clear from his objections to Böhme and Jacobi in the Lectures and elsewhere. Whilst he may not provide us with satisfying answers to the questions he raises, Schelling does offer conceptual means that look interesting in the light of contemporary interests. Before we can begin to assess these ideas, though, we must consider Schelling's next attempt to marry Spinoza and Fichte: the account of the genesis of self-consciousness which he tries to link to the *Naturphilosophie* in the *System of Transcendental Idealism* and other writings at the turn of the century.

3

THE HISTORY OF CONSCIOUSNESS AND THE TRUTH OF ART

THE PATH TO THE SELF

The *System of Transcendental Idealism* (*STI*) of 1800 explicates for the first time in systematic form one of the most influential ideas in modern thinking: the idea that self-consciousness has to develop in stages from a point where it did not exist as such. The *STI* also develops the newly emerged Romantic thought, which we briefly touched on when looking at metaphor in the Introduction, that art can reveal more than philosophy can say. The *STI* thereby helps open the space for the specifically modern versions of aesthetic truth that are central to the work of Adorno, Heidegger, Gadamer and others, which are now even affecting conceptions of truth in certain areas of analytical philosophy.[1]

The *STI* is another expression of the tension in Schelling's work between Spinoza and Fichte, and of a related tension between an Idealist and a Romantic conception of philosophy. The first tension is expressed in the attempt to marry the conception of the *Natur-philosophie* to a Fichtean conception of the I. The second tension becomes evident in the privileging of art above philosophy as a means of revealing the Absolute: Schelling will not sustain this priority in subsequent work, though its implications for his position do not disappear in the later work. These tensions are, again, not merely specialised issues in the philosophy of the period. Schelling is confronted with the fundamental modern problem of how to understand our status as self-conscious natural beings, in the absence of theological support. The danger is that one will either fall into the materialist trap of thinking that by explaining the mechanical functioning of nature we will finally explain ourselves, thus making self-consciousness and freedom merely epiphenomenal, or into the Idealist trap of thinking that self-consciousness is wholly self-grounding, thus making its relationship to nature one of simple

45

domination. The two positions actually tend to be mirror images of each other, in that the *complete* mechanistic explanation would, in Kantian and post-Kantian terms, be a product of absolute subjectivity. Schelling sometimes leaves contradictions unresolved in the *STI*, but in doing so reveals vital issues in modern thought. It is no coincidence that structures which anticipate psychoanalysis emerge in the process, that a new understanding of the significance of art for philosophy is promulgated, and that, in moving away from Fichte, Schelling will in his subsequent work develop an expressly ecological conception of nature.

Schelling begins the *STI* with 'the parallelism of nature with the intelligible' that is familiar from the *Naturphilosophie*. However, he is clear that the *Naturphilosophie* is not complete in itself and that a further transcendental philosophy is required to explicate self-consciousness's higher stages, which are necessary for the move from theoretical to practical philosophy. The tension in the *STI* is a result of Schelling's uncertainty about the priority of the two philosophies. He opts for the transcendental philosophy for good Kantian and Fichtean reasons, but at the cost of a conceptual inconsistency he had evidently been aware of in the *Letters on Dogmatism and Criticism*. In *Of the I* he had, as we saw, changed the Kantian question as to the possibility of synthetic judgements into the question 'How is it that the absolute I goes out of itself and opposes a not-I to itself?' (I/1 p. 175); in the *Letters* this question was put in terms of the Absolute, which was no longer conceived of as an absolute I. In the *STI* he generally goes back to the Fichtean terminology. The problem here has already been suggested: opposing an I to a not-I within an absolute I means using the same term for the subject which is relative to the object as for the whole within which there can be such a relationship. As Hölderlin showed, it therefore becomes impossible to know in what sense the absolute I is an I in the same way as the individual conscious I.

In the *STI* the conceptual structures of the *Naturphilosophie* recur, but as descriptions of the I. Intellectual intuition, the activity of the I upon itself, in which subject and object are identical, is the source of the I in the highest sense, 'to the extent that it is *its own product*, is simultaneously what produces and what is produced' (I/3 p. 372). Nature itself, then, is to be understood via the explication of self-consciousness: 'The concept of an original identity in duplicity and vice versa is therefore only the concept of a *subject–object* and this originally only occurs in self-consciousness' (I/3 p. 373). Instead of a conception in which both nature and consciousness have their source in a higher activity, the Absolute, consciousness is given priority (on this, see Frank 1985 pp. 71–103). This questionable use of the term 'I' leads to what always worries people about Schelling's early philosophy: it seems to understand everything as the functioning of some kind of inflated mind. One should, though, read the text with more hermeneutic sensitivity: with some terminological adjustment, these ideas are not as bizarre as they may sound.

The originality of the *STI* lies in the way in which it turns philosophy into 'a history of self-consciousness' (I/3 p. 331). This history retraces the path leading to the moment where self-consciousness becomes able to write such a history, by seeing what stages the subject necessarily went through to arrive at this moment. Hegel adopts the model for the *Phenomenology of Spirit*, and it can, taken on the level of the individual subject, be seen in Proust's *A la recherche du temps perdu*. It is also a model for psychoanalysis: Lacan clearly uses aspects of the *Phenomenology*, for instance. The stages of development in the *STI* are progressive stages of the absolute I's self-limitation. The lowest stages are those of the differentiation of the natural world from a state of simple oneness. This stage of the limitation, which we can understand via our primitive sense of the resistance of the object world, appears independent of us, because 'the act via which all limitation is posited, as condition of all consciousness, does not itself come to consciousness' (I/3 p. 409). Limitation, the condition of a manifest world, is posited as an 'act' because one cannot give a causal explanation of its occurrence, in that it is the prior condition of possibility of any causal relation between determinate things.

The world of objective nature is, then, an 'unconscious' stage of the I, but it is still 'of the I'. The I at this stage cannot simultaneously become objective by self-division and see itself becoming objective. If Kantian dualism is to be avoided, it must be clear that the sensation of resistance of the other is not of a wholly different order from the awareness of oneself:

> even the judgement that the impression derives from an object presupposes an activity which is not limited to the impression but moves *beyond* the impression. The I is, therefore, not what feels, unless there is an activity in it which *goes beyond the limit*.
>
> (I/3 p. 413)

This conception, derived from Fichte, will be the basis of Hegel's argument against Kant's setting limits on knowledge, and Schelling uses it here against the notion of the thing in itself. Each limit becomes a reason to go beyond that limit, as the awareness of a limit has always already transcended the limit by *knowing* it as a limit. Because each stage of development of the subject becomes a new limit on the infinite activity of the absolute I, it turns into the next object to be overcome. The very emergence of a differentiated world of matter, even prior to organic form and conscious self-awareness, is in these terms a form of 'intuition' of the I by itself. Only because the productivity is inhibited does it manifest itself. The basic structures of the world of objects are nothing but a lower form of structures of mind that the philosopher can understand by reflecting on why the world has come to be felt and thought of as other to herself, even though it must ultimately be the same as herself.

The next stages of development are the constitution of natural organisms, and then the emergence of individual consciousness in the act of 'absolute abstraction', which takes us out of the realm of natural necessity towards self-consciousness and the autonomous will. It is at this stage that the notions of 'unconscious' and 'conscious' productivity begin to become most important. The argument about the emergence of the individual I of consciousness is Fichtean. It is only by an action which takes the I absolutely above the object world that such consciousness can arise. As such it can have no prior cause: 'thus the chain of theoretical philosophy is broken here' (ibid. p. 524) and we must, even to explain theoretical knowledge, move into the realm of practical philosophy, of the I as self-positing spontaneity. How, though, given the absolute transcending of the object world by this action – the subject is again, as we saw in the earlier texts, *unbedingt* – are we to understand the object world without again slipping back into dualism? The answer lies in the fact that the world of nature is the sphere of 'unconscious' productivity, as opposed to the 'conscious' productivity of the self-aware, autonomous I. There is no absolute division of the two: the main problem is understanding how they relate.

'Absolute abstraction' leads to a second phase of development: 'Just as nature developed itself as a whole from the original act of self-consciousness, a second nature will emerge from the secondary act, or from free self-determination' (ibid, p. 537).[2] In subsequent sections of the *STI* Schelling works through the stages of the development of second nature: history and the state. I shall not consider these sections here for reasons of space (on this, see Marx 1984). The argument becomes most interesting when Schelling links conscious and unconscious in his conception of the art-work.

SELF-REFERENCE AND ART

For Schelling, as for Jacobi and Hölderlin, it is clear that the Absolute cannot appear as itself, precisely because it cannot become an object. This might again seem an issue only for those interested in metaphysical exertions of the kind Rorty and others think we ought now to have given up. However, though discussions of the Absolute may sound merely metaphysical, the fact is that the problem involved is central even to philosophies that purport to have finished with metaphysics. The issue is simply the problem of reflexivity, or self-referentiality, which is the key problem of Romantic philosophy (see A. Bowie 1990 pp. 58–80, and Gasché 1986, for a different view), and which Hegel thought he had solved. Novalis says in a classic formulation, in the so-called *Fichte Studies* of 1795–6: 'The essence of identity can only be established in an *apparent proposition (Scheinsatz)*. We leave the *identical* in order to represent it' (quoted in A. Bowie 1990 p. 73). By this he means that in attempting to *say* that something is the same as something else we have to split what is the same to *show* it is the same, as in the proposition A = A, where there are two different As.

In another form this problem is what invalidates correspondence theories of truth. If the first A is an object and the second A a putatively true description of that object, one is left with the problem that identifying the object and the description would require a further perspective that encompasses their relationship. The question is, where would one be able to locate such a perspective? Donald Davidson has recently made a similar point, which, as he suggests, is what makes correspondence theories of truth untenable:

> The real objection to correspondence theories . . . is that there is nothing interesting or instructive to which true sentences might correspond. The point was made some time ago by C.I. Lewis; he challenged the correspondence theorist to locate the fact or part of reality, or of the world, to which a true sentence corresponds. One can locate individual objects, if the sentence happens to name or describe them, but even such a location makes sense relative only to a frame of reference, and so presumably the frame of reference must be included in whatever it is to which a true sentence corresponds.[3]

> (Davidson 1990 p. 303)

This is a linguistic version of the problem Hölderlin had identified in relation to Fichte, which we saw in Chapter 1. Any attempt to encompass a totality must either adopt a perspective outside the totality, and thus include the totality in itself as only a relative totality, or face the problem that totalities cannot describe themselves as totalities, in that the description must then include a description of the description, and so on *ad infinitum*.[4]

Think also, to take an example closer to the world of the *STI*, of the Freudian unconscious. For Freud it is clear that we have no direct consciousness of drives, we only are aware of their 'representations', be it in dreams, fantasies or language. How, though, do we establish the theoretical perspective from which to justify cognitive claims about the relationship between the drive and its representation, both of which must be included in the totality of the psyche? One would have to be in a position which encompassed – in consciousness – both the conscious representation and what it relates to in the unconscious.[5] The issue of metaphor recurs here in a crucial way: in psychoanalysis we only have access to the root of fundamental problems of human existence via the sense of aptness of the metaphors which we use to articulate those problems. The metaphors cannot be finally 'cashed in' in another conceptual, 'scientific' language, because there is no metalanguage in which the truth of the metaphor could be pro-positionally stated. Davidson says of metaphor: 'I hold that the endless character of what we call the paraphrase of a metaphor springs from the fact that it attempts to spell out what the metaphor makes us notice, and to this there is no clear end' (Davidson 1984 p. 263).[6] The psychoanalytical problem cannot appear as itself, then, because it is precisely not an object of conceptual knowledge that could be stated in a proposition: we cannot have access to a drive *as* a drive. The understanding of the workings of the unconscious can, then, only be indirect. The same applies to the Absolute in the *STI*, with the work of art taking the role of metaphor. In Schelling's terms we only ever 'see' products, not the productivity. This does not mean that we think there is no productivity, because our awareness of the limitation of the particular product leads to the desire to articulate our sense of this limitation.

Anything objective must, in the terms of the *STI*, be the result of reflexive splitting of the absolute I. Therefore, 'there can be no predicates at all for the *absolutely identical* which already separates itself in the first act of consciousness, and produces the whole system of finitude by this separation, for it is absolutely simple' (I/3 p. 600). Why bother to try to talk about it, then? The answer is that the absolute presupposition explains the relativity of our knowledge (see Frank 1989 pp. 157–8).[7] In the *STI*, my conscious I has an objective 'unconscious' history which precedes its now being able to make the move to awareness of its freedom. This history, *which also can only be known via its result, not as itself*, must also be integrated into the articulation of the Absolute: hence the need for a narrative presentation. What is being sought is a way of understanding the identity of the subjective and the objective, conscious and unconscious, spirit and nature, which must not be conceived of as theoretical knowledge. Hölderlin and the early Romantics, with whom Schelling was in close contact in Jena at this time, had already suggested that this understanding might be achieved in art.

Schelling sees one form of such identity via organisms in nature, which are 'purposive' in the manner seen in the *Naturphilosophie*, but are not aware of the fact. A tree lacks nothing in being a tree, but is not a tree for itself. Living organisms represent 'an original identity of conscious and unconscious activity' (I/3 p. 610), thus requiring more than mechanical explanation, whilst still remaining in the world of mechanical, determined objects. The task of philosophy, though, is to realise this identity at the level of the self-conscious I. Schelling expresses his aim in a chiasmus:

> nature begins unconsciously and ends consciously, the production is not purposive, but the product is. In the activity which we are talking about here the I must begin with consciousness (subjectively) and end in the unconscious or *objectively*, the I is conscious according to the production, unconscious with regard to the product.
>
> (I/3 p. 613)

The product is supposed to unite conscious and unconscious productivity. However, if they became identical there would be no appearance, because appearance requires that to which it appears and therefore entails non-identity. Absolute freedom, in which the world of consciousness would be wholly reconciled with the world of nature, would ultimately abolish their difference, as Fichte had suggested in his view of practical reason. Freedom, as the ground of identity of the I and the not-I, can here only be conceived of as an infinite progression, a striving, which gives us no objective access to it now. This leads, however, to a sense of dissatisfaction: why do we even think about the Absolute if it is merely a postulate that cannot be fulfilled? Schelling is clear that this problem has a political component: a philosophy that cannot be generally communicated would have no social significance. The fact is that what Schelling needs in order to grasp the Absolute must be an object of experience which is not just an object, but is also not just dependent upon the conscious theoretical subject. He sees this as a work of art.

What makes an object a work of art has nothing to do with the art-object's status as a natural object bound by natural laws. As natural object it is determined by its negative relationship to other objects and means nothing in itself. As a work of art it cannot be finally determined: a work of art is not art because it shares the same attributes as other objects or can be defined in relation to them, but rather because it reveals the world in a way which only it can. There can thus be no science of art. The production of such an object at the level of technique is under the conscious control of the artist; the result, though, is not, because the motivation for that production, the 'drive', is unconscious. The idea derives from Kant's Third Critique, where the genius crosses the Kantian divide between the subject and nature in itself by being 'the talent (gift of nature), which gives the rule to art . . . genius is the innate aptitude (*ingenium*) *through which* nature gives the rule to art' (Kant 1977a pp. B 181–2, A 179). Schelling sees this relationship of nature and mind, unconscious and conscious, as the one place in which the 'Absolute' – he uses the term at this point (I/3 p. 615) – manifests itself:

> As this absolute meeting of the two activities which flee each other is not at all explicable in any further way, but is just an appearance, which, although incomprehensible from the point of view of mere reflection [theoretical knowledge], yet cannot be denied, it is art that is the only and the eternal revelation, and the miracle, which, even if it had only existed once, would have to convince us of the reality of the Highest.
>
> (I/3 p. 618)

The work of art's basic character is an 'unconscious infinity' (I/3 p. 619), because the meaning of the work cannot be exhausted, even though it is manifested in an object, and does not depend upon the conscious intention of the artist.

An apparently limited 'product', then, turns out to reveal the world in a way which conceptual articulation cannot: what we see or hear is an object, what is revealed is not. We do not look at Rembrandt self-portraits aesthetically if we wish to see what he 'looked like'. Only if the object is actually revelatory are we in the presence of a work of art: there can be no rule as to whether a particular product makes this happen. Every definition of what the work is conceals its fundamental character. As Manfred Frank has pointed out, this means that the Romantic Absolute, as Schelling presents it in the *STI*, which can be shown only in art, is very closely related to Heidegger's *Sein* in *The Origin of the Work of Art*: 'both are the ground of the disclosedness of a world, and in such a way that, in showing itself, what shows itself hides itself' (Frank 1989b p. 128). Schelling suggests that science and art are both means of disclosing the Absolute, but science is, as we saw in the *Naturphilosophie*, faced with an endless task of disclosure, whereas art has always already fulfilled this task by the fact of its being art.

Schelling sees the imagination (*Einbildungskraft*) as one key to the nature of art. The argument derives from Kant, and is another instance of the breakdown of the scheme-content distinction. In the first version of the First Critique, Kant had developed the distinction between the imagination's productive and its reproductive aspect. He had, though, then drawn back from the implications of this dual status. The imagination receives images of the object world, which we can then synthesise into cognitive judgements in the understanding, making it an 'unconscious' faculty in Schelling's sense, and it can produce images in the absence of any object, making it a 'conscious' faculty.[8] If art shows the identity of these two sides, then both science and art depend upon the same activity, which is both conscious and unconscious, and we are pushed towards a hermeneutic understanding of science and art as forms of world-disclosure. By determining the object, science also excludes all the object's other possibilities; the work of art does not produce this kind of closure, because it reveals the world in a way which cannot be finally controlled.[9]

The final consequence of the argument of the *STI* is that art is 'the only true and eternal organ and document of philosophy, which always and continuously documents what philosophy cannot represent externally' (I/3 p. 627); or 'aesthetic intuition is precisely intellectual intuition which has become objective' (I/3 p. 625). Philosophy, therefore, cannot positively represent the Absolute because reflexive thinking operates from the position where absolute identity has always already been lost in the emergence of consciousness. Schelling and Hegel will both subsequently attempt to find a way of avoiding this consequence, but Schelling will be led back to a different version of it in his later philosophy. The *STI* ends with the invocation of the need for a 'new mythology', a 'mythology of reason', which would lead the sciences and art back to their common source. This invocation is beginning to look less questionable than it did for much of the time from the publication of the *STI* until recently. The growing conviction in certain areas of both analytical and European philosophy that representational, or correspondence theories, which underlie scientistic views of truth, are failing to give an adequate account of our relationship to internal and external nature is leading in many places to the suspicion that both scientific and aesthetic revelations of truth are only different aspects of the same language-embodied process.

The apparently hyperbolic claims of the *STI* can, therefore, be seen as having real philosophical substance. This is evident if one takes up the theme we considered in the Introduction. One way of re-stating the argument of the *STI* is that the happening of truth is best revealed to us in the continual emergence of new metaphors. Metaphor discloses the world with what, for the conscious subject, is always already there: language. Natural language itself is a result of previous 'unconscious' production: in the form of sound-waves, as marks in the world of intuitions, it appears to be an object. At the same time it is 'conscious' production, in that it has a meaning that no object could have. If that meaning can be made subject to rules, then it ceases to be a metaphor. The motor of poetic language (and of other arts) can be understood as the hope that we might find ways of saying the unsayable, the unsayable being that which cannot be characterised by an objective predicate.[10] The question is, then, whether any work of art can *sustain* its metaphorical potential, thereby remaining irreducible to any final objectification: if it can, the argument of the *STI* has serious claims to philosophical status, even as it is thrown away as the ladder to what is manifested only in the art-work. Schelling will not sustain these ideas in this form, but the problem of whether the Absolute can be articulated within philosophy will repeatedly concern us in examining his later work.

4

IDENTITY PHILOSOPHY

THE IDENTITY OF THE ABSOLUTE

Schelling's 'identity philosophy', which emerges in the period immediately following the *STI*, and culminates in the 1804 'Würzburg System', is often assumed to be the main target of Hegel's famous condemnation in the *Phenomenology of Spirit* of 1807:[1]

> To oppose this one piece of knowledge (*Wissen*), that in the Absolute everything is the same, to differentiating knowledge (*Erkenntnis*) which is fulfilled, or seeks and demands fulfilment, or to present its *Absolute* as the night, in which, as people say, all cows are black, is the naivety of the lack of knowledge.
>
> (Hegel 1970 p. 22)

Schelling's Absolute, as presented in his identity philosophy, has come to be associated with 'immediacy', the failure to carry out the 'exertion of the concept', the articulation of the moments of the process of the Absolute, which is regarded as Hegel's great achievement, begun in the *Phenomenology* and best exemplified in the *Logic* and the *Encyclopaedia*. Here, though, is Schelling himself in 1802, in an early version of the identity philosophy:

> For most people see in the essence of the Absolute nothing but pure night and cannot recognise (*erkennen*) anything in it; it shrinks before them into a mere negation of difference (*Verschiedenheit*), and is for them something purely privative, whence they cleverly make it into the end of their philosophy . . .
> I want to show here . . . how that night of the Absolute can be turned into day for knowledge.
>
> (I/4 p. 403)

55

As Manfred Frank shows (Frank 1975 pp. 68–72), Hegel may even have borrowed Schelling's criticism from this essay, which was directed at those who had misunderstood the notion of the Absolute as the mere abolition of difference in a static monism. What is at issue between Schelling and Hegel is the question of *how* to understand the relative status of particular knowledge without ending in scepticism: hence the reference once again to the Absolute.

Hegel's primary objection to Schelling's identity philosophy was to its use of the notion of 'intellectual intuition', which meant that the beginning of philosophy had already laid claim to a fundamental ground, which Hegel thinks can only be a result:

> only this identity (*Gleichheit*) which *reestablishes* itself or the reflection in the being-other in itself – not an *original* unity as such or an *immediate* unity as such – is the true . . . . The true is the whole. But the whole is only the essence which completes itself by its development. One can say of the Absolute that it is essentially a *result*, that it is only at the *end* what it is in truth.
>
> (Hegel 1970 pp. 23–4)

In the same way that I become there 'for myself' when I move beyond self-enclosure and see myself in a mirror, it is only when the Absolute has become 'for itself' in the process of reflection that it is truly realised as itself: 'If the embryo is in fact *in itself* a person, that does not mean that it is it *for itself*' (ibid. p. 25). The issue between Schelling and Hegel will be whether the Absolute can, as Hegel thinks, be grasped by the process of reflection, thus requiring no presupposition external to reflection. In the *STI* the role of the work of art was precisely to give access to the ground of reflection, which must be presupposed, but cannot appear in reflection. For Hegel being, substance, grounds itself, as Spinoza suggested. Like Schelling, though, he thinks, against Spinoza, that the substance must be active, which is evident in the movement of reflection, the substance's splitting itself to develop itself. Hegel therefore thinks the substance must be 'subject', rather than object, which moves beyond any initial immediacy in the 'becoming of itself' (*Werden seiner selbst*) (ibid. p. 23). In Hegel the grounding can be shown in philosophy by explicating the development of self-consciousness to the point where it understands the movement it has recapitulated as its own history. At times Schelling does come close to Hegel in the identity philosophy, but he also presents the beginnings of arguments that re-emerge in the later critiques of Hegel and form the basis of his significance for subsequent philosophy.

MOVING BEYOND THE I: THE BREAK WITH FICHTE

Before attempting to delineate some of the still viable aspects of the identity philosophy, we need to look briefly at how Schelling completes the move away from Fichte. The way he does so is characteristic of Schelling's main philosophical direction from now on. In *On the True Concept of Naturphilosophie and the Correct Way to Solve its Problems* of 1801 Schelling ceases to equivocate over the relationship between *Naturphilosophie* and transcendental philosophy. The primary philosophy is the *Naturphilosophie*. He has no doubts about what this implies. Although, as Fichte suggests, philosophical thinking has to begin with the free act of the conscious subject, this creates the illusion of this act being the real, as opposed to merely the cognitive beginning of philosophy. Schelling argues that Fichte mixes up 'philosophy' with 'philosophising about philosophy' (I/4 p. 84). Fichte has begun at the highest 'potential', the self-conscious I, without explaining what precedes it, which for Schelling initially emerges in '*unconscious* activity' (ibid. p. 85), not the conscious activity of the philosopher. Transcendental philosophy is a result, not a beginning. Schelling does not regress into dogmatism, though, because he knows he has to account for the conscious subject. He therefore suggests that, having arrived at the subject, philosophy must subtract from the highest point, the self-conscious I, reducing it to the lowest 'potential' in nature, before reconstructing the path upwards.[2] Fichte's philosophy is forced to work within the conditions of already constituted consciousness, where the object always depends upon the subject, but 'in this way it can never get beyond this identity [of subject and object], thus it can basically never get beyond the circle of consciousness' (ibid. p. 85).

Schelling's move beyond the immanence of the I is central to the identity system, and to his significance for modern philosophy, which, as we saw, both Heidegger and Habermas characterised in terms of the primacy of the subject in relation to a world of objects. Schelling now insists that the productivity does not begin as an I, but only *becomes* an I. He can only argue this by an abstraction, which takes away from consciousness in order to reach what precedes it: 'by this abstraction I reach the concept of the pure subject–object (= nature), from which I raise myself up to the subject–object of consciousness (= I)' (ibid. p. 86), which together form the structure of the Absolute. Schelling now insists these stages are 'unconscious' and can only become conscious to an I which has developed out of them and realises its dependence upon them. One must abstract from intellectual intuition in order to arrive at the initial unconscious subject–object, nature. Why, though, call it a subject–object? Schelling's answer is: '*That pure subject–object is already determined for action by its nature* (the contradiction it has in itself)' (ibid. p. 90): without the contradiction between itself as subject and as object, the emergence and development of self-consciousness would be inexplicable. The important consequence of this is that we realise our dependency upon nature in a way which cannot, as Fichte had maintained, be overcome by the imposition of practical reason. For Schelling reason itself is only the higher aspect of nature, which should not be there to enslave what it emerges from.

Schelling makes, throughout his career, many of the moves which are the basis of Horkheimer and Adorno's conception of a 'dialectic of enlightenment', in which reason deceives itself about its relationship to nature and thereby turns into its dialectical opposite. Schelling's objections to Fichte lead him to startlingly 'Green' pronouncements of a kind also seen in Adorno. Here he is in a letter to Fichte in 1801:

> I am thoroughly aware of how small an area of consciousness nature must fall into, according to your conception of it. For you nature has no speculative significance, only a teleological one. But are you really of the opinion, for example, that light is only there so that rational beings can also see each other when they talk to each other, and that air is there so that when they hear each other they can talk to each other?
>
> (in Schulz 1968 p. 140)

By 1806 the gloves are really off:

> in the last analysis what is the essence of his whole opinion of nature? It is this: that nature should be used . . . and that it is there for nothing more than to be used; his principle, according to which he looks at nature, is the economic teleological principle.
>
> (I/7 p. 17)

The reasons for Schelling's harsh judgement have exemplary significance for the history of modernity. One of the disasters in the history of orthodox Marxism, the evidence of which can be found all over Eastern Europe, is its failure to sustain the younger Marx's Schelling-derived concern for non-human nature, in favour of precisely the sort of vision of the domination of nature that Fichte at his worst (e.g., in the last part of the *Vocation of Man*) was capable of, and which is reproduced in other ways in the ravages of modern capitalism.

The significance of the move away from Fichte for the development of the identity philosophy becomes very clear in the *Propaedeutic of*

Philosophy of 1804. Fichte is here seen as really concerned only with 'the origin of finite representations' (I/6 p. 122), which result from the limitation of the infinite activity of the I. Fichte has therefore reduced philosophy to looking merely at the finite, by trying to make the fact of consciousness infinite. Habermas claims of the Young Hegelians that their 'arguments reclaim the finitude of spirit against the self-related-totalising thinking of the dialectic' (Habermas 1988 p. 47). Schelling already begins to move in this direction in his critique of Fichte and he will complete most of the move in the later critique of Hegel. He now sees the consequence of Fichte's position in a startling way, that will affect his thinking from now on. The basic idea with regard to the subject, though without the conception of the Absolute, will reappear in *Dialectic of Enlightenment*, in the conception of objectifying instrumental reason, which represses the fact of the subject's dependence on the Other of nature:

> By positing myself as *myself* I oppose myself to everything else, consequently to the entire universe. *Egoity* (*Ichheit*) is therefore the universal expression of isolation, of separation from the totality (*All*), and as nothing can be separated from the totality, given its infinity, except by its being finitely posited, i.e. with negation, then egoity is the general expression and highest principle of all *finitude*, i.e. of everything which is not *absolute totality*, absolute reality. How the infinite, in which there is no negation, could be the cause of privations, of limitations is absolutely incomprehensible.
>
> (I/6 p. 124)

The freedom of the conscious subject is thus the reason for its *separation* from the Absolute.[3] The subject is therefore faced with the 'necessity of contemplating (*anschauen*) not this absolute totality, but only negations of it' (ibid. p. 125). The constitution of the subject thus depends upon a fundamental repression. As a result of the move away from Fichte in the identity philosophy, Schelling has to deny absolute reality to the finite world at the same time as suggesting that philosophy can move beyond the finite world. This may sound like a regression to the worst kind of Platonism, but the way Schelling carries out these moves points to the future rather than to the past, because he reveals the consequences of the dependence of subjectivity on a ground which it cannot itself grasp.

TRANSITIVE BEING AND IDENTITY

The *System of the Whole of Philosophy and of Naturphilosophie in Particular* of 1804, the 'Würzburg System' (hereafter the *System*), is the culmination of the identity philosophy. The *System* is a mixture of deep philosophical insight and bizarre speculation on the philosophy of nature. Schelling never published it, and he will soon move to a new stage of his thinking, but its specifically philosophical arguments deserve much more attention than they have generally received. The problem with understanding the arguments of the *System* is that they seem at first sight, as Hegel is understood as suggesting, to lead merely to a mystical dissolution of all philosophical distinctions. A careful reading can show that this is not the case. Even though Schelling does hereafter move away from this version of identity philosophy, some of the arguments we are about to consider retain their validity for him until the very end.

The *System* begins in precisely the way which Hegel will come to reject: '*The first presupposition of all knowledge is that one and the same knows and is known*' (I/6 p. 137). Schelling does, though, make it clear that this presupposition has to be explicated. However, it is evident that the explication is only possible because of the *preceding* absolute reality of the ground which is to be explicated. Significantly, Schelling rejects the idea that this beginning will lead to a demonstration of correspondence or *adequatio*. The Absolute is not a result of the *overcoming* of the difference between thought and being, subject and object, which is achieved by arriving at the adequate representation in the subject of the object, or even by showing their mutual interdependence:

> It is clear that in every explanation of truth as an agreement (*Übereinstimmung*) of subjectivity and objectivity in knowledge, both, subject and object, are already presupposed as separate, for only what is different can agree, what is not different is in itself one . . . . We say: nowhere is there a subject as a subject, or an object as an object, but it is rather only one and the same which knows and is known and which therefore is as little subjective as it is objective.
>
> (I/6 p. 138)

The rejection of representation is prophetic. Schelling's proximity to Heidegger here is apparent in Heidegger's remarks on his own *Being and Time* in recently published lectures from 1941:

'Truth' is not something which only arises via the coming together of a thinking subject with an object as a relationship and which is exhausted in the fact of this relationship of *adequatio*; rather the coming together of subject and object (and vice versa) is only possible in that which is already essentially disclosed/opened (*in einem in sich schon wesenden Offenen*), whose disclosure/openness (*Offenheit*) has an essential origin (*Wesensursprung*) which has still never been put in question by all philosophy until now.

(Heidegger 1991 p. 56)

It is plain from this that Schelling does begin to ask the sort of questions normally associated with Heidegger: the *Wesensursprung* is the Absolute in Schelling's particular sense. The crucial thought is that one cannot begin with difference and arrive at identity, unless what differs is already the same: without a ground of identity, which Heidegger understands in terms of 'disclosure', difference ceases even to be recognisable.[4] Something analogous might appear to apply to beginning with identity: how would identity know itself without splitting itself, without making itself different?

The crucial argument to be considered here is that the ground of such a split must be conceived of from the beginning in terms of 'absolute identity': what is revealed in the emergence of the thinking subject is, as Schelling suggested of Fichte, only ever finite difference. Such difference is inexplicable as finite difference if philosophy does not have some way of relating to the infinite (the meaning of which is very specific, as we shall see) in which it is grounded. Well before Heidegger, then, Schelling rejects all 'subjectifying' (*Subjektivieren*) (I/6 p. 142) of philosophy. Like Heidegger he rejects philosophy which operates from a division of subject and object and which leads to domination via the subject's one-sided attempt to overcome that division. He thereby shows ways towards the refutation of the conception of thought as representation.[5] As we saw in the last chapter, the notion of representation gives rise to all the insoluble problems involved in establishing a place from which it is possible to say how the mental representation relates to what it represents.

Schelling's first, thoroughly subversive, move beyond the subject is the following: 'It is not I that know, but rather only the totality (*All*) **knows** in me, if the knowledge which I call mine is a real, a true knowledge' (ibid. p. 140). Schelling makes a clear distinction between the empirical knowledge generated in synthetic judgements and 'knowledge' in terms of the Absolute. He later claims: 'The *I* think, *I* am,

61

is, since Descartes, the basic mistake of all knowledge (*Erkenntnis*); thinking is not my thinking, and being is not my being, for everything is only of God or of the totality' (I/7 p. 148). Real 'knowing' is, then, not what we arrive at in synthetic judgements. In arguing as he does here, Schelling evidently does not privilege the subject. Is the position, though, not just a grandiose tautology, in which the Absolute knows it is the Absolute? Schelling has, to be sure, no doubt that the question must initially be discussed in terms of the statement of identity: $A = A$. The statement and its reformulation are the basis of his rethinking of Kant's question about synthetic judgements which we considered earlier.

Schelling's first move is to deny that, in relation to the Absolute, $A = A$ expresses a relationship of subject to object or subject to predicate. $A = A$ is here, then, *not* just an expression of the most abstract synthetic judgement possible, which would be no more than a tautology:

> In this proposition one can, therefore, abstract from everything, from the reality of A at all, as well from its reality as subject and as predicate; but what absolutely cannot be abstracted from and what remains as the sole reality in this proposition is the *sameness* (*Gleichheit*) or *absolute identity* itself, which is accordingly the true substance of knowledge in this proposition . . . . The *sameness* (*Gleichheit*) does not exist via the subject and the object, but rather the other way round, only in so far as the sameness is, *i.e. only in so far as both are one and the same*, are subject and object as well.
>
> (I/6 p. 146–7)

There is, Schelling claims, a 'doubling of identity', in which the sameness of what is divided is only possible on the basis of a prior absolute identity. This can be explained by pondering the fact that the statement that two things are absolutely different is meaningless, in that if they are absolutely different they are not even two *things*, and the statement refutes itself. If I say that the subject is the predicate, what is on each side of the proposition can change: the same person can be angry and not be angry at different times. What cannot change is the ontologically prior fact that both subject and predicate are. The fact that they both are is the prior condition of their being identified with each other as whatever *kind* of being they may be. This sameness might appear suspiciously like the night in which all cows are black, but the argument does not entail such a result.

Schelling puts Leibniz's question in his own way when he confronts:

> that last question of the understanding which stands dizzily at the abyss of infinity, the question: why is there not nothing, why is there anything at all? This question is eternally banished by the knowledge that *being* necessarily is, i.e. by that absolute affirmation of being in knowledge.
>
> (I/6 p. 155)

The key terms are 'affirmation' and 'knowledge', but what do they mean? Manfred Frank suggests that Schelling conceives of being as the 'transitive relationship of a subject to its predicates' (Frank 1991 p. 141).[6] Instead of 'to be' functioning as an intransitive linking verb, in the Absolute, things are transitively 'been'. Sartre will later use the notion of *être été* to express this; in Schelling's terms, specific existents are 'affirmed'. You or I, as empirical knowing *subjects*, are, therefore, *predicates* of being. Our particular being as you or I, in which my identity is arrived at by my difference from you or all other yous, is 'affirmed' by a being which we cannot *know* as our own because that being cannot *depend* upon difference, which would be the condition of possibility of knowing it. To get to this being we must, therefore, go beyond reflexive knowledge, otherwise we fail to comprehend the way in which we are as everything else is, which is the condition of possibility of predication and truth. How, though, can we do this?

Schelling uses the Spinozist conception of determination by negation in a particular way in the *System*. The Absolute is '*the affirmer and the affirmed of itself*' (I/6 p. 148); it is because of itself, which is why it is absolute. Because it is immanent to itself, all the relations it encompasses *are* itself. The question as to the fact of being can only be answered by being itself, as a question about itself – hence the sense in the answer to the Leibnizian question, that being is there for itself. Being's answer to itself would appear to reintroduce reflexivity into the Absolute, and to lead to the threat of infinite regress: how does what addresses itself as something split from itself know that it is addressing *itself*? The fact is that this is impossible without it already being itself in an immediate fashion before the split. Schelling insists that in his conception of the Absolute 'All regression into infinity is cut off' (ibid. p. 165). The crucial distinction which prevents the regress is, then, between what is the immediate ground of itself, the Absolute, and what is not, the appearing world. Is this, though, not really another version of Kantian dualism?

The position is in fact strictly monist: the appearing world of differentiated nature and the Absolute are the same. How can this be? Schelling relies on a version of ontological difference, difference between 'being' (*Sein*) and 'beings' (*Seiendes*), of the kind associated with Heidegger, the beginnings of which we saw in Jacobi. *Sein*, at least for the early Heidegger of *Being and Time* and the *Basic Problems of Phenomenology*, is that which must already be disclosed before 'beings' can become objects of predication. Schelling puts this in Spinozist terms but the essential idea is the same:

> *Every single being is determined by another single being*, which in its turn is determined by another single being, and so on into infinity. For as a single being it is not determined *by itself*, because it does not have the ground of its being in itself. But it is just as little determined for existence by *God*; for in God lies only the ground of the totality and of being to the extent to which it is in the totality . . . the single being . . . can only be determined for existence by another single being; but the latter must, for the same reason, be determined again by another, and so on to infinity.

> (ibid. p. 194)

As such, what is generally known as true being, the appearing world of objects, is in fact the 'complete negation of *true* being' (ibid. p. 194): it involves what Hegel will term 'bad infinity', and Schelling in the *System* terms 'empirical infinity', an infinity of endless addition, which, unlike true infinity for German Idealism, is not bounded by itself.[7]

The result for Schelling is a reversal of Kant: instead of the only positive knowledge being of appearances, not of the essence, the only positive 'knowledge' — but here lies the crux — is precisely of the essence. Though everything finite is absolutely dependent upon everything else, and requires synthetic judgement to be determinate, the totality of these dependencies, the substance, is not dependent on anything and encloses all the dependencies as aspects of itself. The difference of thought and being is therefore always already overcome, in that it is only if they both already *are* that the question as to their identity can even be asked. Individual thoughts, like individual objects, are not self-grounding, but this means that they must relate to a higher identity, *given our awareness of their failure to ground themselves*.

Schelling puts this in a metaphor, which sees being precisely in terms of a disclosure which always transcends anything particular that is disclosed:

As the eye, when it sees itself in the reflection, e.g. in the mirror, *posits* itself, intuits itself, only to the extent that it posits what *reflects* – the mirror – as nothing for itself, and as it is, so to speak, One act of the eye, by which it posits itself, sees itself, and does not see what reflects, does not posit it; in this way does the totality (*All*) posit or intuit *itself*, by not-positing, not-intuiting the particular; both are One act in the totality.

(I/6 pp. 197–8)

It is this dual action that is the key to the argument. The account of this conception of being from 1806 makes the argument clearer:

for being, actual, real (*wirkliche*) being is precisely self-disclosure/ revelation (*Selbstoffenbarung*). If it is to be as One then it must disclose/reveal itself in itself; but it does not disclose/reveal itself if it is just itself, if it is not an other in itself, and is *in* this other the One for itself, thus if it is not absolutely the living link [*Band*, in the sense of copula] of itself and an other.

(I/7 p. 54)

One could say nothing about being merely in itself: the fact is that it is always already for itself, even as it is in itself: hence its self-affirmation.

Schelling turns the statement of identity A = A into A = B. His explanation of why is worth citing at some length:

The infinite = A is *as* the finite immediately also the finite = B; the expression of this absolute identity A = B. Beginning with B the chain now extends into infinity; the copula itself is not determined; but A cannot determinately = B, except to the extent to which it is also = C = D etc., into infinity. But it can also in this way not = B, i.e. be the finite, without in the same inseparable affirmation (*Bejahung*) also being the infinite, and thus being not only the affirmation (*Position*) of B but also the affirmation of this affirmation .... The difficulty that most people find in thinking the unity of the infinite and the finite, or in thinking that the former is immediately the latter, derives from their misunderstanding of absolute identity, and of the fact that they still imagine being as something different from the substance itself, and as something that really is distinguishable, even though it is precisely the substance itself .... It is evident that A, via the fact that it is the essence of B, i.e. *is* B, for this reason does not become the same (*gleich*) as just B, which everyone, paradoxical as it might seem to them, can try out with any old statement. E.g. the statement this body *is* red. Obviously the quality of the colour red is here what could not be for itself, but is now, via the identity with the subject, the *body*: it is what is predicated. To the extent to which what predicates, the body, is the *Esse* of this attribute, it really *is* this attribute (as the statement says); but it does not follow that the concept of the subject *body* is for that reason (logically) the same as the concept of the predicate *red*. Thus when we say: the substance is, *as* the latter, the finite, as A = B, then it really is this finite attribute and in fact nothing else, without it therefore logically being the *same* as the single thing (*Einzelheit*) (B) for itself.

(ibid. pp. 204–5)

The identity of A and B is not, then, a tautology, such as 'the Absolute is the Absolute', but a judgement that the Absolute, as what transitively constitutes all differences as the same, is the same as the totality of differences. Schelling's statement of identity requires the second term to disclose more than the first term, even as it states they are the same.

To make the admittedly rather difficult point even more emphatically, here is Frank's summary of Schelling's basic notion of identity, which takes up a later clarification from the *Ages of the World*, which we will see in the next chapter, by grounding the relationship of A and B in terms of a third term, X:

Schelling shows that the identity of subject and object may not be thought according to the model of their total lack of difference (or their being just the same) (as if A were *as* A and at the same time and in the same respect not-A, which would be absurd). That does not, he goes on, prevent the apparent subject of the judgement of identity A and the apparent predicate B both . . . turning out to be predicates of a subject = X, which is as much the same as itself as analytical truth or freedom from contradiction demands. Instead of saying that nature is mind (which would be absurd), one must rather say: there is an X (absolute identity, the copula, the link) and this X is on the one hand nature and on the other hand mind (these would be the predicates of X); but that does not mean that mind therefore is as such nature, or nature is as such and in the same respect mind.

(Frank 1990 p. 143–4)

In this way dualism is avoided, whilst the reflexive difference that is required for there to be knowledge can still be articulated.

One vital consequence of this way of seeing the finite world, that has also been implicit in many of the arguments seen so far (particularly those of the *Naturphilosophie*), is that scientific knowledge can only ever be relative. If particular scientific judgements were absolute, they would not say anything, because scientific knowledge would be a series of tautologies, analytical statements of identity, whereas, as Kant had shown, scientific knowledge is necessarily synthetic. The vital point, though, is that this relativity does not entail relativism, because it depends precisely upon a higher absolute principle for relativity to be comprehensible at all. It is the Absolute that explains the fact that knowledge continually changes. As such, it is only by showing the need for the Absolute that we avoid relativism, but in becoming aware of the Absolute via the failure of reflection we make all determinate knowledge relative. We do this, though, without giving up the pursuit of a better account of the world that is inherent in the attempt to say the truth. The notion of truth makes no sense if it is relative. Truth cannot be relative to untruth because the two are asymmetrical: the possibility of lying depends upon already knowing what it is to say the truth, which is inherent in the very act of assertion. This conception of identity and truth has consequences that are still with us in contemporary philosophy.

IDENTITY AND *'DIFFÉRANCE'*

Schelling's conception of identity offers the possibility of a better understanding of a series of concerns in contemporary European and analytical philosophy. It has, for example, become a shibboleth in certain theories that thinking in terms of identity is somehow repressive. Post-structuralism in particular has had a major impact in many disciplines because of its insistence on the dangers of 'identity thinking' (see Frank 1984; Dews 1987; A. Bowie 1990, 1993a). The concern with the supposed danger of identity thinking is, though, often based on philosophical misapprehensions, however much the ethical and political intention of avoiding repression of the Other may be justified. The suspicion of 'identity' derives from the idea that metaphysics necessarily leads to the violence of the general towards the particular, to the repression of the different Other by the Same. It is vital, though, to be clear about what is really in question here. Very often the debate about identity thinking has been reduced to a contest between Hegel and Nietzsche, between the *Aufhebung* of difference at the end of the dialectic and a conception of difference that refuses to resolve difference into identity. The question is both philosophically and historically more complex than this opposition would allow, in that it concerns the very assumptions upon which the debate about Western metaphysics depends. Schelling's role is vital in this respect. The fact is that he seems to qualify in certain ways as a post-metaphysical thinker, thereby rendering the demarcation between the metaphysical and the post-metaphysical more problematic than it has usually been thought to be.

For Jacques Derrida, as for Heidegger and Habermas, metaphysics is linked to the primacy of the subject.[8] The subject 'as consciousness has never been able to announce itself in any other way than as self-presence (*présence à soi*)'; the 'privilege' accorded to the subject as self-presence 'is the ether of metaphysics, the element of our thought to the extent to which it is caught in the language of metaphysics' (Derrida 1972 p. 17). This is already difficult to square with Schelling's statement cited above, that 'egoity is the general expression and highest principle of all *finitude*, i.e. of everything which is not *absolute totality*, absolute reality' (I/6 p. 124) . Schelling's language seems like the 'language of metaphysics',[9] but the core of the argument cannot be, in the terms Derrida has established, because the subject, as a predicate of 'transitive being', of necessity cannot be reflexively present to itself because it is preceded by an origin over which it has no control. In the light of the arguments seen above, Derrida's witnesses for the undermining of self-presence – Heidegger, Freud and Nietzsche – sound familiar in what they say about consciousness. Nietzsche, Derrida claims, sees consciousness as the 'effect of forces whose essence and whose ways and modes are not its own' (Derrida 1972 p. 18), which echoes Schelling's 'The *I* think, *I* am, is, since Descartes, the basic mistake of all knowledge (*Erkenntnis*); thinking is not my thinking, and being is not my being, for everything is only of God or of the totality'.[10] Nietzsche, as seen by Derrida, is actually in certain ways more metaphysical than Schelling. Consciousness for Nietzsche depends upon a force which 'itself is never present: it is only a play of differences and quantities. There would not be a force in general without the difference between the forces' (ibid.). The mechanistic vocabulary makes this in Schellingian terms simply a Spinozist version of the Absolute. Nietzsche's argument is in fact inferior to Schelling's. The notion of such a 'force in general' is, as the *Naturphilosophie* showed, problematic, because it is impossible to suggest that all is force: 'For we can only think of a force as something finite. But no force is finite in terms of its *nature* unless it is limited by an opposed force.

Hence, when we think of a force (as we do in matter), we must also think of an *opposed* force' (I/2 pp. 49–50). This meant it could not be claimed that the Absolute be understood as a force, which is a term that necessarily relies upon its other for it to be manifest at all, thereby rendering it invalid as a term for the totality. The further problem is that a mere opposition of forces is not sufficient to explain the subject's feeling of itself as itself, which requires an immediate moment prior to the opposing forces for them to be identified as constitutive of a subject.[11]

Derrida characterises Nietzsche's thinking in the following terms:[12]

Is not the whole thought of Nietzsche a critique of philosophy as active indifference to difference, as an adiaphoristic system of reduction or repression? Which does not exclude the fact that, according to the same logic, according to logic itself, philosophy lives *in* and *from différance*, blinding itself to the *same* which is not the identical. The same is precisely *différance* (with an *a*) as the detour and equivocal passage from one different element (*différent*) to the other. One could thus take up again all the oppositional couples upon which philosophy is built and from which our discourse lives in order, not to see opposition efface itself, but to see a necessity announce itself such that one of the terms appears as the *différance* of the other, as the other differed/ deferred (*différé*) in the economy of the same.

(Derrida 1972 p. 18)

This 'same', *différance*, plays the same role as the Absolute in Schelling, but entails a problem that Schelling avoids, as we shall see. Metaphysics for Derrida, then, is the attempt, via the subject, to make the absent present, make nature spirit, make finite infinite, make mind matter, or matter mind. The classic representative of this attempt is, of course, Hegel, whose system arrives at a point where negativity is revealed as what had to be overcome in order finally to arrive at the articulation of the Absolute. Derrida suggests that in Hegel: 'The concept as absolute subjectivity thinks itself, it is for itself and next to itself, it has no outside and collects up, whilst effacing them, its time and its difference into its self-presence' (ibid. p. 60). The crucial factor in Derrida's idea of metaphysics is the notion of reflexive self-presence, the *re*-cognition of the Other as ultimately the same. However, even in the identity philosophy Schelling tends not to fit Derrida's model of metaphysics. As such it is hard to draw epochal conclusions from what Derrida asserts about the history of metaphysics. What, though, of Derrida's central term in the attempt to circumvent metaphysics?

SCHELLING AND MODERN EUROPEAN PHILOSOPHY

Différance, which Derrida denies is either a word or a concept, is part of his strategy for avoiding enclosure in the totalising Hegelian 'economy' by the introduction of a temporality which indefinitely defers the return of the different into reflexive identity. Rodolphe Gasché claims:

> Derrida's philosophy, rather than being a philosophy of reflection, is engaged in the systematic exploration of that dull surface without which no reflection and no specular activity would be possible, but which at the same time has no place and no part in reflection's scintillating play.[13]
>
> (Gasché 1986 p. 6)

The idea should be familiar. As Schelling said above:[14]

> the eye, when it sees itself in the reflection, e.g. in the mirror, *posits* itself, intuits itself, only to the extent that it posits what *reflects* – the mirror – as nothing for itself, and . . . it is, so to speak, One act of the eye, by which it posits itself, sees itself, and does not see what reflects, does not posit it.
>
> (I/6 pp. 197–8)

Différance lives from the fact that we cannot identify being as the ground of appearances, because being can never be articulated as itself. Ontological difference means being can never be present as itself and is only manifest in beings. This means that it is actually hidden, leaving us with the question of our access to what is hidden.

Heidegger's sporadic temptation was to suggest *Sein* was once not hidden, and was then forgotten with the rise of objectifying thinking, of the metaphysics that begins with Parmenides' identity philosophy. Often, though, Heidegger talks of *Sein*'s dual nature as disclosed and hidden, which Derrida tends to ignore. Derrida claims:

> being never having had any 'meaning' (*sens*), having never been thought or said as such, except by hiding itself in beings, *différance* in a certain and very strange manner, [is] more 'old' than ontological difference and than the truth of being.
>
> (Derrida 1972 p. 23)

In Rorty's terms that we saw in the Introduction the signifier *Sein* is a metaphor: it does not have 'meaning' and Derrida suggests the same of *différance*. Because any use of the word cannot be finally understood by inference from its use in other sentences, it can be, and, of course, has been, regarded as devoid of meaning altogether.[15] Heidegger was

70

aware of the problem, which is suggested in his contention that *Sein* is always already both disclosed and hidden, and in his occasional use of the word under erasure. Ernst Tugendhat suggests that the basic (and highly problematic) meaning of *Sein* in Heidegger is the 'happening of clearing as such (*das . . . Lichtungsgeschehen als solches*)', the temporal disclosure (*Erschlossenheit*) which is the condition of possibility of the manifest world (Tugendhat 1970 p. 277).

Derrida's mistaken assumption is that previous metaphysics, even including Heidegger's understanding of *Sein*, had depended upon a notion of reflexive 'presence', which meant that philosophy wished to encircle difference – beings – in a totality of the same – being. Metaphysics depends, therefore, upon the elimination of 'metaphor' and the creation of 'meaning'.[16] *Différance*, which denies reflexive presence from the very beginning, is a strategic attempt to escape the encircling trap of identity by removing its ground. It is also a way of skirting the question why being is disclosed at all (the problem which will lead Schelling to his later philosophy) by suggesting it is always already *différé*.

There is not much alternative in this case to thinking that *différance* has the same *function* as the Absolute does in Schelling's identity philosophy.[17] The function of *différance* is to explain why the route to reflexive self-presence is blocked. This is also the function of Schelling's Absolute, which sees reflection as that which gives rise to finite knowledge, knowledge of 'products' rather than of 'productivity'. Though Derrida insists there can be no name for what *différance* is supposed to do or be, this insistence seems to derive from his realisation that if it did have a name it might as well be the Absolute. Any determinate answer to the question of *what* the Absolute is would, of course, introduce relativity. A thing is, as a thing, that which is not other things and can be identified in a predicative utterance: the Absolute is therefore not a thing.

The analogy to Schelling becomes further apparent when Derrida discusses the differential nature of the sign (and, by necessary extension, given Derrida's exclusion of self-consciousness from the understanding of meaning, of any existent). In doing so he uses the Spinoza–Saussure notion of determination as negation in his own temporalised and spatialised manner, which echoes the way Schelling characterises the world of particularity by dynamising Spinozist categories:

> *Différance* is what makes the movement of signification possible only if each element called 'present' . . . is related to something

71

other than itself, retaining in itself the mark of the past element
and already letting itself be hollowed out by the mark of its
relationship to the future element, the trace not relating any less
to what one calls the future than to what one calls the past by this
very relationship to what is not it . . . . An interval must separate
it from what it is not for it to be itself . . . as this interval
constitutes, divides itself dynamically, it is what one can call
spatialisation, becoming-space of time or becoming-time of space
(*temporisation*).

(Derrida 1972 p 13)

Now compare Schelling's conception of space and time (where
'absolutely true' can be understood as 'self-present'): 'Space and time
are two relative negations of each other: in neither, then, can there be
anything absolutely true; rather, what is true in each is precisely that
via which it negates the other' (I/2 p. 368); and, perhaps most
strikingly, his understanding of space in the *System*:

As opposed to life in the totality, particular life can only appear as an
endless disintegration into difference – without identity – *as endless
non-identity, pure extension.* For the inner identity is negated by
the relation of the positions to each other. But this is the
affirmative [i.e. the *Band*, transitive being]. Accordingly, the
particular life of things, as opposed to life in the infinite
substance, i.e. the being-affirmed of things separated from infinite
affirmation, from identity, can only appear as endless difference,
as complete privation of identity, accordingly as a powerless
disintegration, as *pure extension.*

(I/6 p. 219)

If one subtracts the transitive sense of the *Band*, which always subtends
Schelling's conception of difference, the logic of the rest of this passage
is strictly analogous to the spatialised and temporalised conception of
meaning that results from Derrida's accounts of *différance*.

Subtracting the ground of identity leads, though, to problems. If
something is to be *deferred*, it must happen in some way or other:
deferral is not abolition. The fact is that if meaning is always deferred
because there cannot be self-presence, there can be no meaning at all,
merely the 'mediation of signs by other signs' (Dews 1987 p. 30), a
disintegration of sense into indeterminate indifference, into mere
spatiality (cf. A. Bowie 1990 pp. 109–12). The assumption in Derrida
seems to be that 'meaning' must entail the transmission by a sender of
an original content to a receiver: if what is transferred is not intact as

itself, there can be no 'meaning' because the content is not present to the receiver. It is always already *différé*, having lost its 'presence' by being temporalised and spatialised in the signifying chain. The apocalyptic consequences Derrida sometimes draws from this position, which lead him as far as the putative end of Western metaphysics, seem somehow out of proportion to what is at issue. In Schellingian terms the Absolute is the process within which meaning is differentially constituted, but this very constitution means that everything is relative to the infinite context: 'no single being has the ground of its being in itself'. This puts no limit on difference at this level whatsoever; indeed it can, if one subtracts the ground of identity, lead merely to 'powerless disintegration', which is what seems to happen in Derrida. Schelling, of course, does not make the further move that makes Derrida's position incoherent.

Both at the level of the differentiation of the sign and at the level of the differentiation of the world, difference can only make sense via prior identity. The fact Derrida seems to ignore, as Frank has repeatedly shown, is that the existence of series of differing marks anywhere in the world is not sufficient to explain even the most primitive linguistic phenomena.[18] Without that which is capable of interpreting them, differing marks do not *mean* anything: they depend for their meaning upon what links them together, and thus makes them of the same order as each other, as meaningful marks (on this, see Frank 1984 p. 356, and my review essay: A. Bowie 1985). Schelling sees these kinds of difference as non-being, but only as relative non-being, dependent being – what F.H. Bradley later termed the 'unreality' of any 'relation' when it is considered in terms of the totality. At this level there can be no self-presence, thus no absolute knowledge of what a thing is, no 'meaning' in the metaphysical sense. The *prior* ground of relational identity is not something *known*, but nor is it relative: it has to *be* as the link between what differs (which is also itself). Derrida keeps the sense of dependence but thinks it can be explicated negatively without it having to *be* in any positive sense. As Frank suggests, this brings him close to Hegel, because he sees all differentiation as negation without a positive substrate (see Frank 1989a pp. 446–70, and Chapter 6 below). The moves Derrida makes are, then, already part of the history of metaphysics, but he tries to avoid the consequences of the position he establishes by changing absolute identity into *différance*.

In both Schelling and Derrida reflexive identity is revealed to be dependent upon that which robs it of any *knowable* ground, and thus robs it of self-presence. In Schelling this is because absolute identity prevents the particular from being in an absolute way: 'the totality posits or intuits *itself*, by not-positing, not-intuiting the particular' (I/6 p. 198). This is the basis of temporality: 'time is itself nothing but *the totality appearing in opposition to the particular life of things*' (ibid. p. 220). In Derrida *différance*, as what always already (is), renders self-presence impossible. It prevents a return to a ground because that 'ground' is always already split, and, as such, is not a ground in any meaningful sense at all. Schelling's point, though, is that without some underlying absolute identity of all differences predication becomes impossible. If the relative differences are not transitively predicated by the Same, they cannot even *be* differences, because there would be no criterion of difference and the differences could not even be in the relative way that they are.[19]

Schelling's insistence on the *Band*, the transitive copula, is vital, therefore, because it reveals the crucial failure of Derrida's position. Habermas claims: 'Whenever the One is thought of as absolute negativity, as withdrawal and absence, as resistance against all propositional articulation (*Rede*) the ground (*Grund*) of rationality reveals itself as an abyss (*Abgrund*) of the irrational' (Habermas 1988 p. 160). This seems apt in relation to Derrida's *différance*, but fails to take into account how Schelling theorises the ground of rationality as propositionally inarticulable whilst at the same time sustaining a theory of propositionality and reason. The alternative to Schelling's position must therefore, one presumes, make the ground itself rational. This leads of necessity to Hegel, whose conception Schelling will reveal as untenable. Given the evident Hegelian aspects of Habermas's thinking, it can be suggested that Schelling's critique may also be able to suggest ways in which Habermas fails to come to terms with that which cannot be propositionally articulated. I shall briefly consider this question in the Conclusion.

The dizzying aspect of *différance*'s undermining of meaning as 'presence' is a result of taking that aspect of language which leads via its differential constitution into infinity – the semiotic aspect – and ignoring the fact that meaning is constituted at the level of propositions, thus at the level of identity (on this, see Ricoeur 1986 p. 130; Frank 1992a pp. 220–7). It is the structure of 'something as something' that underlies all predicative statements. As Frank puts it: 'The world is not the totality of objects, but rather of what can be established in statements about these objects: the totality of states of affairs' (Frank 1992a p. 220). States of affairs require a ground of identity for their constitution. There is no doubt that one can show that semiotic differentiation cannot be foreclosed: that much is inherent in any moving relational structure, where a shift of one element affects the relations of all the other elements. The supposedly devastating effect of this fact on signification relies, however, on forgetting the way in which the structure of identity that makes meaning possible at all is constituted at the level of propositions, not of signifiers.

This does *not* mean that we therefore have a metaphysically guaranteed semantics: the whole point about the identity necessary for propositions is that it cannot itself be analysed, in that it is the very medium of analysis itself.[20] The identity which grounds propositions cannot itself be said, but must be presupposed: otherwise one cannot even question identity of meaning via such a term as *différance*. If, as Heidegger saw, what is being sought – truth, including the truth about meaning conveyed by *différance* – is not *already* understood in some way, there is no other way that the truth can later be understood in terms of the reflexive or representational relationship between a proposition and a state of affairs, let alone in terms of the chain of signifiers. Without the subject which already *understands* the relationship of the linguistic event to what it *means* there can be no meaning at all, and therefore no question about the subversion of the idea of meaning as presence. If meaning is constituted in the process of communication, and is therefore always revisable, because we can always misunderstand what the other is saying, it is open to the sort of endless transformation with which Derrida is concerned. Once one stops thinking, though, as much modern philosophy has, that language re-presents a pre-existing truth, this is not a devastating insight and does not mean we need to take on the idea of *différance* and the attendant deconstructive baggage. Schelling's identity theory points the way to this non-representational conception in ways which are often more convincing than Derrida's notion of *différance*.

SCHELLING, RORTY AND DAVIDSON

Schelling thinks he has found a way of being a monist without ending up as a static reductionist; in *différance* Derrida wants the advantages of monism – particularly the undermining of dualisms – without having to say that he adheres to it as a metaphysical doctrine. The radically divergent interpretations of Derrida, in which he is seen as a transcendental philosopher, a materialist, or something else that no one seems able to specify, are a result of this equivocation. The implications of these questions about identity are evidently not confined to post-structuralism. Richard Rorty identifies the underlying problem in his discussion of Derrida's ambiguity with regard to whether *différance*, as Rodolphe Gasché suggests, is a 'condition of possibility'. The problem is the ancient one of how monism can even be stated, which leads to another version of the problem of self-reference we considered when looking at the *STI*. Rorty says of most Western philosophers that 'they are continually tempted to say, 'The conditions making an expression intelligible are . . . ,' despite the fact that the proposition itself does not fulfil the conditions it lists' (Rorty 1991b p. 91): his claim is that *différance* plays this role in Derrida. To make the proposition fulfil its own conditions Rorty thinks one would need a closed metaphysical vocabulary, which, as the post-Kantian thinkers realised, means some version of the statement of identity, of A = A.

Even this, though – and this is basically what Derrida has noticed – splits what is supposed to be One, albeit in the attempt to reveal it as One. As we saw Novalis saying in 1795–6: 'we leave the *identical* in order to represent it' (quoted in A. Bowie 1990 p. 73). We therefore cannot *represent* it as the identical which we left. This is the key realisation of Romantic philosophy, which led Schelling in the *STI* to suggest that only art can reveal the Absolute. In the *System* Schelling sometimes equivocates over this problem: Hegel will, as we shall see, come to think that you ultimately can represent the identical as the identical. Rorty suggests:

> Philosophy . . . has to aim at some statement of the form 'No linguistic expression is intelligible unless . . . ' Further, this statement must be part of a vocabulary which is *closed*, in the sense that the statement is applicable to itself without paradox. Not only must a philosophical vocabulary be *total* . . . but it must speak of *itself* with the same 'assured legibility' as it does of everything else.
>
> (Rorty 1991b p. 92)

He thinks that, at his best, Derrida has stopped wanting to be a philosopher, by which he means talking, however disguisedly, such as under the name of *différance*, about the Absolute as the condition of possibility of predication.

Rorty regards ceasing to be a philosopher as a desirable move. Significantly, he connects this to the need to open up a pluralism of vocabularies, as opposed to seeking one true vocabulary. Rorty bases his position on the model of the understanding of literature and art that develops in the modern period, beginning, one should add, with the Romantics, including the Schelling of the *STI*. He wants to move away from the search for any kind of ground in the direction of the free play of different vocabularies. Rorty makes the Wittgensteinian claim, against Gasché's 'philosophical' insistence upon the 'the presupposition of ontological or formal identity of being and thought', that:

> the very idea of a 'ground' for 'propositional articulation' is a mistake. The practice of playing off sentences against one another in order to decide what to believe – the practice of argumentation – no more requires a 'ground' than the practice of using one stone to chip pieces off another stone in order to make a spear point.
>
> (ibid. p. 125)

In the light of Rorty's remarks, then, it seems we should forget the Absolute, the 'ground', and, with it, any problems of metaphysics. Are we, though, not permitted to think – non-theologically, and by staying with Rorty's metaphor – about who or what is holding the stones that are being chipped and is doing the chipping, or about what they are standing on? Put another way: is there no way of relating propositional articulation to any non-linguistic conception of the disclosedness of the world (such as in pre-reflexive self-consciousness), without ending up with a theory of representation or adequation, or without invalidly conflating 'argument' and 'disclosure'? Does Rorty *really* believe concepts are *just* 'the regular use of a mark or noise' (ibid. p. 126), and is there no alternative to thinking what they are, apart from the admittedly untenable idea that they are mental re-presentations of objects? The important fact that makes one sceptical about Rorty's position is that Rorty himself actually does retain a ground, in that he, albeit somewhat inconsistently, advocates a form of physicalism, which involves a questionable ontological commitment of the kind he criticises in others.

Schelling's idea is that we need to think about the nature in which we are grounded, and not think of it merely as an object of knowledge: nature must be conceived of organically, with ourselves as part of it. Out of nature's 'real' material differentiation an 'ideal' form of differentiation emerges: the difference between the two is, though, only ever relative to their both being identical in the sense we have seen. This might sound just like the sort of thing Rorty would treat with anti-metaphysical contempt. The way Schelling puts these issues, though, offers the possibility of an answer to the standard Rortyan objection that in any attempt to talk of grounds we are being offered another version of representational – or 'identity' – thinking, a version of trying to get the relationship between scheme and content, thought and nature, knowledge and its ground 'right'. Rorty is right to be suspicious of epistemological foundationalism, which is based on the impossible task of trying to get beyond such distinctions to a firm *knowledge* of how the two sides of the distinction relate. Schelling, though, simply does not hold to such distinctions, for the reasons we have seen. As he said in the *STI*:

> The question how our concepts agree with objects is meaningless from a transcendental perspective, to the extent that the question presupposes an original difference of the two. The object and its concept, and, conversely, concept and object are one and the same beyond consciousness, and the separation of the two only arises simultaneously when consciousness arises. A philosophy which begins with consciousness will therefore never be able to explain that agreement, nor can it be explained at all without original identity, whose principle necessarily lies beyond consciousness.
>
> (I/3 p. 506)

This clearly excludes a model of representation.[21] The fact that Schelling will end up in a position in some ways closer to Rorty's hero Davidson than Rorty himself occupies makes it worth pondering if Schelling's arguments might not yet lead in new directions. The suspicion, in the light of growing ecological disaster, that now falls on the dominant conceptions of nature in Western philosophy since Descartes makes more sense in Schelling's perspective than in Rorty's. From Rorty's perspective any attempt to talk about nature in itself is doomed to failure. It is for this reason that Schelling's version of identity theory can lead to a more emphatic approach to contemporary fears about the destruction of nature than Rorty's position allows.

When Schelling explicates identity it is, as should now be evident, not a question of sameness, of reflexive self-identification, or of adequate representation. Schelling's identity is a version of the 'identity of identity and difference', in which thinking and being, subject and nature, are both different and the same. Moreover, they are this, *pace* Rorty, without paradox. Schelling's point was that identity, as an ontological question, is not to be conflated with logical non-contradiction: as we saw, it is not a tautological relationship.

Identification means the acquisition of knowledge, synthesis, not analytical sameness: this is evident, for example, in becoming able, after a long period of history, to identify Venus as being both the morning star and the evening star, as Frank suggests of Frege's famous example. Being able to be identical means being able to be different: if this were not the case there would be no need to identify things at all, they would always already be the same and we would be in the night in which all cows are black, 'knowing' everything and nothing. There must also, however, be a sense in which what is different is already the same: otherwise it could not be identified, or revealed as different. This question becomes central in the relationship of the 'mental' to the 'physical'. From what has been said so far it is evident that the mental and the physical are irreducible to each other, are different, but that their difference is relative to the fact that they both are, and are thus the same. The crucial question is how they are the same.

Both Frank and Rorty cite Donald Davidson's theory of 'anomalous monism' as evidence for their case: Frank to justify continuing with a version of Schellingian metaphysics, Rorty as a way of being a 'non-reductive physicalist'. Davidson admits he is committed to

> one important, and, indeed metaphysical thesis. If psychological events cause and are caused by physical events (and surely this is the case) and if causal relations between events entail the existence of laws connecting those events, and these laws are . . . physical, then it must follow that psychological events simply are (in the sense of *are identical with*) physical events. If this is materialism, we are committed to it.
>
> (Davidson 1980 p. 248)

Rorty coopts Davidson as a fellow 'physicalist', and he has some grounds for doing so. The last 'if' suggests, though, that Davidson is actually more circumspect. The reasons for his circumspection bring him very close to Schelling. Like Schelling, Davidson does not adhere to a materialist determinism, in that he does not think there is any possibility of psychophysical laws: 'Anomalous monism resembles materialism in its claim that all events are physical, but rejects the thesis, usually considered essential to materialism, that mental phenomena can be given purely physical explanations' (ibid. p. 214). The physical realm has to be thought of in terms of causal laws, and if mental events cause physical events, they must therefore be physical events, but 'no purely physical predicate, no matter how complex, has, as a matter of law, the same extension as a mental predicate' (ibid.

p. 215). Though we may be certain that there can be no mental events without physical events in the brain, these events cannot be used to predict what a future mental event will be. Causality in the physical realm cannot, then, be used to explain intentional behaviour based on beliefs, so 'psychological concepts have an autonomy relative to the physical with a monistic ontology and a causal analysis of action' (ibid. p. 240). Davidson sees his position as Kantian: it is in many ways closer to Schelling.

Schelling makes the same point as Davidson when he says:

> Between real and ideal, being and thinking no causal connection is possible, *for thinking can never be cause of a determination in being, or on the other hand being can never be cause of a determination in thinking*. For real and ideal are only different views [Davidson would say 'physical' and 'mental' are only different 'descriptions'] of one and the same substance.
>
> (I/6 pp. 500–1)

Rather than reducing the two sides of the identity theory to one of its sides, the physical, as Rorty, despite his claims not to be a reductionist,[22] often does, Schelling insists that the identity has to be understood as the link of the two sides, which cannot be characterised in terms of one of the sides. We are led, therefore, to a notion of substance of the kind Rorty wants to get rid of because he thinks it necessarily raises the problem of how the differing attributes relate to the same substance. In a later piece Davidson himself, though, makes the Schellingian move, when he says: 'I see no good reason for calling identity theories "materialist": if some mental events are physical events, this makes them no more physical than mental. Identity is a symmetrical relation' (cited in Frank 1991 p. 123). Rorty equivocates on this issue, when he says that beliefs and desires:

> are, to be sure, physiological states under another description (though in order to preserve the ontological neutrality characteristic of a non-reductionist view, we must add that certain 'neural' descriptions are of psychological states under a 'physical' description).
>
> (Rorty 1991a p. 121)

Once one has said this, though, one is bound to say something about the identity of the states that is presupposed by Rorty's remarks, which is precisely what we saw Rorty denying was necessary.

Here is the central passage from Schelling, echoing aspects of the *Naturphilosophie*, which suggests why a materialist conception cannot adequately characterise these states, and therefore sustains the arguments about monism in a way Rorty thinks we ought to have left behind:

> *Everything that also seems to develop via freedom in the ideal world* is already potentially in matter; matter can therefore not be the dead purely real essence that it is taken for [in materialism]; it is, as real substance, at the same time ideal and comprehends what the latter comprehends. Extended and thinking substance, as Spinoza puts it, are not two different substances, rather the extended substance is also itself the thinking substance, as the thinking is the extended. Whatever can develop out of the abyss of matter and nature is therefore just as indeterminably infinite as what can develop out of the soul. For every evolution of the soul is necessarily paralleled by an evolution of matter . . . the action of our soul as action is not our action, but an action of the substance.
>
> (I/6 pp. 549–50)

It is not, note, the action of matter. Whereas Rorty often assumes that 'events' are, in the last analysis, physical, both Davidson and Schelling regard this as a one-sided reduction, which is really, despite all, a version of an untenable metaphysical materialism.

Contemporary physicalism tends to assume some kind of identity theory, not least because the theory offers one route out of representational thinking based on a mind–subject and a world–object. Physicalism is, of course, itself the contemporary form of Spinozism. Schelling, as we have seen, is very concerned to avoid the reduction involved in Spinoza's world of conditioned conditions. His identity philosophy is significant because it suggests a way out of the problems that emerge in the attempt to state a physicalist conception of the mental and the physical. It is, as we have seen, no good in Schelling's terms just assuming the mind–subject is actually a world–object. This fails to explain the fact that the world–object is able to become a mind–subject, which is the problem shown by Fichte. If all is matter, then there can be no concept of matter, because we lack any way of *conceiving* of matter at all. Physicalism – reductive or non-reductive – assumes that mental events are in the last analysis physical events, but this actually obviates so much that it becomes hard to understand what it means. If matter has to know itself *as* matter, it needs a criterion to distinguish matter from the all-consuming One about which nothing can be said, that Rorty sees as the necessary result of metaphysics. To be able to assert that mental events are 'really' physical events requires a further ground, that cannot be reduced to either, which is necessary to prevent the assertion just meaning that everything is everything. The point of Schelling's identity theory was to show the necessity of this ground. He thereby shows the impossibility of a coherent version of Spinozism and his arguments also apply to the re-emergence of Spinozism in contemporary physicalism.

The fact is that physicalism is stuck in the problem of reflection that we have repeatedly encountered: maintaining that the mental is really the physical requires that which establishes their identity, which cannot be just one of the two, and must be *prior to* their difference. If this is right, then the position that results cannot be physicalist. Schelling has no desire to underplay the material aspect of nature, but he refuses to be a reductionist about matter. His way round the physicalist problem is the conception of identity in which the difference of mental and physical is grounded in a necessary prior identity. Without this identity one ends up with the impossible problem of overcoming a prior difference (and, indeed, of even knowing it is a difference, which itself requires identity). This does not mean that, having assumed this identity, one can thereafter adopt physicalist modes of explanation, because there is no *causal* relationship between the two aspects of the 'substance'. In this view matter itself must always already be both real and ideal: this cannot be explained causally because the very possibility of *understanding* things causally is not reducible to causality: the causal realm of the physical brain and the mental events of the subject that establishes causal links cannot *be* without each other, and are therefore identical in Schelling's sense, but they are not reducible to each other. For Schelling the 'ideal' and the 'real' are opposed to each other, and absolute in their own terms, in that they cannot affect each other causally, 'and yet each cannot be without the other' (I/6 p. 407). As such, nature itself is the absolute subject, in the sense that the thinking that develops within it is also itself. The thinking subject is identical (in the sense we have seen) with the nature it comes to objectify in cognitive judgements. There is no justification for saying that it is 'really' either 'real' or 'ideal'. Rather it is, in Schelling's terms, the dynamic connection of the two.

ABSOLUTE REFLECTION

How close, then, is Schelling to the idea soon to be explicated by Hegel – which was the prime target of Derrida's objections to identity

philosophy and, by implication, of Rorty's arguments against metaphysical monism — that nature is the other of mind, because the
Absolute is to be understood as the 'other of itself'? There is no simple
answer to this question. As Manfred Frank points out, there is a tension
in Schelling's position in the *System*, between a Romantic position of
the kind we saw in the *STI* and in the analysis of the key thought of the
System, and a version of absolute idealism of the kind Hegel was to
develop in his system. This tension lies in the question whether the
identity of the 'ideal' and the 'real' can be explicated, without already
relying on the inarticulable ground of their identity that Jacobi and
Hölderlin termed 'being'. Frank says of the identity philosophy:

> On the one hand pure identity is moved to a space beyond the
> ideal (the ideal, that which knows, is only one relatum next to the
> real); to the extent to which this is so one can see Hölderlin's
> construction, according to which absolute being cannot be
> deduced from reflection, also shining through Schelling's identity
> philosophy. On the other hand it claims to be able to carry out a
> 'proof . . . that there is a point where knowledge of the Absolute
> and the Absolute itself are one' [I/4 pp. 361 ff.].
>
> (Frank 1989b p. 200)

The second position is where the Schelling of the identity philosophy
and Hegel at times converge. Once one realises the negativity of all
particular knowledge the route to knowledge of the Absolute seems
open. The result is a 'doubling of identity' where 'The real totality is
posited by God's affirming Himself in an infinite manner, the ideal,
though, by the fact that His affirmation is itself affirmed again' (I/6
p. 204). Thinking, properly understood, is an articulated reflex of the
Absolute, and, above all, can *know* itself as such:

> with all knowledge (*Wissen*), apart from the fact that it is a real
> cognition (*Erkennen*) [i.e. what happens in our knowing would
> not happen if in nature that which we can know were not in
> being], the concept of this knowledge is also connected; whoever
> knows also knows immediately that he knows, and this knowing
> of his knowing is one with and immediately connected with the
> first knowledge, all regress into infinity is cut off, for the concept
> of knowledge which is connected with knowledge, which is the
> principle of consciousness, is in and for itself the infinite itself.
>
> (I/4 p. 290)

Schelling terms this an 'identity of identity': 'the sameness of the
subjective and the objective is made the same as itself, knows itself, and

is the subject and object of itself' (I/6 p. 173). Because consciousness knows itself immediately in intellectual intuition, and because what knows itself 'affirms' itself, 'is' in the way everything else is, it can ascend to the notion of the self-affirming totality of all that there is, because the structure of self-affirmation is doubled by its own structure. Epistemology and ontology mirror each other in the overall structure of the Absolute, thereby 'sublating' their difference. As the finite determinations of knowledge reveal what can be variously seen as their finitude, their negativity, their relative status, their not-being, their dependence upon other beings for being what they are, they necessarily lead to the Absolute in which they are grounded. The real question is how this Absolute can be presented in philosophy, which is what is at issue between Schelling and Hegel in the years following 1801.

The future of modern philosophy lies in the implications of this conflict. For the time being we need a schematic outline of the difference between Schelling and Hegel at the stage of the identity philosophy, in order that the significance of the later differences can become clear. We saw the basic point at the beginning of this chapter: Schelling often sees being as 'transreflexive', in the manner we saw in Hölderlin, which Schelling develops in the best arguments of the identity philosophy, whereas Hegel sees it as a 'self-reflexive' totality. Both regard the negativity of the finite as what leads to the infinite, but there is a major difference between them, whose consequences will only really become explicit more than twenty years later. Hegel's objection to Schelling was that he began with a ground that was presupposed rather than articulated. Dieter Henrich makes Hegel's position explicit when he suggests that, in the wake of Schelling, Hegel realised:

> The finite cannot be something radically different from the Absolute. Schelling had for that reason given it the attribute of relative independence, because only in this way did it also correspond in itself to the characteristic of absoluteness. This independence was immediately to be negated (*aufzuheben*). And as this could again only follow internally, Hegel concluded that the Absolute is present in the finite as its own negation by itself. This thought could only be sustained, though, if one could again say, and in a new sense, that the finite is the Absolute and thus the Absolute is also the finite. The Absolute is the finite to the

extent to which the finite is *nothing at all but* negative relation to itself [my emphasis].

(Henrich 1982 pp. 159–60)

The sense in which Hegel's position is 'reflexive' becomes clear when Henrich says of Hegel's conception of the Absolute: 'The Absolute relates *itself* to its Other *as* to itself' (ibid. p. 166), where this relationship to the Other is a cognitive relationship to itself (hence the 'as'). Clearly this is a statement of the 'identity of identity and difference' of the kind we have already seen in Schelling. Where is the great divide?

The key point is again that if the Absolute really is able to relate to the Other as to itself, it would already have to know that the Other *is* itself, *before* the reflexive relationship: I can only see *myself* in a mirror, as opposed to an object which may or may not be me, if I am *already* familiar with myself. This entails a necessary ground which *precedes* any movement of reflection, without which, as was evident in relation to Derrida, difference could not even be known as difference. For Hegel knowledge of the Absolute can only finally be reached at the end of the process, when the relative negations are revealed as the structure of the process which is the Absolute. All finite differences are the Absolute because they are always relative: they are all negative in relation to each other, and result in the (positive) Absolute, as the other of themselves (as negative). The process of overcoming is the Absolute which, so to speak, draws up all the finite negations in a movement towards itself. Schelling's position in the identity philosophy only gives a hint of the problem, and Hegel, of course, has yet to publish his position in this form, let alone in its fully developed version in the *Logic* and the rest of the System, but the potential for revealing the problem is already there.

The key question is how the finite can be *nothing* but 'negative relation to itself'. Frank again:

Negating a not-being (refusing it any being) does not mean: providing it with being. If we encounter a being (*Seiendes*) in the finite world then it is the being of the Absolute. Put another way: if finite being is not wholly and in every respect deprived of being this is because it partakes as such and in its finitude of the Absolute. This minimum of being, without which the finite could not even exist (*dasein*) as finite, is something which is, so to speak, borrowed from the Absolute.

(Frank 1985 p. 127)

Schelling had made this point with regard to the relationship of Fichte's I and not-I, which resulted in the 'striving' for the Absolute expressed in practical reason. This, however, makes the Absolute a postulate: I and not-I are relative negations of each other, so that we are caught in a circle 'inside which a nothing gains reality by the relation to another nothing' (I/4 p. 358). Only if this structure is itself regarded as 'nothing' (i.e. as a relation of dependence, where neither term can be absolute) are we able to understand the need for a positive absolute unity which is the real ground of the reflexive relationship of I and not-I, the relationship within which particular knowledge is articulated. Schelling makes a crucial distinction between the cognitive – reflexive – ground of finite knowledge and the real – non-reflexive – ground that sustains the movement of negation from one finite determination to another. This movement could not be sustained by negation itself:

> reflection . . . only knows the universal and the particular as two relative negations, the universal as relative negation of the particular, which is, as such, without reality, the particular, on the other hand, as a relative negation of the universal. From this standpoint the universal concept therefore appears as completely empty; from the concept of substance, for example, one can never understand *real* substance, something independent of the concept must be added to posit the substance as such.
>
> (I/6 p. 185)

The abstract determinations of thought cannot create their own reality out of themselves: the self-cancelling relations between them have to *be* in a way that thought cannot itself bring about.

What is at issue is, then, in the later terms of Hegel's *Logic*, whether even being, as merely the beginning of the process, is really nothing. Or, in the terms of the later Schelling: is the concept of being real being? For Schelling the ground of finite beings is a being which cannot be *said* to be their own, in that they are negated within it, but which they must also be to be real in any sense at all. Can it, though, as it is in Hegel, be yet another kind of non-being whose real being only emerges at the end of the process? Both Schelling and Hegel are confronted with the question of the transition from the Absolute to the world of finitude because they agree, though not for the same reasons, that finitude, relativity, leads one to the need for the Absolute. In Hegel's terms one can articulate a position which avoids such a transition: thinking is always already in a reflexive relationship to the

Absolute as the Other of itself, as what leads from one finite determination to another, but which is only fully 'for itself', 'self-present' at the end. The finite is therefore actually the infinite, without any transition. Schelling is uneasy about the relationship of finite and infinite, which is why he will become so important for key thinkers after him. Heidegger sees the essential tension that develops in the next period of Schelling's philosophy as between 'freedom [the infinite], as the beginning which needs no grounding [i.e. which is itself the 'ungrounded' ground], and system, as a closed context of grounding/justification (*Begründungszusammenhang*)' (Heidegger 1971 p. 75). This tension begins to show even before the 1809 *On the Essence of Human Freedom*.

THE PROBLEM OF TRANSITION

Two texts of 1804, the *System*, and *Philosophy and Religion*, present opposing views, that suggest what is at issue in Schelling's later philosophy. At the point of transition from the *Naturphilosophie* to the 'ideal' world in the *System* Schelling says that the whole of philosophy is *Naturphilosophie*. One should, therefore, 'not think any hiatus in the transition [from 'real' to 'ideal'] which we shall now make, but rather complete constancy' (I/6 p. 494). Apart from the insistence that this philosophy is *Naturphilosophie* (which in Hegel would be a philosophy of *Geist*) this position largely accords with Hegel: 'ideal' and 'real' are the other of each other, and they do not at this level require a further ground from which their relationship emerges, so there is no need for a transition.

This symmetrical conception, which is almost definitive of what Heidegger and Derrida mean by metaphysics, starts to dissolve for Schelling even in 1804.[23] *Philosophy and Religion* locates the problem at an 'earlier' stage, and introduces a problem which will concern Schelling repeatedly from now on:

> there is no constant transition from the Absolute to the real, the origin of the world of the senses can only be thought as a complete breaking off from absoluteness, by a leap. If philosophy is to deduce the origin of real things in a positive manner from the Absolute, then there would have to be a positive ground in the Absolute .... Philosophy only has a negative relationship to things that appear, it rather proves that they are not than that they are .... The Absolute is all that is real: finite things, on the other hand, are not real; their ground cannot lie in a

87

communication of reality to them or to their substrate, which would have emanated from the Absolute, it can only lie in a *move away*, in a *fall* (*Abfall*) from the Absolute.

(I/6 p. 38)

In the *System* privations and imperfections in the finite, temporal world are seen as merely the result of our temporary failure to comprehend the ultimate infinite unity from which finitude has emerged: 'The finitude in the own being of things is a fall away from God, but a fall away which immediately becomes reconciliation' (I/6 p. 566). This raises a major problem: if the 'fall' from the Absolute is real, there can be no final way of re-establishing the relationship to the Absolute because to do so would mean, as the *System* tries to show, that the relationship was actually always already established, despite its now appearing not to be. However, even to suggest such a fall means that there must be a way in which philosophy has access to a preceding unity. That access, though, can no longer hope to be articulated. The *STI* suggested one approach to this problem by having recourse to the symbolic means available in art: Schelling's later philosophy will repeatedly come up against the problem that access to the Absolute cannot be gained within philosophical reflection.

Schelling's formulations of his view in *Philosophy and Religion* are extreme in a way which will become familiar in his work from the 1809 *On the Essence of Human Freedom* onwards. He now suggests, and thereby already hints at the core of his later philosophy, that:

> the origin of no finite thing leads immediately back to the infinite, it can instead only be grasped via the sequence of causes and effects, which is, though itself endless, whose law has, therefore, not a positive but a merely negative meaning, *that, namely, nothing finite can arise immediately out of the Absolute and be deduced from it.* Whence already in this law the ground of the being of finite things is expressed as an absolute breaking off from the infinite.

(I/6 p. 41)

The target of this is primarily Fichte's I, as we saw it characterised in the *Propaedeutic of Philosophy*. Now this I is effectively the principle of the Fall, the finite world as separated from the Absolute. Schelling next makes a prophetic distinction, between a 'negative' and a 'positive' philosophy. Philosophy which is concerned with explicating the structure of the finite world can result only in a 'negative philosophy, but much has already been gained by the fact that the negative, the realm of nothingness, has been separated by a sharp limit from the realm of reality and of what alone is positive' (I/6 p. 43). There is here no dialectical relationship of the Absolute and the finite world, of the kind expressed in the idea that the finite world, as nature, is the Other of *Geist*. Instead there is a hiatus that separates the two, as well as posing the problem of why they have become separate at all. Though this split may seem merely a theological problem, the difference of negative and positive philosophy will turn out to have substantial echoes in subsequent philosophy, as should already be evident in its relation to the question of ontological difference.

Schelling's route to understanding the fact of the world's being disclosed is via the development of a new notion of freedom. Evidently the notion is no longer the one familiar from Fichte, in that Fichte is seen as leading precisely to the loss of the Absolute, because he regards freedom as the essence of the subject. What is clear even from *Philosophy and Religion*, which does not develop its positions, or even explicate them in a serious way, is that the notion of freedom required to understand the division between finite and infinite cannot be derived from transcendental philosophy. The existential basis of transcendental philosophy, the philosophy whose main function is to give a genetic account of the conditions of possibility of knowledge, cannot itself be included within such an account. In one sense this follows from the *Naturphilosophie*. The major difference will be in the way that this natural ground is conceived.

Philosophy and Religion is an isolated text in this period of Schelling's production. It does, though, point to the end of Schelling's adherence to the kind of philosophy of identity which sees the world of nature and experience as grounded in an Absolute which resolves all divisions into harmony. The problem with such a conception is in many ways an old one, and was suggested when we considered the *Propaedeutic to Philosophy*. Identity philosophy claims it is able to understand human freedom as compatible with an Absolute which transcends the finite human will. The doubling of identity means that thinking beyond the Kantian antinomy of necessity and freedom is possible in a more emphatic way than Kant had allowed:

> This contradiction can only be dissolved by the fact that it is one
> and the same which acts in the body (in the realm of necessity)
> and in the soul (in the realm of freedom), and as this One can only
> be the absolute substance, because only this is itself the absolute
> identity of the real and the ideal — by the fact that *in all action*

[*there is*] *only the absolute substance* (which is neither free nor necessary).

(I/6 p. 550)

This is, despite the Spinozist terminology, compatible with the Davidsonian reading of identity theory we examined above. Whilst the argument may convince at the level of the rejection of dualism, it does not address the issue raised in *Philosophy and Religion*. Schelling suggests that it is only by achieving the highest insight into necessity that one can truly be free, not by the pursuit of desires and goals which depend upon the contingencies of finitude. Because the fact of the world of experience is merely negative, Schelling is led to familiar Platonist, 'metaphysical' conclusions, of a kind that the best parts of the *System* already begin to undermine in the conception of transitive being. He touches on the theme of *Philosophy and Religion* even in the *System*, when he suggests that the 'ground of finitude' can be seen as a 'fall', and that 'sin' is regarding the 'negative' aspect of things as being their reality. The point of philosophy, however, is that it should overcome this limited view in a 'resurrection in the totality' (ibid. p. 552), and the *System* is predicated upon that totality. How is it, though, that the totality involves 'sin'?

As has often been noticed, this makes evil, as it is in Thomism, merely a privation. Why, though, should there be evil, or other privations at all? This question suggests another – Why does the Absolute reveal itself as entailing privation? – which is precisely the question which leads to *Philosophy and Religion* separating the Absolute from the finite world altogether. Furthermore, if freedom is merely the insight into necessity, individual living spontaneity becomes merely appearance, which will eventually be overcome in the totality. Seen in this way the identity philosophy can quickly lead back to the determinist Spinozism that Schelling wished to avoid and which entails all the elements of static metaphysics that he had begun to undermine in many of the arguments we have considered. Underlying all these issues are the questions which will come to form the foundation of the later philosophy and whose ramifications are still with us: why is being disclosed at all and what is the nature of this disclosure?

5

FREEDOM, ONTOLOGY AND LANGUAGE

GROUND AND FREEDOM

From Rorty's standpoint, it is presumably even worse, as Schelling now does, to insist on trying to understand how and why diversity results at all from the unity of the substance, rather than merely trying to show how one might think difference together with identity. One argument from analogy can suggest that the problems Schelling now confronts, though they may seem disreputable to many philosophers, seem not to want to go away. The attention in contemporary theoretical physics to the very emergence of a differentiated universe of space and time from that which involved neither increasingly reveals the limitations of the causal model of physics that served so well until the rise of quantum mechanics and the questioning of existing notions of causality. If one accepts the link between Spinozism and modern science, Schelling's continued opposition to Spinozism, the emphatic nature of which only makes sense if Spinozism entails something of fundamental importance, is linked at least by analogy to a vital shift in modern thinking. Whilst this link clearly cannot be used to legitimate the *philosophical* arguments to be considered here, it may serve to keep open an initial hermeneutic space for such arguments. Further philosophical legitimation of what Schelling attempts to do can also be suggested by its undoubted influence on key questions raised by Heidegger for modern philosophy. Most persuasive, perhaps, is the extent to which Schelling's uncompromising engagement with philosophically problematic issues takes him right to the heart of unresolved tensions in modern thought that are still manifest in areas as diverse as cosmology, aesthetics and psychoanalysis, let alone in theology.

Schelling's move away from the residual Spinozist aspects of the identity philosophy does not, as is sometimes assumed, lead to the abandonment of the idea of an identity philosophy. This is evident in the fact that the philosophy of the *Ages of the World* (*WA* = *Die Weltalter*) is perhaps best understood as a speculative theory of predication, a theory of why there is truth in the world at all. The theory is an attempt to answer the problems suggested in *Philosophy and Religion* that were skirted in the identity philosophy. As we saw in the last chapter, the identity philosophy fails to answer the question of why the Absolute's self-manifestation should entail privation. In the Christian tradition, which from now on plays an increasing role in Schelling's philosophy,[1] this problem is generally linked to the human freedom to do good or evil. Schelling's opposition to Spinozism already suggested the need for a theory which made 'freedom' central. The difference in the *FS* is that freedom is now seen as inextricably bound up with the *active* possibility of 'evil', rather than with philosophical insight into necessity. What Schelling means by 'evil' will become more apparent in a moment. Schelling continues to regard his philosophy as depending upon the demonstration of the identity of the 'ideal' and the 'real', but the ontological accent shifts towards the question of how they become split. This split is no longer the continuous transition of the identity philosophy.

In the recently published 1941 text on the *FS*, which sees it as the 'culmination (*Gipfel*) of German Idealism', Heidegger suggests that the attention to evil in the *FS* is an 'implicit' attempt 'via evil to take the negativity developed in Hegel's *Phenomenology* beyond the "ideal" consciousness-based essence of the distinction between subject and object' (Heidegger 1991 p. 137). Because it is 'consciousness-based', negativity in Hegel still remains within the scheme of self-presence, as that which depends upon the movement of the subject. The fact that evil in the *FS* is spirit, because of its inextricable relationship to freedom, means 'spirit cannot be the Highest. (Against Hegel; the ground cannot be sublated (*die Unaufhebbarkeit des Grundes*))' (ibid. p. 135). Schelling's idea of evil relies on the notion that what impels thinking is grounded in nature. The activity of 'reason', which itself initially depends upon the ground, can become the (ultimately futile) attempt to overcome that in which it is grounded by subordinating it to itself.[2] Schelling claims in the *Stuttgart Private Lectures* of the same period as the *FS*: 'Evil is in a certain respect completely spiritual (*das reinste Geistige*), for it carries on the most emphatic war against all *being*, indeed it would like to negate (*aufheben*) the ground of creation' (I/7 p. 468). What Heidegger does not seem to contemplate is that if in the *FS* the relationship between subject and object is not reflexive, in that the ground cannot finally be sublated into reflexive identity in the dialectic, then the straightforwardly metaphysical understanding of a subject which is mirrored in the world's intelligibility, that he sees as still present in the Schelling of the *FS* and beyond,[3] becomes hard to sustain, even though Schelling himself may make great efforts to sustain it. Heidegger claims the way subjectivity is understood by Schelling makes subjectivity into the precursor of Nietzsche's 'will to power', the will to overcome the Other in the name of the Same. Schelling's argument can surely be read, though, as a *warning* against the potential for domination of subjectivity, which as 'evil' tries to obliterate its relationship to the ground upon which it is dependent. The manifestations of this domination in modern science and technology's relationship to *Sein* are, after all, what Heidegger uses to suggest how far modern metaphysics has gone in the forgetting of *Sein*. In this way Schelling's 'evil' could, in Heidegger's terms, actually be equated with metaphysics itself.

It seems clear to me that Heidegger, after his more sympathetic reading of the *FS* in the earlier (1936) account of it, stylises Schelling into yet another representative of his totalising notion of Western metaphysics, when he claims that Schelling sees being just in terms of subjectivity. Whereas in 1936 he is prepared to make a serious hermeneutic effort to understand Schelling's anthropomorphisms, by 1941 they are merely anthropomorphisms, and are consequently evidence of Schelling as, in the last analysis, merely another part of the process of subjectification which is Western metaphysics. Heidegger thereby fails to see the ways in which Schelling's texts already begin to take one beyond the reflexive schema of Cartesian metaphysics that Heidegger, and Derrida after him, sometimes seem to think is all there is in philosophy until Heidegger himself.[4] Heidegger insists that 'despite all, basically the same passion for the same' (Heidegger 1991 p. 185) – the 'passion' for self-presence – is there in Hegel and Schelling. It will become abundantly clear in the next chapter that Schelling's developed notion of the subject does not depend on self-presence. Schelling's conception of being cannot, therefore, be of a realm of objects opposed to a subject, which is the Heideggerian criterion for a metaphysical conception, because, as was already evident in the identity philosophy, Schelling does not think it possible to make such a separation. The fact that Heidegger, as far as one knows, does not take into account Schelling's critique of Hegel is further reason for viewing Heidegger's account of Schelling with suspicion.

The central issue in the *FS* is again a non-reductionist account of thinking's relationship to being. Spinoza's system, as before, is seen as 'one-sidedly realistic' (in the sense of 'materialist'), and as in need of completion by an 'ideal' aspect 'in which freedom reigns'. Freedom is still linked to the notion of the spontaneous will, which, as in Kant, is cause of itself, but this is now given a much broader ontological base. In freedom:

> there is the last potentialising act, by which the whole of nature is transfigured into sensation, into intelligence, finally into will. In the last and highest instance there is no other being but willing. Willing is primal being, and all the predicates of primal being only fit willing: groundlessness, eternity, being independent of time, self-affirmation.[5]
>
> (I/7 p. 350)

'Idealism' – Schelling is referring mainly to Fichte – has achieved this notion of spontaneous freedom, but, he claims, only for the I. The problem is to demonstrate freedom in the rest of nature, so as to explain the *emergence* of what supervenes on the 'real', which is identical with it, in the sense we saw in the last chapter. This is, then, actually another version of *Naturphilosophie*. The point of the argument now, though, is to encompass a notion of freedom based on spontaneous will that is 'a capacity for good and evil' (ibid. p. 352).[6] This poses the problem of how 'God' can have evil in His world. In line with the key thought of the identity philosophy the *FS* and the *WA* try to answer this question without going back to the dualisms which make the move from God to the world incomprehensible. In non-theological terms the attempt is to show how it is that the world is more than an understanding of it in terms of natural causality can allow.

The crucial fact about identity, as we saw, is that the predicate has more than a tautologous relationship to the subject. For Schelling this is an ontological issue, not one confined to propositions: judgements are real syntheses of what is split in the emergence from the Absolute. Schelling once again explains his notion of identity:

> If someone says the body is a body, he reliably thinks something different in the subject of the sentence from the predicate; in the former he thinks the unity, in the latter the individual qualities of the body contained in the concept of the body, which relate to each other as *Antecedens* to *Consequens*.
>
> (ibid. p. 342)

FREEDOM, ONTOLOGY AND LANGUAGE

The notion of identity is now used to understand 'God'. Schelling insists that 'nothing is before or outside God', which gives rise to the problem of God's relationship to nature. If He *is* nature, the problems of Spinozism seem inescapable: God becomes the sum of the laws of nature. If He is not, dualism seems inevitable and the gap between God and the world becomes uncrossable. Schelling thinks he can avoid these consequences. As Heidegger puts it in the 1936 lectures, for Schelling of the *FS* the identity of God and the universe 'cannot be understood as simple uniformity (*Einerleiheit*), but rather as the belonging together of what is different on the basis (*Grund*) of an original oneness' (Heidegger 1971 p. 103). Much of the argument, one should add, does not depend upon a belief in God in any dogmatic sense. 'God' is here, as Heidegger suggests, Schelling's way of approaching the question of the ground of being, and the fact that being is, to use Heidegger's term, 'disclosed'. Schelling will later talk of God as *'the cause which gives the ideal preponderance over the real'* (Schelling 1990 p. 102): this preponderance can be understood as the disclosure of being. What makes the world intelligible is 'identical' with what becomes intelligible, but this does not mean that it is reducible to it: getting from brain functions to consciousness requires more than can be explained in terms of brain functions, as the critique of Spinozism already demonstrated.

The 'real', then, is in God, but 'is not God seen absolutely, i.e. insofar as He exists; for it is only the ground of His existence, it is *nature* in God; an essence (*Wesen*) which is inseparable from God, but different from Him' (I/7 p. 358). The ground in God precedes God's ex-sistence as 'gravity precedes light as its eternally dark ground . . . which flees into the night as light emerges' (ibid.). The argument is dialectical: the ground can only be *as* the ground because God ex-sists on the basis of it: without the difference between itself and God it could not be as itself. As such, God is actually prior to the ground, even as it is in Him as His ground, which He needs in order to be above it as God. The priority of God at this level is intended to prevent the return to the Spinozist view, which gives no basis for the *emergence* of an intelligible world.

Schelling does not deny the material foundation of the 'ideal' here, but insists that we try to understand how it is that the real must entail the ideal. The key factor, which prevents a static ontology of essences, is 'becoming', 'the only concept appropriate to the nature of things' (ibid. pp. 358–9). The 'real' is 'ungraspable basis of [empirical] reality in things, the remainder that never comes out, that which can never, even with the greatest exertion, be dissolved into understanding, but remains eternally in the ground' (ibid. p. 360). Things, then, 'have their ground in that which in God Himself is not Himself, i.e. in that which is the ground of His existence' (ibid. p. 359). 'Evil' is a higher aspect of the ground:

> For evil is nothing but the primal ground to existence in as much as it strives for actualisation in the created being, and is therefore in fact only the higher potential of the ground which is effective in nature. But as nature is eternally only ground, without itself being able to be (*ohne selbst zu sein*) [i.e. it has the status of relative non-being that we have repeatedly encountered], in the same way evil can never be realised and serves just as a ground in order that the good, by forming itself out of the ground through its own force, can be independent and separate from God via its ground.
>
> (ibid. p. 378)

'Freedom', the capacity for good and evil, depends, therefore, upon a ground from which it can never be wholly separated, lest it lose that via which it can reveal itself and be itself. To realise itself freedom must, at least temporarily, overcome the resistance of the ground. The ground itself involves an inherent lack that forces it beyond itself and which also prevents the circular return to itself that would reveal its essence by self-reflection.[7]

One can here, as with the *STI*, take a parallel from psychoanalysis to clarify the ideas: the structure is analogous to Freud's notion of *Wo Es war, soll Ich werden* ('Where id was, ego should become'). In the *FS* the id is the equivalent of the ground and the ego is God, who develops beyond the id (on this, see Marquard 1987). Though I may be grounded in the id, that does not mean that the reality of my self is reducible to this drive base: the base cannot explain how the 'ideal', my free self, could ever emerge as a subject who is not merely the sum of the objective 'real' processes which I also am. Nor, importantly, can it explain how it is that I can become aware of the id *as* the id in any way at all. For Freud, this awareness itself must depend on the energy of the id being split off from itself as id, which, as I suggested in relation to the *STI*, can only be understood metaphorically. This split repeats the problem Hölderlin showed in Fichte's I, because it demands an account of a relationship which is supposed to be generated by only one side of the relationship: id and ego, like subject and object, demand a whole of which they are aspects. The id is, as such, 'identical', in a problematic

96

variant of the sense we have seen, with the ego. Freud uses a model close to the *Naturphilosophie*, in that the ego and super-ego are the results of the id directing its forces against itself in the interests of self-preservation.

This, though, points to a major difference from Schelling. Freud follows the tradition of Hobbes, which identifies self-consciousness with self-preservation (see Henrich 1982 pp. 83–108), and thereby also subscribes to the materialist conception of the subject which accompanies the demise of Hegelianism. Schopenhauer, one of the first to contribute to that demise, reduces Schelling's argument (with which he was familiar) to the assertion of the primal reality of the 'Will', as the all-consuming ground of appearances (see A. Bowie 1990 pp. 206–14). The importance of Schelling lies not least in the resources he offers for taking on board aspects of the materialist argument without reducing the 'ideal' to mere epiphenomenality, or the ego to being just a mechanism for self-preservation.[8] The parallel with psychoanalysis is enlightening as a way of understanding the relationship of the real and the ideal; does it, though, allow one to move from the level of the self-conscious individual subject to the kind of consequences Schelling wishes to draw for the whole of nature?

This question can be considered by looking at Schelling's notion of 'gravity'. Schelling's insistence upon the identity of mental process with natural process is again the key factor. In natural processes things are formed by forces that oppose each other. The opposition cannot be absolute, as things do not differ absolutely, and only are in an absolute sense to the extent to which they are as everything else is. This fact is one aspect of what Schelling means by 'gravity' (he explicitly distinguishes his conception from what Newton means by the term (I/7 pp. 229–30)):

> The uniting of things in gravity cannot, therefore, have its ground in the things themselves as such, or seen *abstracte*, rather the opposite is the case: things really have their basis in the unity which is the essence of gravity.

> (I/7 p. 228)

'Gravity', then, is the *Band*, the unifying link between, or ground of, the elements of the manifest world. The finite structure of any particular aspect of nature was, as we saw, the *'totality appearing in opposition to the particular life of things'* (I/6 p. 220), or, as Schelling puts it in the 1806 *Aphorisms on Naturphilosophie*: 'The essence of gravity is the principle of not-being-for-themselves of things' (I/7 p. 236). The finitude of things is a result of their dependence on this ground, which ultimately unites them in the process of their revealing their transience.

Any specific existent is, then, 'neither absolutely a being, nor absolutely a not-being, but rather a suspension between the two' (ibid. p. 231). In the form of 'melancholy' (*Schwermut*) the 'lack' is the equivalent in human nature, as Wolfram Hogrebe suggests (Hogrebe 1991), of gravity in the natural world. Gravity prevents all things from achieving self-presence, even as it is also the necessary condition of the movement which gives things their transient determinacy as them-selves – without it the universe, as we saw in the *Naturphilosophie*, would dissipate itself in one go; with it everything must eventually 'go to ground'. The continual overcoming of the ground is, Schelling claims, what gives joy in life, but the ground is the source of the 'veil of melancholy which is spread over the whole of nature, the deep indestructible melancholy of all life' (ibid. p. 399). From the perspective of God, the negativity can be seen in positive terms as the overcoming of any attempt to make the particular absolute (the highest form of which is 'evil'), which thereby allows the continual development of life and spirit. From the finite perspective of the particular individual, though, this leads to 'melancholy'. The challenge is to explain why there should be a manifest, intelligible world of particularity at all. Schelling now tries to avoid the residual Spinozist elements in the identity philosophy, of the kind I have suggested are also present in Derrida, that meant the transition from real to ideal was simply assumed as part of a chain. This requires an ontological conception of the possibility of truth. The fact is that truth depends, as we saw, upon the propositional linking of interpreted signs, in ways for which a merely differential theory cannot account. How, though, does this connect to the intelligibility of the world? The initial problem is understanding why it is that these links come to be made at all: in the *WA* this is a question both of ontology and of language.

WORLD-MAKING

The transition to the manifest world in the *WA* is seen via a genetic theory of predication which tries to explicate the transition whilst acknowledging the major problem it entails: the problem of the 'ground' and the emergence from it. The theory attempts to show nothing less than how it is that we come to say that things are what they are: why does being not remain in a state of inarticulacy, or simply consist in endless chains of meaningless difference? The *WA* offers a chance to ask if it is really sufficient, as we saw Rorty doing, to assume truth is solely an issue of trading sentences in order to establish beliefs, or, for that matter, of evolutionary adaptation.[9]

The implications of this issue can be suggested by looking again at an example of one of the most familiar critiques of metaphysical conceptions of truth. Nietzsche, as is well known, often plays the game of reducing truth to something else, the 'will to power'. Truth in this perspective makes identity out of difference in the name of control or pleasure. Truth is, then, the 'lordly right to give names' of the *Genealogy of Morals* and the 'kind of error without which a certain kind of living being being could not live' of the *Will to Power*; a less melodramatic version of this underlies aspects of Rorty's and other pragmatism. Nietzsche's manoeuvre, though, requires the proposition, however ironically relativised, that the truth is X. The fact is that the possibility of propositionality is prior to the specific predicate – 'power' – for example, that might occur in a proposition about truth. To understand truth as power cannot be done in terms of power itself because, as we saw and will see again in a moment, a judgement always requires a separation between terms in order to establish their identity. Saying 'power is power' is meaningless tautology.[10] The *WA* wants to discover how meaningful identifications come to be made at all. This possibility is prior to any theory that says what those identifications depend on, be it power, force, desire, evolutionary adaptation, or whatever. Such a theory will always rely on the prior condition of what it wishes to prove, namely the very condition of possibility of judgement or predication, which is not itself reducible to a further transcendental condition.[11] As Wolfram Hogrebe (Hogrebe 1989) shows, Schelling wants to ask the question how, given that the fact of being precedes any possibility of meaning, there can yet be meaning at all.

But how can one say anything about what must have been before anything could be said? Schelling often uses the metaphor of the beginning of a line: the beginning of a line is not yet a line, it has no extension, but a point is not nothing at all, in that lines cannot be lines without points. It is this sort of beginning that is at issue here: it can be structurally located, but can only be understood through what it has ceased to be.[12] One condition of it we have already seen: differentiality, reflexivity. Without some kind of articulation there is just One, and this cannot be said. The real issue is getting from this to something else that exists *as* something, which is different from the One, but cannot be without it. As we saw, the 'Spinozist' version of difference leaves one with the problem that saying what *a* is is saying it is not *b*, is not *c*, *ad infinitum*, which means that in one sense *a* is not at all. The way *a* is able to be must be explained by a theory of identity of the kind we looked at in the last chapter.

If the intelligibility of the world in propositions cannot be understood in relation to other forms of articulation, we will be returned to some kind of dualism, which makes the emergence of meaning incomprehensible because it cannot show how matter could ever lead to meaning. Physicalist (reductive or non-reductive) explanations of meaning, which also rely on the 'Spinozist' binary assumption of *a* is not *b* etc. in the notion of the brain as 'super-computer', claim that thought and meaning are relations of matter. This, though, is open to the objection shown in the identity philosophy: it gives one no possibility of accounting for why matter should configure in such a way that it produces language, the *meaningfulness* of which cannot be explained solely in terms of the differentiation of matter or (in the more sophisticated version of the same argument) functional states of a system.[13] Schelling, as we have seen, regards 'matter' as always already 'real–ideal'; we are just a highly developed case of the same. Meaning must, in this view, be part of what is always already potentially present in 'matter' in Schelling's sense. In the FS the 'ground', what the WA will generally term 'being' (*Seyn*), as opposed to 'beings' (*Seyendes*),[14] the manifest world that emerges from it, has an inherent lack that it constantly tries to overcome. The lack opens up the possibility for striving to get beyond it, ultimately to the unity which would overcome it.[15] This structure will be the basis of the dynamic account of truth and meaning in the WA.

One way of understanding the idea of the emergence of meaning in the WA is by thinking about music's relationship to language. Schelling himself uses music to explicate a key aspect of the WA. Music is not 'yet' language, but clearly shares many of the same attributes. It is perfectly possible to give a physicalist description of a symphony, as it is of a sentence. To hear the symphony as music, or the sentence as a sentence, though, one must move beyond descriptions of physical phenomena, to intentionality, and to meanings. Meanings could not exist without their physical manifestation, but if one remains at the level of what can be said in physical terms, the meaning becomes incomprehensible because there is no way of saying how one can get from frequencies to meanings. Meaning depends upon differing elements of the whole being linked as significant. Is it the case, as physicalism would suggest, that music and language are 'really' the sum of their physical manifestations and of the sensory reactions of their recipients? They no doubt are this, but Schelling's argument, like many more recent accounts of truth, is holistic: without the whole the particular element is 'false', as a note or a signifier devoid of context can be determinate as physical phenomenon but meaningless as music or language. The question, as Kant already saw, is how the *connections* between the particular and the whole that make meaning possible come into being. There cannot be a causal explanation of this, as such an explanation would already depend upon what it is supposed to be explaining.

The argument of the *WA* has little chance of even getting off the ground if we cannot accept some interpretation of the following passage, which should give one a feel for the Wagnerian tone of the *WA* as a whole:

> One must allow to man a principle which is outside and above the world; for how could he alone of all creatures follow back the long path of developments from the present into the deepest night of the past, he alone ascend to the beginning of times, if there were not in him a principle before the beginning of times? Poured from the source of things and the same as the source, the human soul has a co-knowledge/con-science/con-sciousness [*Mitwissenschaft*: Schelling does not, as he normally would, say *Bewusstsein*] of creation.
>
> (*WA* I p. 4)

This may sound like metaphysical hubris, but the argument is implicit in the *Naturphilosophie* and the developmental model of the *STI*: if the identity of mental and physical process can be understood in the way that we have seen, there is at least a possibility of making sense of this passage. Hogrebe shows that the *WA* is grounded in a theory of judgement which, as the identity philosophy demonstrated, requires that what is joined in the judgement (which is therefore separate: without the separation it would not need to be joined) must already be the same, as otherwise the judgement would be groundless. The explication of this identity, which now has to be understood via the narrative of how we come to differ from our past, is the key to understanding the *WA*.

The *WA* begins as follows:

> The past is known (*gewusst*), the present is recognised (*erkannt*), the future is intuited [*geahndet*, i.e. not intuition in the technical philosophical sense, but in the mystical sense]. What is known is

narrated (*erzählt*), what is recognised is represented, what is
intuited is prophesied.

(*WA* I p. 3)

The first part of the unfinished *WA* is actually all we get in all the
versions: the past, which has to be narrated. As the past, it is different
from the present: understanding the past requires anamnesia. How,
though, can we understand what we no longer are? The essential point
is that we still are the past, but need philosophy to realise how. This is
not an irrationalist 'intuition' of a primitive, pre-conscious state. The
theory has, like the *STI*, to be able to show the transition from a world
in which there is no knowledge to ourselves, who can think about that
from which we have emerged. The implicit target is again Spinozism
(and the static aspects of the identity philosophy), and the argument
clearly goes back to Jacobi's problem, which we saw in Chapter 1:

> If the world were, as some so-called sages have thought, a chain
> of causes and effects which runs forwards and backwards into
> infinity, then there would be neither past nor future in the true
> sense of the word. But this incoherent thought ought rightly to
> disappear along with the mechanical system to which it alone
> belongs.
>
> (*WA* I p. 11)

Schelling is fully aware that a serious attempt to explain the emergence
of intelligibility has no reason to stop until it reaches bedrock, and this
is what he tries to do:

> But if it is the case that the basis of all knowledge, science . . . is
> deduction from the past, where do we stop? For even having
> arrived at the last visible presupposition the spirit finds yet
> another presupposition which is not grounded by itself, which
> directs it to a time when there was nothing, when the One
> impenetrable being (*Wesen*) contained everything swallowed up
> inside itself, out of whose depth everything developed.
>
> (ibid. I pp. 12–13)

This is all very splendidly rhetorical, but is there a philosophical
argument? The key issue, as we shall see, is the understanding of
'nothing'.

Two sources of Schelling's account of the intelligibility of being
have been pointed out by Frank, Hogrebe and White. The first is Kant's
conception of the 'transcendental ideal' in the First Critique, the second
is a key passage of Fichte's *Wissenschaftslehre* that was already

important for the identity philosophy. Both arguments are concerned with the ground of predication. I shall look at Kant now, and Fichte later. Any *concept*, Kant says, must, as a determinable concept, be able to be characterised by one or other of two contradictorily opposed predicates. This much is obvious from the law of excluded middle and the law of contradiction. 'Determinability' is independent of content: a concept has a priori to be determinable as X or not-X to be a concept at all. The law of contradiction cannot, though, legislate for content. If a *thing* is to be determined, it 'stands under the principle of complete determination'. This means that of all the possible predicates there are, as long as they have contradictories, one of them must be applicable to the thing for it to be something. For a thing to be fully determinate as itself, one would have to go through the list of *all* the possible predicates it is not. The thing must be seen:

> both in terms of its relation to mutually exclusive predicates and in relation to the *total possibility*, as the epitome (*Inbegriff*) of all predicates of things at all, and, by presupposing all these predicates as the a priori condition, every thing is thought of as deriving its own possibility from the part that it has of the complete possibility.
>
> (Kant 1968 pp. B 599–600 A 571–2)

This total possibility, the 'transcendental ideal', which is the 'material for all possible predicates', suggests an affinity between all things. The consequence is that 'to know a thing completely one must know everything possible . . . complete determination is consequently a concept that we can never represent *in concreto* in its totality' (ibid. p. B 600 A 573).

Kant makes a strict distinction between negation and affirmation, of the kind which we saw Schelling using against Fichte (I/4 p. 358), and which Schelling will later use against Hegel. Logical negation can only take place within a judgement, where one concept is related to another. Negation therefore says nothing about the content of a concept: the concept of a not-something is only the privation of a something: 'nobody can think a negation determinately without having the opposed affirmation as its ground' (ibid. p. B 603 A 575). As such: 'All true negations are, then, nothing but limits, which they could not be called if the unlimited (the totality (*All*)) were not the ground' (ibid. p. B 604 A 576). This ground is the ground of the content of all thought about things:

103

all negations (which, of course, single predicates are, whereby everything else can be distinguished from the most real being (*Wesen*)) are just limitations of a greater and finally of the highest reality; therefore they presuppose this reality and their content is simply derived from it.[16]

(ibid. p. B 606 A 578)

Determinacy is the attribute of objects of the understanding. The transcendental ideal is the condition of possibility of things being determinate, so it cannot itself be determinate, because determinacy depends upon predication, and predication is limitation. What *is* the transcendental ideal, then? The simple answer is 'absolutely anything', and thus 'nothing in particular'. Most importantly, it cannot be considered to be negative, which is the attribute of what is determinable. For Schelling this immediately raises the question we have already seen: if it is nothing in particular, how is it that we have a world of experience which is divided into particularity? As we saw, Schelling added an ontological and genetic side to Kant's philosophy from the very beginning. This is again what he does in the *WA*.

What Kant explains as a necessary *theoretical* condition of predication, Schelling, in later lectures in 1847 and 1850, which clearly derive from the ideas of the *WA*, sees as itself being a *real* condition of a world of which things can be predicated. It is not that Schelling does not understand Kant's strictures on the making of the transcendental ideal into something determinate, but he understands the strictures in an ontological manner, not in transcendental terms. As Hogrebe suggests (Hogrebe 1989 pp. 66–71), Schelling turns the transcendental ideal from a final transcendental possibility into the original onto-logical possibility of the predicative world of articulated and known nature – a world which, of course, can give rise to Kant's theory but must first be there to do so. Schelling repeatedly stresses in his later work that '*being* is the first, thinking is only the second or what follows' (II/1 p. 587). The crucial issue is now to consider the different 'kinds of being' (ibid. p. 288) that are the correlates of Kant's theoretical possibilities.

The first being must have everything swallowed up in it: even saying this is too much, but everything must be able to have come out of it, inasmuch as it has. The question, of course, is how and why it has, which takes us to the central issues of Schelling's later work. In the *WA* the past is the ontological ground of the present, but the past itself depends upon a ground where there was no time at all. One task will, therefore, be to explain time's emergence. Each phase of the *WA* carries within it the necessity which preceded it:

> man learns that his peaceful dwelling place is built on the hearth of a primeval fire, he notices that even in the primal being itself something had to be posited as past before the present time became possible, that this past remains hidden in the ground, and that the same principle carries and holds us in its ineffectiveness which would consume and destroy us in its effectiveness.
>
> (*WA* I p. 13)

The world whose origins we are to understand must entail the *same* conflictual forces as still act, though not necessarily in the same *form*, in this world: this much ensues of necessity from an identity philosophy. Above this temporal world is 'the Highest ... which is above all time and wishes to reveal itself in every development' (*WA* I p. 14). The Highest is 'pure freedom', the 'will that wills/wants nothing', notions that seem as meaningless as it is to try to talk about the world before there was meaning. As we have seen, though, that which has no 'meaning' is one way of conceiving of metaphor: it does not depend upon preceding rules or determinacies of context, and we cannot know what it 'means' until it ceases to be a metaphor.

Schelling appeals to an intuitive sense of what a being could be like which is not subject to the inherent lack that will characterise all other forms of being that can develop into determinacy, and which thereby depend on what is not yet themselves. 'Pure freedom' must be devoid of desire, because it would otherwise be beholden to what it desires. Schelling uses the image of a child who is purely happy with itself and 'enjoys its being', not as this or that, but as just being. Talk of 'just being' can only be understood by metaphors. Another example would be what it must be like to be in a happy pre-conscious state in the womb: clearly it is not like anything we can *know*, because our knowledge is based on separation from such states. (In the sense in which it is concerned with what precedes the separation which makes truth possible – the insertion into the 'Symbolic' – Lacan's 'Imaginary' plays a rather similar role to what is intended here, though its structural role in Lacan's overall theory is different.) The question is really whether we can write off all the aspects of the history of mythology, religion, art and psychoanalysis, which depend upon some such intuited being, without repressing more than we gain in the demonstration of the logical impossibility of knowing or saying anything about it. Schelling makes a vital point when he insists that 'pure freedom', despite its necessary indeterminacy, cannot be equated with absolute nothingness:

> The meaning of negation is generally very different, depending on whether it is related to the inside or the outside. For the highest negation in the former sense must be One with the highest affirmation in the latter. If something has everything in itself, it cannot for that very reason have it at the same time externally.
>
> (WA I p. 15)

The key structural factor is, then, that 'the will which wills/wants nothing' can remain negative, in that it is absolutely within itself, because it does not entail any sense of possibility or development, but as such also does not entail any lack in itself, which is the highest affirmation. The move to determinacy in the WA entails conflict, of a kind that is there in all forms of being that we know: it is *also*, though, our awareness of the desire to move beyond conflict that constitutes our access to this preceding state.

The vital question now addressed by Schelling is 'By what was this happiness (*Seligkeit*) moved to leave its purity and to step out into being?' (ibid. p. 16): the problem of *Philosophy and Religion* that echoes through the later work. If pure actuality really is pure, there can be no reason for it to move beyond itself, because that would entail a sense that it has potential that can be actualised, which would make it dependent upon actualising itself to be fully itself. This suggests two possibilities: either that there is no 'Highest' because the idea of it leads to this impossibility, which Schelling sees as making the world's life and intelligibility inexplicable; or the possibility that the move does not happen for a reason, in the sense of that which would ground the move.

Schelling is now clear that the transition from the infinite to the finite is inexplicable as a logical necessity: this point will later become vital in relation to Hegel. To sustain the anti-Spinozist position, a duplicity has somehow to arise, which entails a fundamentally new situation, but which must not entail an absolute difference from the initial situation: the same has to be both infinite and finite. Becoming something which is not the undifferentiated One is, Schelling argues, explicable as an act of 'freedom', which can have no prior causal explanation. However, becoming something entails necessity: the necessity of being that something. This leads back to the impossibility of knowing why the Absolute should become something, in that it thereby ceases to be

106

absolute. Schelling moves towards the idea that God makes a free decision to create the world but that He does not have to make the decision: it is only the fact of the manifest world that is our evidence of the decision.[17]

We can only understand this notion of freedom if we are, as the *FS* suggested, able to acknowledge a groundless freedom in ourselves. This freedom is not Kant's practical reason, which postulates our higher purpose as the higher aspect of nature, but rather freedom to take on all that we are as beings who are always already driven by the same forces as nature, the ground, and have the capacity for good and evil. Schelling suggests that nobody

> has chosen their character; and yet this does not stop anybody attributing the action which follows from this character to themselves as a free action. Here, then, everyone acknowledges a freedom which is in itself necessity, not freedom in that later sense, which only takes place where there is opposition [i.e. a choice between alternatives]. Common ethical judgement therefore recognises in every person – and to that extent in everything – a region in which there is no ground/reason (*Grund*) at all, but rather absolute freedom . . . . The unground (*Ungrund*) of eternity lies this close in every person, and they are horrified by it if it is brought to their consciousness.[18]
>
> (*WA* I p. 93)

God has to take on the ground if there is to be a creation, as otherwise He remains just pure freedom, but He, unlike us, does not have to take it on.

From this period onwards Schelling repeatedly uses the example of 'love' to explain this relationship of God to nature. As opposed to the Hegelian dialectical model of love as a relationship of free mutual dependence, which enables me to be myself by the reflection in the other, in this model the relationship is not reflexive. The following passage from the 1810 *Stuttgart Private Lectures* suggests why:

> God Himself is linked to nature through voluntary (*freiwillige*) love, He does not need it, and yet does not want to be without it. For love is not when two beings need each other, but where each could be for themselves . . . and does not see it as a privation to be for themselves, and yet does not wish to be, morally cannot be without the other. This is also the true relationship of God to nature – and it is not a *one-sided* relationship.
>
> (I/7 p. 453)

There is no *reason* for an autonomous person to love somebody, precisely because they are autonomous, and love is seen as only fully realised when it is not a result of dependence. In the terms we have seen, such dependence would deprive one of the ability to be as oneself by making one's being dependent: what is required, then, is a relationship where the positive identity of the subject is sustained, rather than it being 'negative', a case of relation to the other. The point is to suggest that 'love' between two people cannot be seen as a symmetrical relationship: it is not reducible to a form of self-reflection in the other, and, as such, it is not a dialectical relationship.

This is, of course, both a point about love, and a metaphor for a central metaphysical issue. Hegel uses the metaphor of love to explicate the 'concept' (*Begriff*) and its relation to reality, where the structure, as Michael Theunissen puts it, is such that 'the one does not experience the other as a limit, but as the condition of possibility of their self-realisation' (Theunissen 1980 p. 46). The world's intelligibility thereby becomes the result of an inherent necessity that is always already built into its relational structure. Schelling increasingly comes to suspect that this model just assumes a relationship of 'ideal' and 'real' without actually coming to terms with the fact that there is an irreducible facticity involved in the emergence of the relationship. This suspicion will become central to his critique of the transition from the *Logic* to nature in Hegel's system.

Despite the fascination of some of these ideas, none of Schelling's attempts to deal with the fact of the finite world is satisfactory as an answer to the fundamental metaphysical question. Schelling obviously knows this: he keeps going back to these issues until his death. Let us, though, consider how Schelling tries to develop the argument. Though Schelling has made vital new moves, we are still, then, left with the old problem of monism. As Hogrebe suggests, once we talk of the One in any sense, we have divided it: like Heidegger's *Sein* it can never be *said* as itself, in that propositions require duality:[19]

> the original fiction of an absolutely indeterminate and thus diffusely unified something or other has immediately decayed into a duplicity: into a something or other which we call *pronominal being*, and Schelling elsewhere [in the *Philosophy of Revelation*] calls *quodditative being*, and that which something or other is, which we called *predicative being*, and Schelling elsewhere correspondingly calls *quidditative being*.
>
> (Hogrebe 1989 pp. 83–4)

The *WA* works with a model in which opposing principles which at first sight appear completely to exclude each other have to co-exist. This model was suggested in Schelling's notion of 'love'. 'Pronominal being' is required for determinacy, for things to have a specific 'quoddity', but if it were an absolute and exclusive force this would mean we were stuck with the One that has everything swallowed up inside itself in a pre-'big bang' state. Even at the level of the emergence of a nature, there must be more than this. There must be 'predicative being' which 'flows out, spreads out, gives itself', what the *WA* calls 'love' (in a slightly different sense to the one just outlined); this is opposed to 'being', 'egoity', 'selfhood' (I/8 pp. 210–11), which is, like 'gravity', the contractive force of pronominal being. 'Love' without egoity to anchor it is like the infinite force of the *Naturphilosophie*, which would dissipate itself at one go – and not even know it was happening – if there were not something to prevent it. These forces are, Schelling insists, not *connected* to each other, they are ultimately the *same*, as otherwise all the problems of dualism arise. This version of identity seems impossible, but we have already seen a possibility of making sense of the problem in aspects of the identity philosophy. It was Fichte who articulated the structure of this possibility.

In the *Wissenschaftslehre* Fichte, as we saw, was faced with the following problem: the infinite is the I, but the finite world, the not-I, has to be explained. There cannot be one without the other, but they are not the same. This would seem at the same time to mean that they are the same, as for the not-I to be the not-I it needs the I, and could not be without it. The structure should be familiar from the identity philosophy. It leads Fichte to the following important conclusion, in which he himself implicitly suggests the problem that Hölderlin revealed in his trying to characterise the totality as I:

> Everything which is opposed to something is the same as what it is opposed to in one characteristic = X; and: everything the same is opposed to what it is the same as in one respect = X. Such a characteristic = X is the ground, in the first case the ground of *relation* in the second the ground of *difference*; for identifying (*gleichsetzen*) or comparing (*vergleichen*) what is opposed is called relating; opposing what has been identified is *differentiating* them.
>
> (Fichte 1971 p. 111)

How does this apply to the *WA?* We have seen that two essential forces are at play: a contractive, pronominal, form of being, and an expansive, predicative form. The intelligibility of anything depends upon its relations to other things in judgements. In the signifying chain, where A is not B is not C, etc., there can be no meaning if what is different is wholly different, as Fichte suggests, and as we suggested earlier in relation to structuralism and Derrida. Even to discriminate that A is not B is actually a proposition, a judgement which must be grounded in identity, in that A *is* that which is not B, C, etc.

The two forces, which he terms A and B, are regarded as identical by Schelling, in a passage which sums up the essence of the identity philosophy:

> The true sense of every judgement, e.g. that A is B can only be this: *that which* is A is *that which* is B, or *that which* is A and *that which* is B is the same/one (*einerlei*). Thus even the simple concept is grounded in a duality: A in this judgement is not A, but something = x, which is A; thus B is not B, but something = x, which is B; and not this (not A and B for itself) but the x that is A and the x that is B is the same, namely the same x. In the proposition cited three positions are really contained, first A is = x, second B is = x, and only out of this follows the third, A and B are one and the same, both namely x . . . the properly understood law of contradiction really only says that the same cannot be *as the same* something and also the opposite thereof, but this does not prevent the same, which is A, being able, as an other, to be not A.
>
> (I/8 pp. 213–14)

For something to be *as* something, it must both be in the positive sense in which everything is, which means that it is swallowed by this all-embracing positivity, and in another sense which cannot result from positive being, because it negates that positivity as quoddity in order to have quiddity. What starts as the necessary positive basis ceases to be what it was, but does not therefore cease to be. Once predicative being is initiated, the other being becomes a negative force, in that it strives to keep everything as one against the centrifugal differentiating tendency of the other force. This reversal can itself be reversed, as will be evident in a moment.

The two forces are as follows:

> first, negating force (B), which forces back the affirming being (A) and posits it as internally inactive (*unwirkend*) or makes it hidden, second, expansive, communicative being which does exactly the

opposite by holding down the negating force in itself and preventing it from having any effect on the outside.[20]

(I/8 p. 215)

The conflict of these forces, though, does not obviate the need for their identity, in that for each force to be itself it needs the other to be opposed to it. At this level the argument echoes Hegel's — and Schelling's (see Frank 1991 pp. 94–5) — notion of the identity of identity and difference, in what Schelling calls 'the One indivisible primary being (*Urwesen*)' (I/8 p. 217). This primary being is 'first nature' which is 'in contradiction with itself/contradicted by itself (*von sich selbst im Widerspruch*)' (ibid. p. 219). The contradiction is what gives rise to life and development. We now come back yet again to the problem of the transition from unity to contradiction.

Why not just assume that there always already is contradiction? We have just seen the answer to this in Fichte's argument: logically, and ontologically, there must be a ground of identity which is the prior condition of contradiction. The trouble is that this assumption leaves us with the transition beyond the One. Schelling's theory of identity in difference here (and elsewhere) has much to be said for it once the transition has been made, but not much as far as the transition itself is concerned. This failure is essentially why Schelling leads to the end of German Idealism, the end of the hope for a self-grounding system of reason. In the next chapter we shall look at whether Hegel's attempt to avoid such a transition, by regarding the infinite and the finite as always already the 'other of themselves', really escapes Schelling's problem.

The transition in the *WA* can perhaps best be understood as a kind of 'singularity': cosmology can deal with the results of a singularity, but not, by definition, with its facticity as singularity. That this has fatal consequences for the *WA* as closed metaphysical system is clear: though the *WA* can claim to show what results once a world emerges, it cannot finally explain that emergence itself, though it repeatedly tries to do so. This should not make us therefore write off the *WA* as mere speculation which lacks any legitimation at all: contemporary cosmology is, after all, in something of a similar situation (see, e.g., Penrose 1989). The *WA*'s strength lies in at least giving what Hogrebe calls a 'heuristics' for thinking about issues that are prior to any possible scientific explanation: namely, about the origin of the very possibility of explanation, the grounding of judgements in ontological difference. What is once in contradiction must, as Schelling suggests, try to achieve unity, in that the contradiction would otherwise not be manifest in any way at all, and thus could not even be said to *be* a contradiction. Judgement, non-tautological identification, thus depends upon an ontological fact—contradiction – which demands to be overcome at all levels, from physical processes to cognitive processes.

Given the *manifest* fact of the world, the attempt to answer the question of why there is being rather than nothing at all, which itself already entails the contradiction of being and nothing, becomes inescapable. The contradiction of being and nothing does not entail thinking absolute nothingness: the nothing which leads to the question of being is, as should already be clear, 'at the heart of being', as it is in Sartre's *Being and Nothingness*. For Schelling the positive and negative sides of the contradiction cannot in themselves ever be absolute: the positivity of pronominal being becomes, as we saw, the negative force in relation to predicative being. They are both carried by the *Band*, the process of their identity. At this stage of the *WA* the relationship of forces leads to an 'alternating positing' (I/8 p. 220), where the differing moments keep replacing each other. When pronominal being becomes negative it does not cease to be, and the same applies to predicative being: if they did cease to be, the process would stop. The negative belongs to the positive: although pronominal being is unknowable, knowable kinds of being cannot be without it: 'For it [pronominal being] is not non-being (*nicht nicht Seyendes*) because it completely lacks light and essence, but rather because of active closing off of essence, thus because of effective power' (ibid. p. 223). Schelling now tries to suggest why the process moves beyond this stage, in the theory of the 'potentials', which he will retain in varying forms for the rest of his life as a key weapon against Spinozism.

So far the account has given us two forces of the same being: one which contracts, another which expands. In the identity philosophy the magnet was the model for such relations of forces, in that even at the poles the opposite force had to be present. Now, though, there is a more dynamic relationship between the opposites. At this stage, which is the first potential, the contractive force has predominance. Schelling makes a brave and interesting attempt at showing why the development begins at all, by maintaining that the closing off of B means that A is inside what is closed off. He suggests that a 'being cannot deny itself without making itself internally into the object of its own wanting and desiring . . . positing oneself as not being and wanting oneself are one and the same' (ibid. p. 223–4), because what posits itself as not being must still be in some way. What is required to reveal this is a beginning: the stage we are at here is not anything in a 'predicative' sense, but at the same time not not-being in an absolute sense (it reflects Schelling's ontological understanding of Kant's transcendental ideal). A beginning is a lack, in that it dialectically requires its other to be a beginning at all. If there were no beginning, being would not be manifest, for it to be manifest it must initially be hidden, but it must still be. The second potential is where A gains preponderance over B, which leads to manifest, predicative being (*Seyendes*, as opposed to *Seyn*, which is pronominal). Schelling makes an important further move in characterising manifest being:

> For it admittedly has the fact that it is manifest being from itself, but the ground of the further fact that it is as manifest being, that it is effective, that it reveals itself as manifest being, lies in the negating potential.
>
> (ibid. p. 227)

The negating potential gives the expansive potential a ground against which to manifest itself. Given the necessity of this interdependence for them to be *as* anything, the two forms of being must be grounded in a third potential which is above their opposition.

The final realisation of the third potential – the process of which is the process of *Geist* as the dialectic of B and A – would be the end of the overall process. We have, though, only just reached the beginning: we are not even at the stage of the beginning of time. Just how problematic it is to reach the third potential Schelling demonstrates in his account of the 'rotating movement': B and A could simply go on replacing each other indefinitely, which would preclude a creation that developed at all, because the development would just be swallowed again at each replacement of A by B. This stage will be vital in Schelling's later conception of mythology: mythology ends when this process of rotation, which he thinks also takes place in the history of consciousness, is overcome.[21] For Schelling the 'rotating movement' involves a being which strives 'to be, and yet cannot be, so it remains in the state of continual desire, as an incessant seeking, an eternally unquenched thirst (*Sucht*) for being' (ibid. pp. 231–2). The anthropomorphic vocabulary might again make one suspicious, but we must remember that Schelling is concerned to understand ourselves as the result of processes which still underlie our being, and to which our '*Mitwissenschaft der Schöpfung*' gives us access. This leads him to ideas that are usually seen as characteristic of the period towards the end of the nineteenth century.

The following metaphors suggest a structure that will later become almost definitive of 'modernism':

When the abysses of the human heart open themselves in evil
and those terrible thoughts come forth which ought to remain
eternally buried in night and darkness; only then do we know
what possibilities lie in man and how his nature is for itself or
when left to itself.

(ibid. p 268)

Such remarks could be directly applied to Conrad's *Heart of Darkness*,
where Kurz is precisely concerned to find out 'what possibilities lie in
man'. Conrad's work owes much to Schopenhauer, and consequently
owes much to the Schelling of the FS, which Schopenhauer had clearly
read.[22] Schelling also invokes Dionysus as an image of what had to be
overcome for us to be what we are now. He thereby lays the ground
for what will, in a more crude and reductive version, become the world
of Nietzsche's *Birth of Tragedy* and of its irrationalist epigones. Music,
as what is not yet language but shares attributes with language, is a
recurrent metaphor from Romantic philosophy onwards (see A. Bowie
1990) for our access to pre-propositional being: 'For because sound
and note only seem to arise in that battle between spirituality and
corporeality, music (*Tonkunst*) alone can be an image of that primeval
nature and its movement' (*WA* I p. 43). Music is the result of the
relationship between 'gravity' and 'light', which correspond to
contractive and expansive being. The same relationship will be
fundamental to Schelling's view of language.

Unsurprisingly, given such metaphors, the model of the *WA*, like
the *FS*, also prefigures aspects of psychoanalysis. The common factor is
the understanding of opposing forces whose opposition leads to
consciousness of the world, but to which consciousness cannot have
direct access because it is itself the result of their opposition. The
recourse to metaphor in evoking this state follows, both at the cosmic
level and at the level of the psyche, from the non-empirical nature of
what is evoked. The *WA* links the continuing potential for madness in
the individual subject to this cosmic state. A world of experience can
only come into being by overcoming the dominance of the 'rotating
movement', by the development of 'propositional being'. One cannot
say what precedes this, as this depends upon propositionality, which is
only possible after the emergence of 'propositional being'. At the same
time, our initial relation to anything in the world, the world's
Erschlossenheit, is, as Heidegger shows, itself pre-propositional. The
key philosophical question is how we come to terms with this fact.

Schelling, unlike some of his later imitators, is not concerned to
celebrate the state of 'rotation', the Heraclitean flux, or whatever one

114

wishes to call it: the result of the conflict is pain and *Angst* (*WA* I p. 41). His concern is with the necessity of acknowledging that the world of truth, of *Geist*, has to be founded in what opposes it. Otherwise we are left with a groundless Idealism, that makes the emergence of truth (and the living world) pointless (he will suggest that this is really also the case in Hegel): 'for in what should understanding prove itself, except in the overcoming, command and regulation of madness?' (I/8 p. 338). The opposite problem is assuming that the ground, in whatever version, exhausts the question of ontology, as happens in most forms of materialism. Spinoza's materialist world is seen as only knowing the forces at the stage of their 'existential identity' (*WA* I p. 45), which is only the stage of the first potential. This stage has, though, to be able to lead to the later world of consciousness and feeling, the possibility of which develops via the continual 'separation and re-unification of the forces' (ibid. p. 39), and the 'eddying movement which always appears to be the beginning and the first appearance of creative forces' (I/8 p. 250). How, though, does this world reach 'articulation' (*WA* I p. 39)?

WORD-MAKING

Schelling characterises this move as a move to the 'word':

> existence (*das Existirende*) seeks nothing but the word in the increasing fullness of its inner being, via which it can be expressed, liberated, unfolded, and everywhere it is only the created or discovered word which solves the inner dispute.
>
> (*WA* I p. 57)

The 'word' results from mediation of the conflict between the contractive and the expansive force:

> It seems universal that every creature which cannot contain itself or draw itself together in its own fullness, draws itself together outside itself, whence, e.g., the elevated miracle of the formation of the word in the mouth belongs, which is a true creation of the full inside when it can no longer remain in itself.
>
> (ibid. pp. 56–7)

This happens both at the level of the material cosmos, and at the level of conscious beings. This may again sound merely theological or anthropomorphic. The fact is, though, that accounting for the emergence (as opposed to the transmission) of structures in the natural world, including the emergence of language, is, as we saw in the

Naturphilosophie, impossible in reductionist terms. Kant's denial that a mechanistic science could ever explain even a blade of grass applies even more emphatically to the explanation of language. Most analytical philosophy has assumed that the origin of language is not a problem about which philosophy has or could have anything interesting to say, and, in its own terms, this is right. It has been psychoanalysis and certain areas of hermeneutics that have kept alive such questions by attending to the issue of world-disclosure, as opposed to the analysis of truth as the making of validity claims.[23]

Clearly one cannot explain from within a language what that language is or how that language came to be. The circularity that results repeats the problem of reflexivity: from Romanticism to Wittgenstein's *Tractatus* and beyond, the basic structure of modern philosophy, with the major exception of Hegel's system, has more and more been determined by the realisation that totalities cannot describe themselves as totalities. What is often ignored is that this idea is also part of older and more obscure traditions of Western thought, of which Schelling was obviously aware. Here is the ninth of Gershom Scholem's 'Ten unhistorical propositions about kabbala':

> Totalities are only transmittable in an occult fashion. The name of God can be addressed but cannot be said. For it is only what is fragmentary in language that makes language sayable. The 'true' language cannot be spoken, just as little as what is absolutely concrete can be understood (*vollzogen*).
>
> (Scholem 1970 p. 271)

Before this is dismissed as wholly irrelevant to contemporary philosophy, here is Hilary Putnam on 'Why there isn't a ready-made world', making much the same point as Kant does in the notion of the 'transcendental ideal', and suggesting something actually not that far from Scholem (note the 'perhaps' at the end):

> Analytic philosophers have always tried to dismiss the trans-cendental as nonsense, but it does have an eerie way of reappearing. (For one thing, almost every philosopher makes statements which contradict his own explicit account of what can be justified or known; this even arises in formal logic, when one makes statements about 'all languages' which are barred by the prohibitions on self-reference. For another, almost everyone regards the statement that there is no mind-independent reality, that there are *just* the 'versions', or there is just the 'discourse', or whatever, as intensely paradoxical.) Because one cannot talk

about the transcendent or even deny its existence without
paradox, one's attitude to it must, perhaps, be the concern of
religion rather than rational philosophy.

(Putnam 1983 p. 226)

The initially bizarre conception of the 'word' in the context of the WA
appears less strange if we are aware that the problem it deals with is
actually constitutive for almost any area of modern philosophy.

Kant's transcendental ideal is one evident source of Schelling's way
of considering the 'transcendent'. Schelling did also have contact with
the tradition of the kabbala via Franz Baader, as well as by reading
Hamann and Böhme (see Brown 1977).[24] Schelling's conception of
language does seem to owe something to his awareness of the mystical
tradition of the kabbala, in that it shares a fundamental idea with that
tradition. Scholem suggests that in the tradition of the kabbala 'the
movement in which creation takes place is . . . interpretable as a
movement of language' (Scholem 1970 p. 33), and that the 'essence of
the world is language' (ibid. p. 10).[25]

The basic idea here is also familiar from Gadamer's notion that
'Being that can be understood is language' (Gadamer 1975 p. 450).
Schelling had already talked in the *Philosophy of Art* of 1802–3 – during
the period of the identity philosophy – of language as the expression
of the ideal in the real: language, as inseparable material signifier and
ideal signified, is like the world of which it forms a part:

> In the same way as knowledge even now still grasps itself sym-
> bolically in language, divine knowledge grasped itself symbol-
> ically in the world, so that the *whole* of the real world (namely to
> the extent to which it is itself again the unity of the real and the
> ideal) is itself also an originary speaking. But the *real* world is no
> longer the living word, the speaking of God Himself, but only
> the spoken – congealed – word.

(I/5 p. 484)

In the *Stuttgart Private Lectures* Schelling says of the *Band* of A and B
that it is:

> very expressively termed the word, a) because in it and with it all
> capacity for differentiation begins; b) because in it being-self and
> not-being-self . . . are organically linked . . . the being which is
> dumb for itself is first raised to comprehensibility by the ideal.

(I/7 pp. 442–3)

117

Though the *WA* has made the relationship of the ideal and the real more conflictual (as suggested in the links between Dionysus and music), and the relationship of God, the principle of intelligibility, to the ground far more complex, the conception is in essence the same as in the *Philosophy of Art*. But can we make sense of it?

The theory is clearly not a theory of language as correspondence or representation. Language, the 'living word' as opposed to the 'spoken', 'congealed' word, is *poiesis*, that which makes a manifest world possible. Language does not create the existence of the world (Putnam's 'discourse independent reality' which must, of course, include the discourse of which it is independent) – that existence, for Schelling, is the X that grounds the theory of predication. However, language, understood as constituted like the rest of the world of which it is an aspect, is the condition of possibility of things being manifest as things. The accent lies on the 'living word', which corresponds to the expanding force; the material signifier corresponds to the contracting force that allows meaning to be determinate at all by articulating the infinite multiplicity of the world's possibilities via a finite number of fixed and iterable signifiers. The real, finite world inherently becomes 'congealed', and the ideal must continually strive against this for the developing truth of the world to be manifest. Without the real to strive against there could be no meaning, because language would have no medium in which to exist; at the same time the real has no *reason* to be manifest and, in the way we have repeatedly seen, always poses the question as to how it is that it *is* manifest.

The question is not just a concern of this particular part of the history of metaphysics. A related conception recurs, for example, in key aspects of Jacques Lacan's work on language, which owes much to Heidegger, who evidently owes much to Schelling. Here is Lacan on the issue of language and the real, echoing Novalis's notion that we leave the identical to represent it: 'no language could say the true about the true, since the truth is founded in that of which it speaks and it has no other means of saying the true about the true' (Lacan 1971 p. 233). There can, for Lacan, be no meta-language which would represent the whole of the truth, because the meta-language itself is made up of what it would 'represent'. In the *Philosophy of Art* Schelling also suggested that language, as 'the direct expression of an ideal – of knowledge, thought, feeling, will, etc. – in something real', was, as such, a 'work of art' (I/5 p. 358) in the sense we saw in the *STI*, where art revealed the unity of conscious (ideal) and unconscious (real) production (see A. Bowie 1990 pp. 108–9). Manfred Frank describes Schelling's idea of language in the *Philosophy of Art* as follows:

> even if one defines the world in the traditional way as the totality of objects, one must see that, according to Kant, objects are contracted statements (judgements), in which something is not directly represented, but is, rather, expressed as something. For Schelling the situation is even clearer. In his view there is nothing in heaven or on earth which does not consist in a synthesis of the real and the ideal activity. This synthesis (which has the structure of a judgement) in the natural realm – as Schelling puts it – is under the function (*Exponent*) of reality, whereas in the spirit world it is posited under the function of preponderant ideality. What alone *exists*, as the ground, both in the natural and the ideal world, is the absolute identity of the real and the ideal, only the separation of which brings forth the finite world in its relativity and its transient appearances (*erscheinungshafte Nichtigkeit*).
>
> (Frank 1989b pp. 182–3)

The difference of the *WA* from the identity philosophy, as we have seen, is that the separation of 'absolute identity' into the real and the ideal has become the central problem.

It is not the case, therefore, that the ideal reflects or represents the real *as* the real. We cannot say that the 'ideal' manifested in the judgement is the reflection of the 'real' without adopting a third term, which would have to be the absolute 'viewpoint'. This, though, cannot itself be a viewpoint, a position defined in relation to another position, because if it were we would be led into an infinite regress. What would make possible the identification of the reflection with what it reflects would here already have to be identical with itself: this prior condition cannot be stated in propositional form.[26] Language, as material signifier and ideal signified, is itself dependent upon the prior identity of real and ideal: the signifier does not represent or reflect the signified, but if it is to be a signifier and not just an object, it must entail the ideal. What is manifested as something in the judgement becomes what it is via a pre-propositional synthesis of the kind that Schelling sees in all of nature, not by being a true representation of a language-independent world of fixed objects. The central point for the *WA* is that without living language, which is itself 'real–ideal', the real would not be manifest at all, though it would still be. Living language, as the realm of the sayable, is what opens up the possibility of propositions, the world of apparently stable objects. Such propositions, though, exclude the

119

other sayable possibilities. The resultant 'contraction', the WA suggests, involves a lack: the sayable is reduced by the said to finite determinations which cannot exhaust the sayable. This leads to the attempt to overcome the lack that is constitutive of all determinate being that we already saw in relation to 'gravity' in the FS. This position is not just theologico-metaphysical speculation, in that its implications are still being explored in key areas of philosophy.

The dynamic structure present here is still a vital issue in both psychoanalysis and hermeneutic philosophy, as well as in that side of analytical philosophy that takes metaphor seriously. Ricoeur's view of how metaphor allows us to redescribe the world in unheard of ways is, for instance, dependent upon a similar conception. Like Schelling, Ricoeur sees the ' "place" of metaphor' – and by metaphor he clearly means the same as the 'living word' – as the 'copula . . . . The metaphorical "is" means "is not" and "is like" at the same time' (Ricoeur 1986 p. 10). The tension between pronominal and predicative being repeats itself at the level of the living as opposed to the 'congealed' word. The key fact in the WA, then, is that the world of 'rotation', of inarticulable chaos, can become a dynamically articulated world, the highest aspect of which is language:

> If there were nothing but that blind necessity, then life would remain in this dark, chaotic state of a movement which eternally begins and thus never begins, eternally ends and thus never ends. But the highest aspect of nature is elevated to freedom by the sight of eternal freedom, and with it all other forces come at the same time to consistency (*Bestand*) and essence.
>
> (I/8 p. 252)

The concept of 'freedom', like the concept of 'love' we considered earlier, is understood as that through which pronominal, predicative and propositional being each gain their own status as part of a whole.

They do this by now allowing the others their own place in the whole, rather as the same elements which can be combined to make explosive material can also come to form living organisms. The differing kinds of being therefore become what they could not be if they were to remain in the chaotic rotation. Subject and predicate become more than they would be in isolation from, or conflict with each other, by being linked in the proposition. Hogrebe suggests the metaphor of a film projector as a way of understanding the point of Schelling's conception. The projector could either remain stuck with one unmoving image (pronominal being), or could run the film at the speed of light so that nothing is seen but a flash (predicative being), or could establish a dynamic which allows the intelligible unfolding of the differing dimensions. It does so by moving the static image via the force that would produce the flash, which is itself thereby prevented from dissipating itself in one go (propositional being). At this level the theory is reflexive: the moments become the 'other of themselves'. However, the linkage happens even though there is no necessary reason for the moments to be linked in an articulated manner: Schelling deliberately uses the metaphor of 'longing' as the basis of the move to articulation, to suggest that this is not a causal or logical move. The 'lack of being' in the ground, that leads nature beyond itself into articulated self-revelation, cannot finally be understood. Articulated understanding itself depends on the move from chaotic undifferentiated identity to difference, and it can therefore only establish the fact of the lack, not comprehend it from a position beyond it.

The fact of the emergence of an articulated world, the emergence of the 'word', cannot, then, be explicated causally. We are left with the notion that something was lacking for things to have had to become 'sayable' (*aussprechbar*), for them to have to be disclosed, rather than remaining unarticulated. This is, of course, a version of the question which Schelling asked about Kant from the very beginning. The disclosure cannot be explained in terms of causal necessity, as otherwise the whole system goes back to Spinozism, whose notion of identity is empty, tautological, 'because it lacks opposition' (I/7 p. 443). Schelling's concept of identity is bound up with the attempt to overcome ontological difference, but it thereby also requires ontological difference as its basis: if it did not, it would also just be tautology.

The process beyond rotation to articulation leads to the third potential: 'the eternal link (*Band*) both between nature and the spirit world and between the world and God' (I/8 p. 252). How, though, can there be the – now articulated – world of finitude as God's creation without God having to be wholly separated from it in order to retain His divine status? Schelling stresses that God is 'that which is above being' (*das Überseyende*). As such, God can only be manifest 'in relation to an other . . . which can only stand to Him in the relation of [pronominal] being (*Seyn*)' (ibid.). This other seems thereby to take on the status of non-being because it is dependent on its other, God, to be itself, 'and yet it cannot be something which is not at all' (I/8 p. 257): it is only dependent in relation to the Highest. If there is to be intelligibility God must manifest Himself – 'An eternal *being*-conscious

(*Bewusstseyn*) cannot be thought because it would be the same as unconsciousness' (I/8 p. 262); once He does manifest Himself (the reasons will concern us in a moment), He must take on this other being.

If this again seems too theological, linking the argument to language can help to suggest a way of making more secular sense of it. Schelling, one should remember, whilst insisting upon the ineliminability of the real, is primarily concerned with the emergence of intelligibility, of a world of which we can speak, not with the reduction of the ideal to the real so prevalent in contemporary physicalism. The mere materiality of the signifier, which is the 'ground' of language, has to be negated if language is to enable us to articulate a world of interpreted states of affairs. If the sign remains mere matter, it is not a sign at all, but without the material of the sign there can be no 'ideal' meaning. The material of the sign cannot be a guarantee of meaning, because meaning depends upon the *idealisation* of the material of the sign: the same meaning can theoretically be carried by electro-magnetic charge, carbon stain, moving airwaves, etc. Meaning also depends upon the synthesising movement beyond the static signifier to propositions, and upon the consciousness that can carry out new syntheses.

In the *Stuttgart Private Lectures* Schelling suggests the analogy of becoming conscious to the 'transition from identity to difference' in God. The developed stages of the process of consciousness are inseparable from, though not reducible to, the acquisition of language. Even though Schelling does not directly make this link, it is implicit in the conception of the 'word'. Becoming conscious is not a negation (*Aufhebung*) of identity, he claims, but rather a 'doubling of the essence':

> If we now become conscious of ourselves – if light and darkness separate in us – then we do not go *out of ourselves*; the two principles remain in us as their unity. We lose nothing of our essence, but instead just possess ourselves now in a double form, namely once in unity, the other time in division. So with God.
>
> (I/7 p. 425)

The child that becomes aware of itself as itself by entering the differentiated world of the symbolic order does not cease to be the same child, even though, in Lacan's terms, its identity may be 'defiled' by entering into that order. This structure involves a necessary tension between the consciousness of the individual subject and language, which Lacan sees as inevitable if we are to articulate the truth. Consciousness, Schelling emphasises, prefiguring the notion of intentionality, has to emerge from its other:

There is no consciousness without something which is both excluded and attracted. That which is conscious of itself excludes what it is conscious of as not itself, and yet must also attract it as, precisely, that of which it is conscious, thus as itself, only in another form.

(I/8 p. 262)

The ground that consciousness emerges from has to be unconscious, and once consciousness has emerged the ground becomes the past, via its ontological difference from living consciousness. At the same time consciousness could not *be* itself without that past: it is different from it, in that it cannot encompass it, but its own identity is dependent upon its identity with its ground. Processes of consciousness have their correlates in the real world because of this structure of 'identity' – difference from and dependence on – the ground.

The basis for Schelling's idea of our *'Mitwissenschaft der Schöpfung'* lies, therefore, in the identity between our unconscious past and the nature of our present consciousness, and in the identity between the ground and manifest nature, as well as in the absolute identity of these identities. In both cases the fundamental process is the attempt to overcome the lack of being in the ground by a development that is drawn to the future as the place where identity could be realised as a totality rather than as a succession in time. Time in the WA is, therefore, understood via ontological difference, in the light of Schelling's theory of identity and predication. Without the relative non-being of the other dimensions of time, each dimension of time could not be differentiated and there would be no time, as there is not at the stage of the rotating movement. For there to be time there must be an organised totality:

> every single [moment of] time presupposes time as a *whole*. If the whole of time were not to precede the single moment as an idea, it could not posit the whole of time as future, i.e. it could not posit itself, because without this determinate future it could itself not be this determinate time. But it only presupposes the whole of time as an idea; for if the idea were posited in it as real, then it would not be the single, determinate time which it is.

(WA I p. 81)

The 'ideal' conception of time has to articulate time as a dynamic tripartite totality if any particular moment of time is to be seen as past present or future: i.e. if there is to be time at all.

123

The whole of time as an idea is a result of 'spirit', the third potential, in which the preceding two potentials come to their truth via their orientation to the future, where they would cease to be opposed. The move to difference is therefore towards a future that would overcome the difference which is the condition of the manifest, and thus temporal, world. This move from identity to difference, as we saw, led to a past that is the condition of consciousness, but it also separated consciousness from direct contact with its ground. In the real the contracting force, which becomes the past, and the expanding force are mediated by the third potential into the future-directed flow of time (cf. Hogrebe's projector metaphor). As real, finite beings we experience time as lack – our being is never complete for us because it is temporal – even though we can explicate its ideal structure as a totality. The differing dimensions of time can only be understood as different via this structure. The awareness of time depends upon an identity which is sustained between the differing moments, otherwise we would have a version of the rotation, in which each moment simply swallows the other. My consciousness must sustain an identity which is prior to the difference of the moments in order for them to be my experience of time at all; it must also, though, already potentially contain the structure of difference within itself.[27]

Despite such insights into the philosophical understanding of time, and despite the profundity of many of the conceptual resources he mobilises in understanding the past, Schelling's attempt to give a philosophical presentation of the *content* of all three temporal dimensions is never completed. The articulation of the Idealist aim of the systematic unification of subject and object, by understanding the real development of history from the very origins of being, founders on problems of the relationship between philosophical system and historical contingency which do not admit of solutions (on this see, e.g., Habermas 1973). To conclude this chapter, let us briefly look at one central problem before moving on to Schelling's later struggles with these ideas.

The key to the *WA* is the identity theory, in which the ground and what is beyond it are irreducible to each other but cannot be without each other. The theory is used to explicate ontological difference, again in terms of language. The divinity '*is* as the One, and, precisely because it is the One, both the No and the Yes, and the unity of the two' (I/8 p. 299). If the divinity were to negate pronominal being by incorporating it into itself, then the divinity would not be able to manifest itself as free; if it were to leave pronominal being independent of itself the divinity would deny its essence as 'the equally eternal no and the equally eternal yes' (ibid. p. 300). It must, though, 'reveal itself as that which was free to reveal itself and not to reveal itself, as eternal freedom itself' (ibid.), by having the 'no' as the preceding ground of the succeeding 'yes', by having the inarticulacy of matter as the basis of language. By taking on the 'no', the ground, God shows that He is above it, but He also needs it if He is to *show* this superiority. If God had of necessity to create the universe, He would be faced with the inevitability of taking on something determinate, the ground, and thereby being forced to be it. The taking-on of the ground must therefore be free of such necessity. However, this suggests a fundamental problem.

Schelling will in the last analysis assume an a priori theological basis for his argument, which he spends much of his later work developing, despite all his later demonstrations of the inadequacy of the onto-theological arguments of Descartes and Hegel. This will finally make his overall project unworkable. The trouble is that if one does not presuppose a theological understanding of ontological difference, the idea of freedom suggested here can easily become indistinguishable from the idea that the emergence of a manifest universe is inexplicable or merely contingent. If there were actually nothing in our world that can make such freedom intelligible, then the Idealist idea that the intelligibility which is our highest aspect is the universe's own intelligibility becomes untenable. The highest principle in Idealism is the uncaused spontaneity of the I, and Schelling's system depends, as we saw, on showing how this principle is inherent in the rest of nature. The strongest part of Schelling's argument is the attempt to re-define the idea of freedom so that it can accommodate the 'real' aspect of nature whilst making it clear that nature's being manifest as something cannot be explicable via this aspect. This argument, already given an initial form in the *Naturphilosophie*, is made more convincing in the *WA* by its being linked to the emergence of language, the 'word', seen in the light of the further development of identity theory.

The danger lies in the insistence that God's 'freedom', which is conceived of as a spontaneity in the Idealist manner, is, as it has to be in order to avoid Spinozism, beyond the principle of sufficient reason: 'one cannot give a further ground/reason for an action of absolute freedom; it is so because it is so, i.e. it is absolutely, and, as such, necessarily' (I/7 p. 429). Schelling is aware that he would be returned to all the problems of dogmatic theology's attempt to prove the existence of God that Kant had so effectively demolished if he had to give a reason for the manifest world. At the same time the inability of the principle of sufficient reason to ground itself without paradox, that Schelling associates with God's freedom, will become the route to the end of onto-theology which goes, via Schopenhauer, to Nietzsche, Heidegger and beyond. Schelling is situated between the Kantian and the proto-existential positions, which is not the least reason why he is so important in the history of modern philosophy. This situation is precisely what will distinguish him from Hegel.

Despite the failure of the system as a whole, the account of the genesis of the very possibility of predication given by the *WA* points, then, to resources for the debate over 'Western metaphysics' which are far from exhausted. The advantage of the theory of the *WA* is that its understanding of identity theory and of language does not entail the kind of reduction of truth to power that has become so popular in the wake of Nietzsche. One can hardly consider the world of the *WA* as a world lacking in force, difference, and conflict, but the *WA* does not surrender the possibility of a conception of reason which comes to terms with the conflicts rather than regressively glorying in them. Schelling does not give up on the idea of the *Ages of the World*: he still gives his system this name in 1827, for instance, and the *Philosophy of Mythology* and *Philosophy of Revelation* are essentially attempts to complete such a system. His awareness of the dangers he is courting, which he will try to overcome in his later philosophy, are perhaps best illustrated in the following passage (from the lectures given in Erlangen in 1821 to be considered in the next chapter), which can serve to lead us to the later philosophy. Here the identity between the finite and the infinite becomes only a 'potential', in that it cannot be realised by the finite. Hegel's claim that he can realise this identity in philosophy is what Schelling will come to contest:

> Why is what nature is nature, and what God is God; as both are really (*an sich*) the same? This question is the same as if I were to ask: why is the left the left and the right the right? One cannot get to the bottom of this (*Hier ist auf keinen Grund zu kommen*). It is just their lot. God is not God for particular reasons but rather because He is God *jure positivo*. The ancients were already more familiar with this view, and there are echoes of it in the oldest Greek tragedy: for it is the mourning/tragedy (*Trauer*) of everything finite that in itself it is the same as the infinite, but not to be the infinite, but rather not to be it. It is only to be in *potentia*.
>
> (Schelling 1969 p. 90)

6

SCHELLING OR HEGEL?

INTRODUCTION

The later Schelling's significance in the history of philosophy depends on the reasons for his critique of Hegel. Why, though, should Schelling's critique of Hegel still be important? The historical demise of Hegelianism was the result of powerful historical and scientific forces, rather than of the attacks of the embittered Schelling on his former friend, which he began in the 1820s and carried on, directly or indirectly, until his death in 1854. Hegelianism was doomed even if there had been no Schelling: the dominance of a philosophy in the public sphere is not just a matter for philosophers. However, Hegel's philosophy has proved in recent years to be much more durable than might have seemed possible in the second half of the nineteenth century, or in the light of analytical philosophy. Versions of Hegelianism flourish in the German- and English-speaking worlds, as well as elsewhere. Key aspects of Hegel's thinking seem more able to stand up to scrutiny than was assumed to be the case at many times after the initial demise of Hegelianism. Hegel's development of a method that can avoid static categories, his rejection of rigid distinctions between subject and object, his contextual approach to questions of ethics, his account of the development of the subject's identity via its interaction with the Other, and many other aspects of his thought, are rightly the object of continuing philosophical debate and form the basis of many contemporary conceptions in psycho-analysis and social theory. Hegel has also been the main point of orientation, as I suggested at the very beginning, for many of the recent attempts to overcome 'Western metaphysics'.[1] I do not in any way wish to underestimate Hegel's significance in all these areas. However, if it is the case that Schelling's objections to Hegel have real philosophical substance, they must also be relevant to those areas where Hegel is regarded as a living philosophical option rather than as the dead representative of the metaphysics of presence. As such, the detailed exploration of some at first sight rather abstruse points in Schelling's later philosophy can reveal issues that have been neglected in contemporary theory.[2] The fact that patterns of thinking close to Schelling's have played a significant role in post-structuralism is already evidence of the continuing actuality of Schelling's thought in the debate about the nature of reason in modernity.

Modern accounts of Schelling's critique, which really got under way in the 1950s with Walter Schulz's new approach to the later Schelling (Schulz 1975),[3] are faced with the task of trying to give an account of Hegel and of Schelling that does justice to both. The fact is that there are really two debates involved here: one concerns the question of whether Schelling understood Hegel correctly, the other whether Hegel or Schelling is actually right. Unsurprisingly, adherents of Hegel tend to suggest the real issue is the former, in that if Schelling misunderstood Hegel his criticisms will be unfounded. It seems clear that Schelling sometimes did not get Hegel right. At the same time, though, some of his critique is so fundamental that it cannot just be a matter of technical questions about moves in Hegelian philosophy, in that similar issues to those raised by Schelling against Hegel have become the life-blood of much subsequent philosophy. I want to suggest that Schelling reveals a fatal problem in Hegel's philosophy which has consequences for all subsequent philosophy. The detailed defences of Hegel against Schelling of Alan White and Klaus Brinkmann do not take on this problem, and Schelling's case has not been adequately presented in English, least of all by post-structuralist critics of Hegel: hence my extended attention to it here.

The basic issue is whether the aim of German Idealism, the grounding of reason by itself, may not be a form of philosophical narcissism, in which reason admires its reflection in being without being able to give a validable account of its relationship to that reflection. In a later version this issue re-emerges in Heidegger's concern with the development of the 'subjectification of *Sein*', which begins with Descartes and continues until his own attempt to find a way of doing philosophy that does not have its ultimate ground in subjectivity. The issue of the self-grounding of reason is the philosophical crux of Schelling's later philosophy. The validity of Schelling's Hegel-critique depends on the validity of key assumptions concerning the relationship of abstract philosophical concepts, such as freedom, reason, or being, to what they are concepts of. It is the articulation of this relationship that is at issue between Schelling and Hegel. Although central aspects of Schelling's 'positive philosophy' are determined by theological concerns, the best arguments stand without theology, which is why my account will only consider certain aspects of the later philosophy in detail.

I spent a considerable amount of time examining the WA in the last chapter because much of the substance of the later philosophy is already present there. In the WA Schelling increasingly moved away from the idea that one can give a philosophical reason for there being a manifest world, towards a conception which relies upon a new notion of 'freedom' to explain the fact of the world's being disclosed. This line of argumentation becomes part of his move towards the 'positive philosophy', which concerns him until his death, and which is the major philosophical addition to the ideas of the WA in the later work. The distinction between a 'negative' and a 'positive' philosophy briefly surfaced in *Philosophy and Religion*, as we saw. There Schelling already suggested that a philosophy which reveals the structures of the finite world can only reveal the relative non-being of every determinate thing, and thus cannot explain why there should be such non-being at all, rather than the positive Absolute. One way of trying to overcome this split is to suggest, as do aspects of the identity philosophy, that relative non-being is itself the Other of the Absolute, so that the two are 'identical' in the identity of identity and difference. The Absolute is therefore a process in which everything finite reveals its finitude by its self-cancellation, but thereby necessarily leads to the infinite as the inherent 'Other of itself'. This is the conception which Hegel will bring to full methodological expression in the *Logic*, and concretise in his System. The success of the enterprise depends upon articulating the knowledge that what appears finite is actually infinite, because we can know its finitude in philosophy, and thus transcend finitude within thought. By the early 1820s Schelling was fully aware that Hegel had developed and articulated such a conception, which purported to solve the major metaphysical problems involved in the relationship between the finite and the infinite, without requiring a prior positive foundation of the kind which raises all the problems of the transition to negativity that we have repeatedly encountered. Schelling himself, of course, had from the very beginning insisted that one start with the Absolute, thereby ensuring that the problem of the transition did not go away. If such a beginning could be avoided, Hegel would be right and philosophy could claim to have overcome the distinction between thought and being by revealing the *nature* of their identity in a self-bounded philosophical system.

The ability to grasp such an identity in thought requires thought to reflect what it is not – being – as really itself, even as it appears not to be itself. This problem was already evident in Fichte's attempts to characterise the 'not-I' whilst sustaining the primacy of the I, and is the crux of German Idealism. If the 'substance' is to be 'subject', then negativity, the finitude of the particular subject, must turn out to negate itself, and thereby lead to the infinite. The infinite should then be evident in speculative thinking's moving beyond any determinate category to the philosophical insight into why all determinate thoughts come to be negated. This final insight is absolute knowledge. It is this conception that Schelling, whilst accepting its force as an immanent methodological account of how thought can progressively articulate conceptual knowledge, comes to reject in the 'positive philosophy'.

REFLECTION AND INVERSION

The reasons for such a rejection are already evident in lectures Schelling gave in Erlangen in 1820–1.[4] In these lectures, which Horst Fuhrmans published in 1969 on the basis of notes taken by a member of the audience, under the title *Initia Philosophiae Universae*, and part of which Schelling's son published under the title *On the Nature of Philosophy as a Science*,[5] Schelling tries, like Hegel, to explicate how philosophy can give a systematic articulation of knowledge. He acknowledges the necessity, which we saw in the identity philosophy, for the system to be able to encompass the propositions A is B and A is not B by showing how change must be incorporated into truth. This requires a ground of identity if such opposed propositions are to find their place in the system despite their difference. The difficulty lies in giving an account of such a ground. Nothing that emerges from the ground can of itself explain what is required, because what emerges from the ground is determinate and thus dependent upon an other. What is needed here cannot be dependent upon anything. Schelling terms this the 'absolute subject', which, as the name suggests, is the condition of all predicates and therefore cannot itself be characterised by a predicate:[6]

> this One subject must go through everything and remain in nothing. For if it remained anywhere, life and development would be hindered. *To go through everything and to be nothing,*

130

namely not to *be* anything such that it could not also be otherwise – this is the demand.

(Schelling 1969 pp. 16–17)

This ground would appear to have to be God, but Schelling insists, in order to escape pantheism's failure to account for privation, on making a further distinction, which goes back to the refusal in his early philosophy to regard the Absolute as a 'thing', as well as to the *FS* and the *WA*: 'We said: there is nothing that the absolute subject is *not*, and there is nothing which that subject is. Namely, the absolute subject *is* not not God, and it is yet also not God; it is also that which God is not' (ibid. p. 18). This system, then, demands the renunciation of any positive conceptual determinations at the outset.

The fact is, though, that we live in an articulated world, albeit one whose articulations do not have any ultimate stability. Schelling characterises the 'absolute subject' in a manner which is vital to the later philosophy:

> in order to enclose itself in a form (*Gestalt*) it must admittedly be outside all forms, but it is not its being outside all forms, being ungraspable [i.e. as itself] but the fact that it can enclose itself in a form, that it can make itself graspable, thus that it is free to enclose itself in a form and not to do so, that is positive about it.

(ibid. p. 21)

The essential idea is, then, as in the *WA*, 'freedom', in the sense of that which cannot be expressed by any determinate predicate but which gives rise to a manifest world of determinations. Schelling is careful not to suggest that freedom is a predicate which defines the 'absolute subject': 'For then this freedom would appear as an *attribute*, which presupposes a subject which is still different from and independent of it – rather freedom is the essence of the subject, or the subject is itself *nothing other than eternal freedom*' (ibid. p. 21).[7] The idea that freedom is not an attribute but is rather the necessarily prior ground of the world's being disclosed will be echoed in Heidegger's assertion in 'On the Essence of Truth': 'Man does not "possess" freedom as an attribute, instead at the most the opposite is true: freedom, ex-sisting (*ek-sistente*), revealing *Da-sein* possesses man' (Heidegger 1978 p. 187). The question for Schelling is how this 'freedom' has taken on the determinate forms of the existing world, including ourselves. He describes a process of 'knowledge', by which he means becoming articulated, in the manner of the emergence of the 'word' in the *WA*.

131

He expressly says that this is not a question of human knowledge, for reasons we shall see in a moment.

Schelling appears next to make a thoroughly Hegelian move, by pondering the beginning of this process of 'knowledge':

> That which is the absolute beginning cannot know itself; by going over into knowledge it ceases to be the beginning and must therefore progress until it finds itself as the beginning again. The beginning which knows itself as the beginning, the restored beginning is the end of all knowledge.
>
> (Schelling 1969 p. 25)

At the end the beginning looks back at the process of knowledge in which it appeared to cease to be itself, and now sees that it is really the moving reflection of itself in the object. In Hegel's *Logic* the analogous process begins with (1) 'being' as the 'indeterminate immediate', which is then (2) 'reflected' in the subject, that thereby becomes reflexively determinate *as* subject because being becomes *its* object; in a further movement the mediation between subject and object is grasped in (3) the 'concept', which is the subject's realisation that the process of mediation, in which the opposition of subject and object is finally overcome, is the truth of its own development as both subject and object. Here Schelling seems to concur with such a conception, in which what he calls 'wisdom' must be 'in the beginning, the middle, and the end' (ibid. p. 27). There is, though, a crucial difference.

In the Hegelian conception the knowledge which reveals the truth of the beginning at the end is the truth of what at the beginning was 'immediate', and, importantly, *knows* it is that truth.[8] The concept of being, when it has been fully articulated, is the truth of being and reveals that its beginning is 'negative', dependent, in the sense we have repeatedly seen. The problem, which I shall analyse in detail later in the chapter, is that in moving from (1), the initial immediacy of being, to (2), the stage of reflection, Hegel fails to deal with the difficulty of how what is mediated can know itself to be identical with what is immediate without simply presupposing this identity. The fact is that the truth of being, which is supposed to be a *result*, would have already to be there at the beginning, thereby posing the question of how it could be known at all as itself (i.e. in the way I see myself, rather than a random object, in a reflection). Schelling now makes moves which explicitly put the validity of Hegel's structure in question: we have already analysed some of the reasons for this questioning in relation to Jacobi and to Hölderlin's *Judgement and Being*, and in Schelling's questioning whether finite beings' self-cancellation is sufficient to arrive at a positive Absolute.

In reflexive knowledge the difference between the subject and the object of knowledge gives rise to the need for this difference to be cancelled out: by understanding what the object opposed to me is, I both go beyond the immediacy of the object's resistance to my thought and go beyond the immediacy of myself by engaging with the Other, the object of knowledge. Schelling now separates this process of reflection from its basis, which he denies can be understood in the way the relationship of subject and object in specific knowledge can be understood. He does so by suggesting that the real process of dynamic development, of 'freedom', is only *repeated* in thought, rather than being the immanent truth of that process itself. This means that philosophy cannot grasp the 'absolute subject' within thinking: 'Now in man, however, this wisdom is not present anymore, in man there is no objective bringing forth, but rather just ideal imitation (*ideales Nachbilden*) . . . in him there is only knowledge' (ibid. p. 27). Schelling thereby moves towards a fundamental critique of Idealism, of the kind Habermas suggests is characteristic of key aspects of modern philosophy:

> Idealism had deceived itself from the very beginning about the fact that the *formae rerum* actually always already contained in themselves and merely repeated what they were supposed to have expelled as the material and the absolutely not-being – namely the material content of those empirical single things from which the Ideas had first to be derived by comparative abstraction.
>
> (Habermas 1988 p. 38)

Schelling would not accept Habermas's notion of 'material', but the basic move against Idealism is as Habermas describes, in that the primacy of the subject is undermined by the realisation of the dependence of its thinking on what is itself not the result of thinking.

Although man is where living 'wisdom' is still possible, 'what was deed and life in that objective movement is in man now *only* knowledge' (Schelling 1969 p. 28). What exactly does this mean? The answer lies in the notion of reflection. Though knowledge is conceived of as a dynamic process, it entails a reflexive structure of knower and known, whereas the 'absolute subject . . . can also be called *pure* knowledge and cannot as such be what is known' (ibid. p. 29). The absolute subject cannot be split into subject and object without losing its fundamental nature as freedom, the freedom 'to enclose itself in a form and not to do so', because freedom is not a determinate predicate, in that it entails both A and not-A.[9] One can only know freedom via its self-objectifications: 'we see it in all its forms but not as the eternal freedom, not as subject, not *as it is in itself*' (ibid. p. 30). The very fact that there is the philosophical question as to how we could know the Absolute means that we could only know it in a mediated fashion. We do not know it as itself, but only as it is for us in reflection, in considering what determinate things in the world are: 'The absolute subject is only there to the extent to which I do not make it into an object, i.e. do not know it, *renounce* knowledge' (ibid. p. 38). The argument sounds very much like the arguments of the early philosophy in which the Absolute was only available in intellectual intuition. This gave rise to Hegel's accusation that the Absolute thereby became indeterminate because the unity of subject and object was given from the outset rather than revealed in the process of the beginning's coming to its truth at the end. Now Schelling sees access to the absolute subject in terms of 'ekstasis' (*Extase*) (ibid. p. 39), in which the thinking subject ceases to regard the manifest world as some kind of not-I, and thus as in a reflexive relation to itself, and moves beyond itself, thereby allowing the absolute subject to be as itself and not an object of knowledge. This sounds suspiciously mystical; the fact is, though, that the argument moves in a logical manner.

Schelling is concerned to show that consciousness attributes the world to its own activity when in fact it is the prior activity of the world that is consciousness's condition of possibility (on this, see Frank 1975 pp. 123–30). Though any discussion of being only seems possible by making being a determination of thinking, this is actually an *inversion* of the real situation. Whilst the world may seem only to become determinate by being incorporated into the other – thought – this incorporation depends upon the activity of what cannot itself be *shown* to be thought. Schelling argues as follows: the absolute subject in the state of inwardness (what Schelling here terms A), prior to any self-manifestation, prior to anything that could be thought of as a world, corresponds to the state of consciousness as absolute unknowing externality (B) in 'ekstasis': i.e. nothing can be known about it, both are 'immediate'. When the absolute subject manifests itself it becomes B, as the now external, mediated object world. As such it can correspondingly become internalised by that which now knows it, consciousness, which was B, but has now taken on the status of A. Objectivity, but not being, as Kant had shown, depends upon the priority of the thinking subject. Kant had then argued that this implied that the subject could not know things in themselves, thereby introducing a non-reflexive third term into the structure of knowledge.

Schelling's point is in a way quite simple. What was wrong with the Kantian argument was that it actually introduced a reflexive moment into the third term, by suggesting that what we could not know were still in fact things. This entails a concept of reflection because the thing 'in itself' is that which is differentiated from thinking. As Schelling bluntly puts it in the later Lectures: 'to the extent to which [the thing in itself] is a thing (object) it is not in itself, and if it is in itself it is not a thing' (I/10 p. 84). The point for Schelling is to show, at the most fundamental level, that the structure of reflection cannot apply. This realisation can, it is vital to remember, only come about for us by reflection, in thought. Gasché therefore is mistaken when he says in defence of Hegel: 'Any attempt to challenge absolute reflection through some notion of immediacy is bound to fail . . . insisting on the immediate is a reflexive act' (Gasché 1986 p. 74). Gasché's mistake, as we shall see, is to ignore the distinction between the cognitive ground and the real ground of knowledge that Schelling had already made in aspects of the identity philosophy. The difficulty in understanding Schelling's position is evident: the demand is to think something unthinkable. We can, though, meaningfully talk of what we think are not thoughts: things, for example. To be a determinate thing the object must be determined in a proposition by the subject, thereby involving it in the structure of reflection. It is a key aspect of the notion of reflection that leads Schelling to a vital insight:

> The transition out of the subject into the object reflects itself via the transition out of the object into the subject. As the object reflects itself in the water, in the same way the absolute subject stands in an inverted relationship to consciousness. The absolute subject only leaves behind absolute non-knowledge. But if A becomes B, in the same relationship B becomes A, i.e. knowledge.
>
> (ibid. p. 44)

How is this to be understood?

Being in itself encompasses the potential for thought within itself: it can become for itself. As soon as there is thought it appears to be able encompass the world, but *this* is the inversion that Schelling is concerned to correct. It *appears* that the truth of being lies in its internalisation by consciousness: what could we say about being if it were not in some way present to consciousness?[10] But now Schelling makes the vital third move, in which the absolute subject reasserts itself as subject, as A, thus as the real ground of the process. 'A' leads to consciousness and reflective knowledge but is not any conceptually articulable thought or thing:

> only now it is A that has been restored from B [from its being an object of knowledge]. Correspondingly the knowledge that stands in relation to it will also change its relation; as the absolute subject is restored, knowledge must die off into non-knowledge, B which became A must again become B, i.e. *non-knowledge*, but as it is brought back from knowledge it is no longer simply non-knowledge, but it is knowing non-knowledge; it is non-knowledge but no longer externally, as at the beginning, but internally.
>
> (ibid. p. 45)

This is, then, as Manfred Frank makes clear against the standard misinterpretation of Schelling (Frank 1975 p. 129), not a dogmatic assertion involving knowledge of the transcendent basis of thought: the realisation is a product of reflection's attempt internally to ground itself, not of a primary mystical intuition of the Oneness of being. As Frank puts it, 'there is no concept of being outside the concept which appears on the horizon of a self-cancellation (*Selbstaufhebung*) of reflection' (Frank 1984 p. 354).[11] One cannot positively say what being is, but this does not mean that it disappears from philosophy: it is the dependence of reflection on what cannot appear as knowledge that means that being must be prior to knowledge. Being cannot appear as itself precisely because something appearing *as* something is what defines the structure of reflection and knowledge.

Schelling understands the Socratic *docta ignorantia* by the fact of the movement of knowledge, in which, as in Hegel, there is 'constant change'. However, against Hegel, this change cannot be explicated from within the process of reflection. The identity of thought and being for Schelling is ontologically, not logically, prior to consciousness's attempt to show this identity: 'This relationship, this interchange could not take place if our consciousness were not eternal freedom which has come to itself, and vice versa, or if eternal freedom and our knowledge or consciousness were not originally One' (ibid. p. 47). Showing the identity after the separation of thought and being – the separation required for there to be a question as to their identity – thereby becomes impossible: it must be presupposed.

One arrives at the awareness of what cannot be conceived of in terms of reflection precisely via the correction of the inversion entailed in the reflexive attempt to grasp the nature of consciousness, thus via the realisation that being must precede reflection, even as the opposite necessarily *appears* to be the case to the conscious subject. In the process of realising that particular knowledge is always overcome I seek a principle of that overcoming. This seems to be the reflexive activity of consciousness itself, which tries to fix the object world by internalising the external object in the concept, thus by representation. Consciousness also tries to fix itself as the principle of this process, thereby putting itself in a reflexive relationship with the object as the necessary Other of itself.

The idea that thought is the underlying principle turns out, though, to be a misapprehension, since if knowledge is continually changing it cannot finally know itself *as* itself because the fact of its identity – which, remember, Schelling does not question – depends on an other that it cannot encompass within itself: namely, the principle of *change*, 'eternal freedom', the absolute subject:

> α) Knowledge is continually changing, it is always an *other and yet the same* [i.e. as Hegel also made clear, if it is to qualify as knowledge at all, something must remain identical between what is refuted and what is now asserted], but β) it is not my knowledge that changes its form, rather it is changed; each form it takes is only the reflex (the *inversion*, hence reflection!) of the form in eternal freedom, and γ) I perceive that form [i.e. of eternal freedom] immediately via the reflex in myself, i.e. via the change in my knowledge.
>
> (ibid. pp. 47–8)

It is not the particular manifestation of knowledge that tells me the truth about the world, but rather the necessity of movement from one piece of knowledge to the next. Thus far Hegel would concur. However, a logical reconstruction of the process of knowledge can, for Schelling, only be a reflection of thought by itself: the real process cannot be described in philosophy because the cognitive ground of knowledge and the real ground, though inseparable from each other, cannot be shown to reflect each other.

Schelling, then, undermines the idea that the truth is dependent upon a relationship of correspondence or representation between thought and thing, because a cognitive perspective on this correspondence could not be articulated[12] – this was already the case in aspects of the identity philosophy. The fact that there is knowledge, reflection, cannot be deduced from knowledge itself. As Frank suggests, what makes the world intelligible, thinking

> cannot enlighten itself about its own facticity (*Bestand*), about the contingency of what imposes itself as a law of thought upon it; it *experiences* its necessity every time de facto. As such one can say that the a priori status of the logical is . . . not itself logically grounded.
>
> (Frank 1975 p. 139)

It is this insight that has prophetic import for the future of philosophy.

What is at issue is a new version of the ontological difference of the kind encountered in the identity philosophy and in the *WA*. This version of ontological difference is another challenge to a vital aspect of Heidegger's account of the history of philosophy. Discussing the role of the copula in logic, Heidegger claims that philosophy has been cut off from the question of *Sein* in the following way:

> The problem will remain immobilised as long as logic has not been taken back again into ontology, i.e. as long as Hegel, who on the contrary dissolved ontology into logic, has not been grasped and that always means has been both overcome and at the same time appropriated by the radicalisation of the question. This overcoming of Hegel is the internally necessary step in the development of Western philosophy, which must be made if it is to stay alive at all.[13]
>
> (Heidegger 1989 p. 254)

We shall in a moment consider in more detail whether Schelling really does overcome Hegel. For the moment we have established how Schelling makes a clear distinction between the ontic, the knowledge of B, and the ontological, A, thereby making sure that logic cannot swallow ontology.

Heidegger claims in the same text that in all previous philosophy:

> Either everything ontic is dissolved into the ontological (Hegel) without an insight into the ground of the possibility of ontology itself; or, on the other hand, the ontological is completely misrecognised and explained away ontically, without an understanding of the ontological preconditions which every ontic explanation already carries in itself.[14]
>
> (ibid. p. 466)

It is clear from this passage that Heidegger is ignoring essential philosophical moves in the later Schelling. This is not merely a scholarly point. Much recent post-structuralist theory in particular has relied explicitly or implicitly on Heidegger's assertions about the history of philosophy, as a way of seeking to circumvent the supposed monolith of Western metaphysics. The target of that history is usually Hegel, for much the same reasons as Hegel becomes the target of Schelling: he tries to establish a self-enclosed system in philosophy. Schelling explicitly rejects the possibility of a self-reflecting dialectical system when considering the transition which we repeatedly considered in the *WA*:

> Here nothing more can be explained by necessity; rather, the transition into being is a free deed. Here all deduction ceases, to the extent to which *it* is a deduction of something absolutely given from premises which have been determined in advance. Here we separate ourselves from the concept of the dialectician. Here is the point where not the concept but only the deed is decisive.
>
> (Schelling 1969 p. 116)

What emerge in the most interesting aspects of Schelling's later work are arguments which reveal the consequences of ontological difference. These arguments reveal the need for a different understanding of the history of Western metaphysics from that offered by the adherents of post-modernity. However, if Schelling already makes certain of the philosophical moves necessary for a post-modern or post-metaphysical perspective, what status are we to attribute to him? There cannot be any exceptions in such a view of the history of philosophy, particularly in the later Heidegger's conception of the history of *Sein*, as that would mean the story loses its point as an account of the forgetting of *Sein*.

Let us pursue Schelling's argument further, in order to begin to understand his peculiar status in modern thought. The absolute subject, 'eternal freedom', having manifested itself, cannot manifest itself *as* itself. This is so even if what it becomes must, despite this, also be itself in the way we saw in the *WA*'s theory of identity. Any determinate manifestation contradicts its freedom from finite determination:

> Eternal freedom thought it could finally ground itself. But what now becomes objective to it is only an illusion/appearance (*Schein*) of its form, an artificial fantastic self. It is not in fact/deed

139

(*in der Tat*) as that as which it knows itself: and vice versa, it does not know itself as that which it really is. Here, accordingly, the difference between knowledge and being emerges for the first time. Eternal freedom is an other 'in itself' and an other 'for itself'.

(ibid. p. 138)

For Schelling we cannot think of 'eternal freedom' in any other way than as the 'Terminus *a quo* of our thinking . . . . Eternal freedom is the unthinkable, that which no one can think of as ever being, but *eternally only as past/having-been been [sic] (gewesen)*' (ibid. p. 92).

Schelling plays on the etymology of the past tense of *sein* (*gewesen*), and of *Wesen*, usually translated as 'essence', but which in German also has the sense of that which has been 'been' (Sartre's *être été*), in a transitive manner. *Wesen* will be the central category of the 'Logic of Reflection', the middle part of Hegel's *Logic*. What carries *Wesen* in Schelling is pre-reflexive being: as such, *Wesen*, reflection, is now the *lack* of full being.[15] *Wesen* tries to overcome this lack in the concept, but necessarily fails to do so because of its dependence upon the being that precedes it. It is thereby condemned to a constant striving to overcome this lack in the future. This leads Schelling to a structure that has again become familiar in recent European philosophy, the structure of the inherent lack in the subject, whose very nature is determined by this lack. The proximity of pre-reflexive being to Lacan's Real can suggest another way of understanding this.[16] Here is Malcolm Bowie on Lacan's Real: 'The Real . . . is the irremediable and intractable "outside" of language; the indefinitely receding goal towards which the signifying chain tends; the vanishing point of the Symbolic and Imaginary alike' (M. Bowie 1988 p. 116). This goal is the goal of what Schelling terms 'negative philosophy'.

Rather than this goal, as it is in Hegel, being realisable in philosophy, the fact is that it involves the same inversion we saw above: the Real is actually always already lost as that from which the subject emerges. The hope of attaining it seems to be in the future, but this is only the way it appears to thought's self-deception. Schelling's interest for us, then, lies in the way in which he questions the last great attempt at positive metaphysics: that of Hegel. The continuing power of the conception of ontological difference in Schelling, evident in the re-appearance of Schellingian arguments in recent theory, makes it perhaps more appropriate to regard him, rather than Hegel, as the archetypal philosopher of modernity. If this is the case, then we may well do best, as I think we should, to dispense with the very idea of the post-modern, at the very least in philosophy.

THE LIMITS OF NEGATIVE PHILOSOPHY

The project of Schelling's later philosophy is to make Christianity into a philosophically viable religion. It would, however, be invidious in a philosophical account of his work to focus primarily on this question, given the complexity of the issues involved.[17] The arguments of the later philosophy that need not be couched in theological terms are, it seems to me, most in need of re-assessment. The problem of Schelling's theology is important here, though, because the most important defences of Hegel against Schelling insist on it. Alan White claims: '*If* Hegel's first philosophy is taken to be metaphysical theology, then his system is completely vulnerable to Schelling's critique' (White 1983b p. 74). White goes on to maintain: 'For Hegel first philosophy is transcendental ontology, the science of the determinations fundamental to things and to thought; for Schelling, it must be transcendent theology, the science of the highest being' (ibid. p. 99). Klaus Brinkmann suggests, in a similar vein, that 'Schelling's objections [to Hegel] would only be acceptable if one could opt for the position of the late philosophy' (in Hartmann 1976 p. 208), by which he means the late philosophy in all its theological splendour.

Looked at in this way the question seems simple: unless we accept his theology, Schelling's objections to Hegel are invalid. Evidently the question is more complex than this. The key issue involved here has already been outlined and can be summarised in the question: is a 'transcendental ontology' really possible? The condition of its possibility is the demonstration that determinations of thought are really determinations of being, thus that ontology, as Heidegger put it, can be dissolved into logic. I shall try to show that Klaus Hartmann, and White and Brinkmann, who rely on Hartmann's position, simply assume determinations of thought are the reflexive determinations of being, by uncritically relying on Hegel's conception of the negation of negation. As such, for reasons we have already considered in the *Initia*, White and Brinkmann largely miss the philosophical point of Schelling's later work.

Brinkmann sees the basis of Schelling's critique of Hegel as the idea that 'there is something which is wholly other . . . in relation to thought, which cannot be represented conceptually'. He objects that 'This other, which is called the reality of the real (*Wirklichkeit des Wirklichen*) in Schelling, is naturally itself a category, which, as it means absolute otherness in relation to thought, is normally designated by "being" ' (in Hartmann 1976 p. 131). Gasché, as we saw, says much the same: 'Any attempt to challenge absolute reflection through some notion of immediacy is bound to fail . . . insisting on the immediate is a reflexive act' (Gasché 1986 p. 74). In consequence, thought knows what this absolute other is in relation to itself. The problem with this argument lies in explaining how thought can encompass its own relationship to what is *absolutely* other to it in a 'category' which *identifies* it. The only way a category can be determined is by its *difference* from other categories in thought – we already encountered this issue in relation to Kant's 'transcendental ideal' – but *this* difference has to be absolute: there cannot *be* any other 'category' of this kind. Such a category requires the articulation of a structure which includes (a) this particular *thought* (of absolute otherness, or 'being'), (b) what really *is* the absolute other of thought, (c) that which encompasses both as negatively related but actually identical aspects of itself. In fact to have such a thought presupposes the success of the whole of Hegel's System, in that the ultimate difference of thought and being must be overcome in the Absolute, *and be known to be overcome*, if such a category is to be legitimated. Brinkmann admits as much when he claims that 'apart from the final category no negation of the negation is complete' (ibid. p. 198). Gasché claims:

> Yet these contradictions [between reason and its Other] are not final obstacles to elaborating the self-reflection of the Absolute, because they seem to be moments in self-knowledge as a process. The Other, which the self can only know itself as, thus becomes the result of the self-alienation of the self before it recognises this Other as itself again.
>
> (Gasché 1986 p. 67)

The problem, as we shall see in detail in a moment, is simply this: how can something *re*-cognise itself without *already* knowing itself before ceasing to be itself? The attempt to use the negation of the negation as the immanent principle, which is behind both these arguments, will invalidate Hegel's whole attempt at a self-bounded metaphysical system.

Schelling's positive philosophy attempts to suggest a different path for philosophy, in the face of the impossibility of reason *knowing* what is absolutely other than it as ultimately itself. The interest of this philosophy lies not least in the fact that, despite this impossibility, it does not renounce an emphatic conception of reason. The difficulty in assessing the positive philosophy as a whole does lie in the fact that Schelling conceives of it as a theology which regards the question of creation as central, as Brinkmann and White claim. However, one does not need to accept Schelling's theology for the main philosophical point of the later philosophy to remain valid. The positive philosophy is for Schelling the necessary result of the limitations of 'negative philosophy'. By 1827/8, as is shown by the publication of the *Nachschrift* of Schelling's Munich lectures entitled *System of the Ages of the World*, Schelling thought he had found the 'common mistake of every philosophy that has existed up to now' (Schelling 1990 p. 57). The problem was what he termed the 'merely logical relationship of God to the world' (ibid.), which entails a reflexive relationship of the two, in which the world necessarily follows from the nature of God, and God and the world are therefore the 'Other of themselves'. The target is still initially Spinoza, but now Hegel is also attacked, somewhat cursorily and unfairly, though a key idea is already present. The beginning of the *Logic* with 'the most abstract of all, being' leads to the problem that:

> This being had to transform itself for no reason into existence (*Dasein*) and the external world and then into the inner world of the concept. The consequence was that the living substance, as a result of the most abstract concepts, was only left in thought.
>
> (ibid. p. 58)

Like all 'negative philosophy', then, Hegel's will be understood as inverting the relationship between thinking and being by making the truth of being a necessary consequence of thinking.

This inversion, which we saw identified in the *Initia*, is what makes something into negative philosophy. Any system which is self-contained, in which each proposition follows necessarily from the preceding proposition (one model is evidently Spinoza's *Ethics*), cannot by definition be wrong within itself, and Schelling is emphatic that this is the case, but it cannot fulfil the aim of philosophy. Schelling illustrates this, somewhat shakily, by the case of geometry (one has to assume he is talking about the geometry of his day, which was still basically Euclidean). If all the propositions follow as axioms in a system, the system is ultimately a grand tautology, like the fact that every triangle must have three sides:

> Knowing a truth whose opposite is impossible cannot be called knowledge, e.g., that $a = a$. Everyone will say that they thereby know just as much as they did before: nothing. In knowing a truth, then, the opposite must be possible, $a = b$ cannot also $= c$; and by saying a is not $= c$ but $= b$, I know something.
>
> (ibid. p. 18)

We saw the basis of this conception in the identity philosophy, where the X that grounded predication could be as A and as not-A. As Schelling puts it in the 1830 *Introduction to Philosophy*, in an 'emphatic' philosophical proposition: 'the subject must be such that it could equally well be and not be, a is b if it could also not be b' (Schelling 1989 p. 57). Sciences like geometry, which do not allow of the possibility of the opposite of their propositions because their object is a priori, are 'negative' sciences, whereas 'philosophy . . . has as its object that of which one can only say that it is' (ibid.). This might appear just to be an argument in favour of the empirical sciences, a kind of early positivism.[18] Schelling does term what he is doing 'philosophical empiricism', but what he means by this is clearly not positivism.

The positivity of the positive philosophy lies in the demand for an explanation, even in the case of geometry, or logic, of the fact that there can be self-contained a priori systems of necessity.[19] Such systems cannot, and this is the fundamental point, explain their own possibility: whilst geometry maps the structure of space, it does not account for the existence of space. Schelling does not deny the internal necessity in geometry or logic, but demands to understand why it is necessary. The only possible answer to this is the fact that it is necessary, which does not allow of a further *logical* explanation. Whilst Hegel agrees that philosophical propositions cannot be statements of identity, because they must move beyond the subject in the predicate, he thinks that the explication of this movement as a whole can be grounded in reason, thus that the *Logic* can ultimately articulate identity within itself.

Schelling cannot accept this conception of reason, as he suggests in the following startling passage, whose implications for any theory which regards its object as ultimately knowable are still often ignored:

> could not, just as easily as reason, unreason rule? As the world is at present reason does admittedly rule. The laws of thought are *positive* [in the sense of 'binding'], logic is a positive science and can only be understood by the positivity of reason. Now it admittedly seems easy to put reason first. But if pure infinite being [which plays the same role as 'eternal freedom'] is nothing more [than reason], then we have already finished in philosophy. All we need to do is assume that, to pass the time, reason posits itself and its opposite, in order then to have the pleasure of finding out the reason once again from this nature [that it has posited]. If we free ourselves *of all partiality* then we have to say:

this assumed relationship of both sides, where the preponderance is on the side of the ideal, is not something that
follows as a matter of course, but is something contingent and
really posited, something that can be, but, as such, that can
absolutely not be, and is in this sense contingent, because it
presupposes a true cause.

(Schelling 1989 p. 101)

What we are able to know about particular causes in nature cannot tell
us about the *Ur-sache*, which for Schelling means the 'cause' but also,
following the etymology, the 'primal matter', of nature as manifest
being. This cause is what 'gives the ideal preponderance over the real'
(ibid. p. 102), which brings us to one version of what Schelling means
by 'God'. Schelling's argument again need not succeed as theology to
be philosophically valid. There is no doubt that Schelling's aim is to
answer the question of being by establishing the basis of a
philosophical religion, but, for instance in the 1842–3 *Introduction to the
Philosophy of Revelation or Foundation of the Positive Philosophy*, he
himself emphasises that certain key moves in his argument do not
depend upon this aim:

I do not begin with the concept of God in the positive
philosophy, as former metaphysics and the ontological
argument attempted to, but I must drop precisely this concept,
the concept *God*, in order to begin with that which just exists, in
which nothing more is thought than just this existing – in order
to see if I can get from it to the divinity. Thus I cannot really
prove the existence of God (by, for instance, beginning with the
concept *God*) but instead the concept of that which exists before
all possibility and thus without doubt – is given to me.

(II/3 p. 158)

To appreciate why he argues in this manner we must now consider
how and why he makes the move from negative to positive
philosophy.

In order to understand this better, we first need a very brief outline
of the pattern of Schelling's later attempts at a philosophical system.
The basic pattern of the system remains from the early 1830s onwards,
although the relative weight given to the different parts changes, so
that the historical review of philosophy[20] becomes reduced in size in
the later versions, where Schelling tries to work out the way to link
negative and positive philosophy into a whole system (on this, see
Fuhrmans's introduction to the *Foundation of the Positive Philosophy* of

1832–3 (Schelling 1972)). Schelling begins with an introduction which reveals the limitations of 'logical' – negative – philosophy, shows these limitations in the history of modern philosophy, then attempts to give a theory of creation as the free act of God, thereby trying to skirt the traps of Spinozism and its perceived successors, including Hegel; this introduction was then followed by the *Philosophy of Mythology*, and the *Philosophy of Revelation*. The overall pattern of the early version of the introduction, of *c*. 1832–3, is most clear in the volume edited by Fuhrmans, that of the later version of the whole system in the 1841–2 *Philosophy of Revelation*, edited by Manfred Frank (Schelling 1977), which contains the whole system in outline. The point of the introduction is to establish the need for a historical philosophy, which is then attempted in the analysis of the history of mythology and of Christian revelation. In mythology:

> the ideas (*Vorstellungen*) are products of a necessary process, or of natural consciousness which is left to its own devices, on which there is no influence of any free cause; on the other hand *revelation is thought of as something which presupposes an* actus *outside consciousness and a relationship which the freest of all causes, God, has himself freely given to mankind.*
>
> (Schelling 1977 p. 250)

Mythology repeats the patterns of the basic processes of the *Naturphilosophie* and the early stages of the *WA* in consciousness; revelation parallels the break in the *STI*, when free consciousness develops, and also parallels the later stages of the *WA*. Schelling has therefore concretised the Idealist model of his early philosophy by trying to show its workings in historically attestable manifestations of thought. The reasons for this change lie in the move from negative to positive philosophy.

I shall concentrate now on the philosophical introductions to these texts, which contain the real substance of the late philosophy. In the introductions Schelling gives varying – not always fully compatible – versions of the move from negative to positive philosophy. Much of the argument is centred round his reinterpretation and refutation of the ontological proof of God. This reference to apparently dead theology, like much of the work of the later Schelling, should not allow one to ignore the issues raised. Over 130 years later T.W. Adorno will also say of the ontological proof, in his lectures on *Philosophical Terminology*, that it is 'a question which appears to me, the more I think about it, as really the centre of philosophical reflection' (Adorno 1973 pp. 97–8). The fact is that the ontological proof is a route to matters concerning ontology in general. I shall concentrate on three texts, in order to make the presentation more accessible: the *Foundation of Positive Philosophy* of 1832–3 (*GPP* = *Grundlegung der positiven Philosophie*), the *Introduction to the Philosophy of Revelation* of 1842–3 (II/3), and the 1841–2 *Philosophy of Revelation* (PO = *Philosophie der Offenbarung*). I shall also take in other points from the Lectures (I/10), a version of which anyway formed part of the 1832–3 lectures, as well as from other texts when they make issues clearer.

POSITIVE PHILOSOPHY

Schopenhauer once suggested, with characteristic lack of charity, that Hegel's philosophy is one long version of the ontological proof of God. One might correspondingly suggest that Schelling's later philosophy is one long investigation of ontological proofs in philosophy. The reasons for this derive from some of the arguments we have already considered: if philosophy is to avoid the traps of inversion that Schelling had revealed in the *Initia*, the relationship between thought and being will be changed in ways that affect any attempt at a philosophical system, not least, of course, that of Hegel. The fact is that discussion of the ontological proof of God can easily become a discussion of ontological difference, which is what it often does for Schelling.[21]

When he begins the *GPP* he is quite emphatic about what he is looking for:

> for to the extent to which logic and dialectic themselves can be established as sciences, to that extent they rather presuppose philosophy, they are themselves possible as sciences only within philosophy, for the primal kind of all being (*Urtypus alles Seins*) must be achieved.
>
> (Schelling 1972 p. 67)

Why, though, is the 'primal kind of all being' so central? The argument proceeds in an apparently theological manner, but if we take Schelling's conception of God as that which gives preponderance of the ideal over the real this allows us initially to consider the questions at issue here in terms of thought's relationship to being. Schelling suggests that the relationship can be looked at in one of two ways, which correspond to negative and positive philosophy. In the 'regressive', negative, form of philosophy the essential factor comes at the end. In a dynamic philosophical system, the final result would clearly seem to be what matters the most. This is why God is often considered to be the final thought of philosophy. Kant had regarded the hope for such a positive final result within philosophy as involving an invalid 'transcendence', in that philosophy would have to claim positive knowledge of the intelligible if it wanted to complete itself. For the purposes of *philosophical* thinking, therefore, Kant's God becomes a postulate. Schelling largely concurs with Kant's suspicion of transcendence, to the extent that transcendence is the result of logical necessity, and must therefore be present within thought. He does not, however, think that this settles the issue of thought's relationship to transcendence.

His initial contention, which is also adopted by Feuerbach and the early Marx, is that any philosophy whose end is included within itself excludes real historical development. The alternative to this approach is the 'progressive', positive form of philosophy. Here the beginning becomes crucial, in that thought itself cannot create it, so it must in some way precede philosophical reflection. The real problem is how to get to this beginning philosophically. The aim is to find a defensible conception which countenances the idea that thought cannot sustain the illusion of its own omnipotence. The structure of Schelling's arguments leads to the basic structure of the positive philosophy.

The arguments derive from the ideas of the *Initia*: the ability of thinking to go beyond immediacy cannot be explained by thinking itself because thinking, as Schelling had already argued against Fichte, is not the ultimate ground of itself. The easy response to this fact might appear to be the following: because finite thought has within it the idea of the infinite it already provides the foundation for a proof of God's existence, because the concept of God cannot itself be the result of finite thinking. Schelling, though, wishes philosophy to come to terms with a different conception of existence, which he again suggests via the contrast with mathematics: 'But what philosophy has over mathematics is the concept of the subject of that which *can be* something *and can also not be something*' (Schelling 1972 pp. 97–8). Philosophy becomes the science of 'that which can also *not* be, of which one can only say that it *is* – in a word it follows that philosophy must be *positive science!*' (ibid. p. 98). Schelling denies that the world emerges via any kind of logical necessity:

> what we call the world, which is so *completely contingent* both as a
> whole and in its parts, cannot possibly be the impression of

something which has arisen by the *necessity of reason* . . . it
contains a *preponderant* mass of *unreason*.

(ibid. p. 99)

Whatever necessity reason can give us, therefore, is not to be
grounded in the necessary operations of thought, because the
necessity of *that* necessity is precisely what is at issue in the positive
philosophy. Schelling does not, though, think that this fact invalidates
what can be achieved by negative philosophy, only that such
philosophy cannot finally explain itself. It is when negative philosophy
tries to suggest that it can be positive, as he thinks it does in Hegel, that
Schelling considers it mistaken.

Schelling begins with the doubt about the reality of 'external things'
that is constitutive of Western philosophy from Parmenides onwards.
His basic point, already familiar from the identity philosophy, is that if
'external things' are not real, they must still *be* in some way if they are
to be doubted; this, though, means that 'what is a being (*Seiendes*) in a
certain way is also a not-being in a certain way' (ibid. p. 106).
Philosophy's task, as it was for Plato, is to arrive at what truly and
completely is. This evidently locates Schelling at the heart of 'Western
metaphysics', but the way he pursues this aim does not. The simple
point is that philosophy cannot *know* a priori what true being is. If
philosophy makes a claim to such knowledge, all it has done is to
assume that a certain kind of existence – the existence of an a priori
concept in thinking – is the absolute kind of existence. Schelling uses
his objection to this claim, which is what defines the 'metaphysics of
presence', both against the *cogito* and against the ontological proof of
God. He will use it by extension against Hegel.

The highest being of negative philosophy must be characterised by
necessity, otherwise there is no way in which thinking could arrive at
the notion at all, without surrendering its claims to logical and
systematic status. Dieter Henrich suggests why in relation to the
ontological proof:

The second [Descartes's as opposed to Anselm's] ontological
argument assumes that we think of God, as opposed to
everything finite, as a being which is necessarily there. What is
necessary is that which only depends upon itself in its being and
effect. If it were created by an other then it would be in its power,
if it were there by coincidence then it would have no power over
its existence. Hence this God is also said to be *causa sui*. He exists
by His own power and can be known without relating to

anything else. But if something is ground of its own being then it can only be thought simultaneously with the thought of its existence. It is on this argument that the second ontological argument is based. Moses Mendelssohn skilfully compressed it into a short formulation: 'I cannot separate existence from the idea of the necessary being without destroying the idea itself. I must think concept and thing or drop the concept itself' (*Morgenstunden* p. 319).

(Henrich 1967a p. 4)

Schelling, though, suggests that Descartes's use of this argument as a proof of God fails to make a key ontological distinction because it confuses a form of existence in thought – necessary existence – with the fact of existence, which, as he has made clear, is not logically explicable in the same way:

But it is something completely different whether I say: God can only exist *necessarily*, or whether I say: He necessarily exists. From the First (He *can* only exist necessarily) only follows: therefore He exists necessarily. N.B. *if He exists*, but it does not at all follow *that* He exists.

(I/10 p. 15)

The problem is both whether the *concept* of necessary existence really has, as Mendelssohn suggests, a different status from any other concept, and whether this is the only way in which we can approach the question of necessary existence and of God. Schelling will, it is true, attempt to salvage the ontological proof by inverting it, but what matter for subsequent philosophy in this context are his albeit not always consistent moves beyond the Idealist paradigm of the articulable identity of *thought* and being. This paradigm includes the thought of God, which necessarily entails His being, that Hegel sees as the 'self-determination of the concept'.

Schelling's ontological reflections are, significantly, also applicable to the *cogito*. Both in the case of the ontological proof and in the case of the *cogito*, existence and essence, 'that' and 'what', seem to be coextensive. Heidegger makes this point whilst arguing in 1941 that the Schelling of the *FS* is really just part of Western metaphysics:

already, together with the securing of the certainty of the *ego cogito* (*sum cogitans*), goes the *pre-givenness of God* which itself offers the last securing of certainty (Descartes, Medit. III). This context of securing of self-re-presentation (*des Sich-selbst-*

Vorstellens) is then grasped in German Idealism from within itself in its absoluteness.

(Heidegger 1991 p. 119)

Clearly this Schelling cannot be understood in such a manner:[22] self-representation is the paradigm of reflection whose failure was shown in the *Initia*. Schelling arrives at his key point by distinguishing differing kinds of being, so that even the – albeit limited and punctual – absolute certainty of the *cogito* to which Descartes lays claim turns out not to be absolute:

> this *Sum cogitans* cannot . . . mean that it is as though I were *nothing* but thinking, or as if thinking were the substance of my being . . . . Thinking is, therefore, only a determination or way of being . . . . The *sum* which is contained in the *cogito* is, therefore, only *sum qua cogitans*, I am as thinking, i.e. in that specific way of being which is called thinking . . . .. The *sum* that is contained in the *cogito* does not, then, have the significance of an absolute 'I am', but only of an 'I am *in one way or another*' namely as just thinking, in that way of being which one calls thinking.
>
> (I/10 p. 10)

The argument can be taken a stage further: the *cogito* itself is, as such, no more absolute than the ideas I have of things, which, even if they do not exist absolutely, are '*not not at all*', in that they must, in the same way as the I, *be* in thinking if they are to be doubted: 'For what is not at all in any way also cannot be doubted' (ibid. p. 11).

Schelling further 'decentres' the Cartesian subject by exploring one of the key insights into subjectivity at which Fichte was the first to arrive, and which was developed by the Romantics (on this, see Henrich 1967b, and A. Bowie 1990 chapter 3):

> I think is, therefore, in truth in no way something immediate, it only emerges via the reflection which directs itself at the thinking in me; this thinking, by the way, also carries on independently of the thinking that reflects upon it . . . . Indeed, true thinking must even be independent of the subject that reflects upon it, in other words, it will think all the more truly the less the subject interferes with it.
>
> (ibid. p. 11)

Schelling, then, makes the distinction which Sartre will later also make, between reflexive and pre-reflexive consciousness. This distinction is vital to the Hegel-critique. Like Schelling, Sartre is aware of the problem of how the subject could recognise itself in reflection, either upon itself or in an other, if it did not already have a pre-reflexive familiarity with itself which is ontologically prior to any kind of self-*re*-cognition. It is this kind of ontological priority that, Schelling realises, is the real challenge to Idealist philosophy.

Heidegger's claim that the basic Cartesian assumptions about the absolute certainty of self-consciousness form the ontological basis of all modern philosophy is, then, clearly not valid for the later Schelling. Thus Heidegger:

> A Cartesian basic attitude in philosophy cannot at all fundamentally question the *Dasein* of man . . . . It, and with it all philosophising in the modern period since Descartes, risks nothing at all. On the contrary the Cartesian basic attitude knows in advance, or thinks it knows, that everything can be proved and grounded in an absolutely strict and pure manner.
>
> (Heidegger 1983 p. 30)

The Cartesian attitude is based, as we saw, on the notion of self-presence. On the basis of 'I think, I am', thought is supposed to guarantee an epistemological and ontological certainty which nothing else can. The right of thought to subject *Sein* to itself then supposedly becomes the motivation of all metaphysical reflection, culminating in Nietzsche's claim that the will to power is the hidden basis of the subject's certainty. Schelling, though, does not conceive of the subject in terms of the metaphysics of presence. *The attempt to reach the true being of the subject in reflection, he maintains, is precisely what prevents an adequate understanding of the nature of subjectivity, and of being.* What is to be understood must already be there before it can understand itself: such an existence is not something that can be proved, in that it is always already in existence and cannot, as the *Initia* showed, claim itself as the necessary ground of its being. The focus now turns, therefore, upon the differing kinds of being in the preceding history of philosophy.

Schelling's initial task is to look at the history of ontology after Descartes, in order to show how ontological difference has only ever been understood in terms of 'negative philosophy'. This leads him to some of his most productive conceptual differentiations. Spinoza's advance over Descartes, he maintains, depends upon his not giving absolute status to the *concept* of being. Schelling tries to show how the orientation to the concept of being necessarily leads to a point where philosophy needs to realise the dependence of the concept upon what precedes it. One must, Schelling suggests, initially get to 'what absolutely cannot not be' (Schelling 1972 p. 133) by subtracting all possible predicates in order to give one the *mere subject of being*. This conception of being, which is logically analogous to the 'pronominal being' of the *WA*, is, remember, still the kind of being that results from negative philosophy, in that it is the result of an operation in thought. Although it is negative, this does not mean it does not have any kind of being. It cannot be denied, in that thought necessarily presupposes it even in the process of revealing its negativity. As such, that which 'cannot not be' initially has no objective being because it is just the logically prior condition of objectivity: Schelling plays on the etymology of *Gegen-stand*, 'ob-ject', in the sense of that which 'stands against' a subject, and contrasts it with this kind of being, which is just *Ur-stand* 'primal-standing', because it, as the 'mere subject of being', has no reflexive relationship to an object-other. To counter the objection that Spinoza's conception of God is of 'infinite substance' – i.e. that it is the really existing substratum of all objective attributes – Schelling makes a distinction between the 'mere subject' of being, and substance in Spinoza's sense, which is 'being that is completely *objective* and without thought (*besinnungslos*)' (Schelling 1972 p. 137). The abstraction of 'mere subject of being' cannot be sustained because any attempt to say anything about it immediately moves one beyond it into predication, into the 'blind being', the 'pure objectivity', that is its correlate and is the beginning of Spinoza's system.

The point is, though, that Spinoza himself has excluded that which explains development by beginning on the object side, which Schelling, in line with his early philosophy, shows cannot come first. This involves the following, in order that the division between Idealist and Realist positions can be overcome:

> The subject of being is precisely not yet being in the transitive sense. But its positive concept is to be the being which *can* be (*das* **Seinkönnende**). In the concept of being we therefore have double being: namely (1) *that* being of which it is the possibility or the presupposition [i.e. transitive being, which has not yet been reached], and (2) *that* being of which it is not the presupposition but with which it itself is and which is for this reason the merely essential (*Wesende*), intransitive being.
>
> (Schelling 1972 p. 137)

The important claim is that 'negative philosophy' can only ever have an a priori access to being: it shows the possibility of something which

SCHELLING AND MODERN EUROPEAN PHILOSOPHY

it cannot itself provide. It is 'being which is merely in thought'. Because it involves both a subjective and an objective aspect, it is admittedly 'unity of thinking and being'. It is, though, not 'transitive' being, being which sustains the movement of a differentiated world of which thought is one aspect, and is therefore only 'immanent' in thought (I/10 p. 34).

Being which is only immanent in thought is what Schelling now (usually) means when he refers to *Wesen*, which is intransitive and will rely on transitive being for its reality. Even attempting to think the subject of being – that which cannot not be in a logical sense – leads in Spinoza to that which cannot not be in a real sense:

> and however early I may arrive, before I have had time to think, so to speak – *before* all thinking, it is to me, or I *find* it already, as being, because it, as the subject of all being, is precisely that which is according to its *nature*, and is never to be thought as not being.
>
> (ibid. p. 34)

What, though, makes this being, which is *still*, then, really the result of a logical deduction, into an articulated, living world? Spinoza's system fails to give any account of why the differentiated world can become disclosed as differentiated, because the relationship of attributes to their ground is merely necessary, in the same way as the attributes of the triangle follow from its a priori nature. The objection is familiar from the earlier Schelling, and so far Schelling has just reformulated the early philosophy in a more cogent manner, without reaching the new aspect, the 'positive'.

In the later philosophy Schelling wishes to understand the facticity of the world, but he tries to square this facticity with the Idealist conception of the subject's capacity for self-determination, which cannot be derived from anything we could know about the world as object. Achieving this will depend in the last analysis upon the success of Schelling's attempt at a philosophically viable theology. First, however, Schelling further develops aspects of negative philosophy's relationship to the question of being. Though the power of the Fichtean subject has been undermined by Schelling's revelation of its ground, the importance of that which is *unbedingt*, in the sense we saw in earlier chapters, remains constant. Unsurprisingly Fichte is now mobilised as the key figure in the move away from Spinoza's necessitated notion of being: 'Fichte's true significance lies in the fact that he was the opposite of Spinoza' (II/3 p. 54), in that he 'determined the infinite substance as I, and correspondingly as subject–object', via his notion of intellectual intuition. Here the argument is the same as in the *Naturphilosophie* and in the *WA*, where Schelling insisted that the spontaneity of the conscious I had to be extended to the whole of nature, in order to explain the development of consciousness from unconscious nature. His aim is now to show how even his own account of this development is lacking in a fundamental respect. In doing so, however, he already arrives at conceptual resources that suggest how he has moved beyond Hegel.

This is evident in one of the most remarkable aspects of the late philosophy: Schelling's reformulation of the ideas of the *Naturphilosophie* in terms of his new understanding of 'negative philosophy' and of the necessity of the transition to 'positive philosophy', particularly in the *GPP* (pp. 184–213), and in the Lectures (I/10 pp. 99–125). The initial premise is compatible with a Hegelian position, in which the 'substance is subject'. As we saw, neither Hegel nor Schelling can accept Spinoza's conception of substance because each regards it as resulting in a static system, in which development becomes inexplicable. The insistence on the priority of what can explain development, the movement of negation, means that a system like Spinoza's lacks that which can continue to posit itself in objective forms without finally being fixed in any of these forms. Both Hegel and Schelling therefore insist on the necessary priority of the 'subject', in the sense of that which can assume predicates as manifestations of itself, but which cannot be reduced to any predicate. The task of philosophy is to explicate the overall process of development of the world, both in terms of the world's determinacy as object of knowledge and in terms of the finitude of any particular determination. The subject's movement is the process of a dialectic between itself and its Other, the object. The aim is to discover the identity of the object with the subject, thereby making the overall process, in which everything finite is ultimately *aufgehoben*, intelligible as the movement of the Absolute. For Hegel the subject is the 'other of itself': without the movement beyond itself the subject cannot even be itself, in that it has no means of knowing itself. Schelling's description of the subject's move into objectivity, though, whilst seeming to follow such a conception, actually undermines it.

The initial status of Schelling's subject is a version of that which 'cannot not be'. Whereas in Spinoza this subject automatically led to the necessity of the object world because 'being belongs to the concept' of what 'cannot not be' (Schelling 1972 p. 136), in Schelling the initial subject must be able to allow one to account for the continuing development of subjectivity. As such the subject must be *more* than that which of necessity leads to the objective attributes of the world: it must be able to account for the fact that the world is not a completed object. In one sense Hegel would agree, but the way in which this lack of completion is understood is what counts. For Schelling the determinacy of the subject entails a fundamental dissonance, in that the subject's essential nature is precisely *not* to be any *thing*. It is here that the importance of Schelling's differentiations in the notion of being become central. To begin with the subject must be '*as* nothing', in that it does not, for lack of an other, have any objectively determinable status. The question is what happens for the subject to take on attributes.

Schelling gives a striking description of this move, which will later have echoes in Freud, Lacan and others. In order to be 'as something' the subject must become what it was not.[23] Schelling sees this becoming-something in terms of 'attracting' (*anziehen*). The word's multiple meanings in German lead him to a play on these meanings, which reveals the impossibility of self-presence. This is perhaps the most impressive case of Schelling's apparently anthropomorphic metaphors leading to philosophically legitimable insight. Besides meaning 'attract' in all its senses, *anziehen* means to 'put on', both in the sense of clothing, and in the sense of artificially 'putting on' character attributes. By trying to be sincere, as is well known, one is condemned not to be. The subject must, however, sustain itself: otherwise it will be swallowed by objectivity, and development would be incomprehensible. As such it must 'attract' – *anziehen* – itself.

The crucial problem is that, for the process to be transparent, it would have to attract itself *as* itself, thus be in a reflexive relationship to itself. This, though, is a priori impossible, in that the subject is 'as nothing'. The 'as-structure' is the prior condition of stating the truth about something. Predication becomes possible by the ex-sistence of an identity – 'A as B' – of the kind that we saw in the identity philosophy, which is more than tautology. The assumption has to be that there is A before the judgement but that its determinacy makes it more than it was prior to the judgement. In the case of the subject, though, A is *not* something before the judgement and cannot therefore be *re*-cognised in it because it would have to be already known for this to be possible. This leads to the following, which will be essential to Schelling's demonstration of the necessary failure of Hegel's attempt to show that the substance is subject:

But the subject can never grasp itself *as* what it Is, for precisely in attracting itself (*im sich-Anziehen*) it *becomes* an other, this is the basic contradiction, we can say the misfortune in all being – for either it *leaves* itself, then it is as nothing, or it attracts itself, then it is an other and not identical with itself. No longer uninhibited by being as before, but that which has inhibited itself with being, it itself feels this being as alien (*zugezogenes*) and thus contingent. Note here that correspondingly the first beginning is expressly thought of as a contingent beginning. The first *being*, this *primum existens*, as I have called it, is, therefore, at the same time the first contingency (original coincidence). This whole construction therefore begins with the first contingency – which is not identical with itself – it begins with a *dissonance*, and must begin this way.

(I/10 p. 101)

What is infinite, as we saw in the *Initia*, cannot reflect itself *as* infinite in the finite.

The demand there was that the absolute subject should not be anything such that it could not be otherwise. This means that there cannot be a *concept* of the infinite subject because the concept would be that which allowed us to see it *as* something. The movement is therefore a result of the impossibility of the absolute subject definitively 'inhibiting' itself with a determinate form of being that would finally be itself:

> But it is the *infinite* subject, i.e. the subject which can never be destroyed by anything, and, accordingly, as it is *something* it is also immediately again that which goes beyond itself, thus that which grasps and knows itself in this being-something.

(ibid. p. 103)

In these terms the process of knowledge is a dialectic, in which the absolute subject reflects itself as the manifestations of the real world, beginning with 'matter' and going through the stages of the *Naturphilosophie*, and of the development of consciousness we have considered in previous chapters. Schelling claims that his philosophy is, as such, always already within nature, thereby avoiding the problem of the transition from the *Logic* to nature that he will show in Hegel. The main point to hold on to, though, is the fact that the absolute subject 'wants itself as such, but precisely this is not immediately possible' (Schelling 1972 p. 190). Schelling has, then, characterised the essential moves in the *Naturphilosophie* and the identity philosophy in a way which brings him very close to Hegel, in that subject and object are inextricably bound up together once the process has begun. In certain key respects, though, he has suggested a fundamental problem. The absolute subject is either immediate and unknowable, or mediated and thus lost as itself. The awareness of the problem of reflection – the problem of how that which relies on the other of itself for determinate being, can see itself, *as itself*, in the other of itself – is once more the crucial issue.

Schelling maintains that the system he has just presented in outline avoids the Spinozist trap of making the determinations in the world merely necessary consequences of God's nature: 'by the subject which goes through everything declaring itself as God it appears *above* the world, whereas in the doctrine of Spinoza God falls *into* the world' (Schelling 1972 p. 211). In this system 'there is no point where God could, as it were, be stopped. One only ever finds His footsteps, and no longer Himself' (ibid.). The very description of the highest principle in these terms suggests the new version of the continuing problem: it depends upon negativity. Schelling claims that this system, like Kant's, still ends with God as a result, in this case of an objective process, in which He goes through the stages of objectification and emerges as Himself at the end, thereby proving His ability not to be subject to what He becomes.

The ability to describe this system, however, means that the highest form of reflection must be able to show a priori the necessary process through which the absolute subject must go. The result must, then, already be *presupposed* at the beginning for it to be able to be *known* as the result of the process. If this is so, God cannot be *as* God during the process because He is alienated from Himself in the process; He is only really God at the end. Stated less theologically, one could say that the system produces a Spinozism which admittedly makes the development of an articulated world into something 'subjective', but still entails a process in which the end has to reflect the beginning as the logically necessary Other of itself. Schelling suggests that the only way to sustain this conception is to regard it as an 'eternal happening' (I/10 p. 124) (Schelling 1972 p. 213), in which the nature of the world continually emanates from God's nature. Once more this is a logical, reflexive, relationship, and therefore *'everything* only happened in thoughts and this whole movement was only a movement of thinking' (I/10 p. 125). Having undermined the concept of reflection in quite devastating fashion, Schelling has shown how it will always recur as long as what is demanded is a completed, closed system of philosophy.

This is the point at which Schelling demands the positive philosophy, which must concern itself with '*existence*' (ibid.). Schelling sees this in terms of a 'free creation', by which he means a creation which did not have to happen and cannot be deduced from anything we know about the world, apart from the undeniable fact that it is. If there were necessity in the creation itself the first cause would itself be necessitated and we would repeat the problem we have just encountered. The requirement is the production of 'a being which is not its [the 'complete cause's'] own being' (Schelling 1972 p. 214). At this stage of the argument Schelling has little more to say about the matter, and moves to his critique of Hegel, whom he sees as producing a negative system of the kind whose limitations he has just shown. The fundamental idea should, though, already be evident: any attempt to reduce the being of the world to the way philosophy can conceptualise it fails to deal with the fact that the world is at all: *Wesen*, the being known in reflection, requires transitive being, whether this is being that is dependent on the transitive creator, or, less theologically, being which transcends the concept we have of it and is the existential condition of the possibility of the concept.

The standard Hegelian objection to this, as we saw, is that the transcendent being, like Kant's 'thing in itself', is actually a determination of thought, which can only be arrived at by a process of subtraction of what one always already knows of the object. The object as object of knowledge must, however minimally, always be already determined in the process of its relationship to the subject: it can never be pure object. At the level of describing the process of development of knowledge Schelling would not disagree. The problem that concerns him is the fact that there is the object at all. The final aim of Schelling's philosophy is, therefore, to reveal that the fact of manifest existence is the result of God's freely decided creation. Even though he fails in this aim, he does succeed in revealing the fundamental problem with Hegel's system.

CONCEPT AND BEING

Klaus Hartmann sees the aim of Hegelian philosophy as 'grasping what there is in concepts' (in Hartmann 1976 p. 2). The structure of Hegel's philosophy depends upon the fact that 'being's not-being-alien to the concept is represented in the relationship of negation between concept and being, which is brought back to unity by negation of the negation' (ibid. p. 7). Hartmann, Brinkmann and White think that this side of Hegel's philosophy can be legitimated, without reading it in theological terms, by the demonstration of philosophy's ability to reconstruct the categories necessarily entailed by the fact that it is always already engaged with its object. The 'negative' relationship of thought and being is a result of the object appearing opposed to thought. By *appearing* opposed to thought, though, the object reveals its dependence upon thought, as the condition of its being *known* as opposed to thought. The opposition is resolved by the fact that thought and being must, therefore, be the 'Other of themselves', in the 'identity of identity and difference'. There can be nothing which does not involve a relationship to an other, except the Absolute Idea itself, which finally reveals the identity that each determinate moment failed to achieve and which led it beyond itself. At the end the determinations of thought and the determinations of being can be shown to be identical. McTaggart claims that the proof of the Absolute Idea 'must always remain negative', and that the Absolute Idea's finality 'rests on our inability to find . . . an inadequacy' in it (McTaggart 1910 p. 308). Schelling's argument in the positive philosophy, though, begins at the other end: the inadequacy of Hegel's position will lie in the characterisation of the very movement which eventually leads to the Absolute Idea. What Hegel means can be interpreted in a multitude of ways, but all of them, from the theological to the 'categorial', are open to Schelling's fundamental objection because the notion of reflection, at whatever level, is inherently problematic.[24]

Having analysed the significance of the ontological proof for Schelling, we can usefully consider Hegel's account of it because it makes a fundamental difference clear. Hegel does not accept Kant's refutation of the proof. Kant, he claims, shows that in relation to any finite particular there is a necessary difference between the thing and its concept which prevents one moving from the concept to the existence of anything. For Hegel, though, the very definition of the finite, is: 'that the *existence of it is different from its concept*' (Hegel 1959 p. 78), in that the concept in Hegel's particular sense must be the articulation of the dynamic totality of the object and its relations, which cannot be reduced to a finite, empirical manifestation. God, however, is supposed to be precisely that whose nature is the *unity* of the concept and of being:

> This is admittedly still a formal determination of God, which for this reason only contains the nature of the *concept* itself. But that the concept already includes being in its completely abstract sense is easy to see. For the concept, however it may otherwise be determined, is at least what emerges by sublation (*Aufhebung*)

of mediation, thus is *immediate relation* to itself, but being is nothing but this either. It would be . . . very strange if this most inward aspect of *Geist*, the concept, or even if I or especially the concrete totality, which is God, were not even rich enough to contain in itself a determination which is as poor as *being*, which is indeed the most poor, the most abstract.

(ibid. p. 78)

The idea that being is the most abstract category is, of course, what sets the *Logic* in motion. Indeed Hegel's argument about the ontological proof, cited here from the *Encyclopaedia Logic*, is couched in terms of key aspects of the *Logic* as a whole. Clearly his conception of the relationship between thought and being is at odds with what we saw in Schelling's questioning of the ontological proof, in that Hegel does not regard the move from 'existing necessarily/in a necessary manner' to 'necessarily existing' as a problem. For Hegel the articulation of the unity of thought and being is the necessary result of the unsatisfactory nature of the unmediated concept of being.

The point of the *Logic*, in line with Hegel's whole system, is to avoid a founding presupposition: everything in the system must be justified within the system, as otherwise what founds the system is, like the thing in itself, left outside it. The way to avoid the problem of the founding presupposition is to reveal that it depends upon something else. What appears as 'immediate', absolute within itself, can thereby be shown to be 'mediated' and brought within the system by showing its dependence on the other elements of the system. The complete revelation of interdependence is the Absolute Idea, which has taken up into itself the truth of all the preceding elements. The apparently most immediate − being − is in fact the most abstract and in need of concretisation by showing what it really is. Whereas being is presented by the likes of Schelling as immediate, for instance in 'intellectual intuition', where it is 'as though shot from a pistol' (Hegel 1969 I p. 65), it actually must be understood like everything else: 'there *is* nothing, nothing in heaven, or in nature, or in *Geist*, or wherever, which does not contain both immediacy and mediation' (ibid. p. 66). We shall look in more detail at Hegel's development of this point in a moment. Schelling's basic thought is, of course, that being cannot be ultimately considered to be mediated in this way. The difficulty for Schelling is that what he is trying to do cannot be achieved conceptually, in reflection.[25] In Hegelian terms, then, he is invoking an invalid immediacy, as Brinkmann suggested when he maintained that 'being' is just the category for 'absolute otherness in relation to thought'. Another term for this is the Kantian 'thing in itself', which Hegel sees as an abstraction produced by thought. Kant's objection to talking about the noumenal was that it involved a move from ideas that result logically from necessities in thinking to the dogmatic assertion of the *existence* of what is posited by thought. Schelling argues in a similar way in relation to the ontological proof. He agrees with Kant against Descartes that although the idea of the highest being follows of necessity from the 'nature of reason' (II/1 p. 284), this does not make the existence of such a being necessary. At the same time he draws different conclusions from Kant about the implications of this argument.

The most powerful arguments of Schelling's later philosophy concern the difference between thought and being, *Wesen* and *Seyn*. In Hegel's *Logic* one begins with being, but is forced to move beyond it into *Wesen*, and finally into *Begriff*, 'concept' or 'notion', in order to overcome the fact that being is 'the most poor, the most abstract'. Schelling wishes to show that this structure cannot fulfil what it promises. He does so by exploring the implications of the relationship between *Wesen* and being, between what things are and the fact that they are. The crucial move, which Schelling repeatedly carries out, is the demonstration that a system of reason cannot finally explain the fact of its own existence. It is this failure that leads to a different conception of being, which is perhaps Schelling's major contribution to modern philosophy.

There is no mistaking the gravity of this issue for Schelling; the tone of the late philosophy is increasingly existential. The same question as the identity philosophy had asked is now repeated in a different context:

> Far . . . from man and his activity making the world comprehensible, he is himself what is most incomprehensible, and continually drives me to the opinion of the unhappiness of all being . . . . Precisely he, man, drives me to the last despairing question: why is there anything at all? why is there not nothing?
> (II/3 p. 7)

Without an answer to this question 'everything else sinks for me into the abyss of a bottomless nothingness' (ibid. p. 8). Schelling's search for an answer to the question is directly connected to the need for a positive philosophy that will not be open to the problem he reveals in Hegel. In Hegel, and in the systematic version of the 'science of reason', the 'negative philosophy' which Schelling, with more help from Hegel than he often admits, outlines in the Lectures and in the *Presentation of the Purely Rational Philosophy* of between 1847 and 1852, reason works from the position of the 'subject of all being'. By this he means that philosophical reflection can work independently of experience by presenting what necessarily ensues, given the necessities to which reflection is led in any articulation of what there is. In this sense Schelling still adheres to German Idealism's project of a transcendental philosophy which would complete what Kant had begun. Schelling rejects the idea that 'reason', as the 'infinite potential for cognition', must establish the prior existence of the 'infinite object of cognition' in order to legitimate itself: 'there is no question whether there could be a potential of infinite cognition – for this would be to ask whether there *could* be a reason, which no one thinks of asking, everyone presupposes that there is reason' (ibid. p. 74). The crucial point is what status we can attribute to the undeniable necessities of thinking.[26]

Central to this is the question how potentiality and actuality are conceived:[27] reason can deal with the former, but not finally with the latter. Schelling concurs with Kant that the fact of being is not something established by reason, whose realm of legislation is 'the question as to *what*' there is: 'Kant shows . . . how vain is the attempt of reason to arrive by conclusions beyond itself at existence' (ibid. p. 83). The fact of existence is something that can only be established by 'experience' (ibid. p. 58). This may seem a trivial point, or just a kind of empiricism, but in the context it is clear that more is at stake. Experience for Schelling is that which cannot ensue from an a priori necessity. Reason can legislate what must be the case *if* something exists, but not whether something really *does* exist, which was the point of Schelling's refutation of the ontological proof.

Schelling makes the importance of ontological difference very clear when he explains his conception of being against that of Parmenides and Spinoza. The ability to arrive at the abstract general thought of being can be demonstrated by the subtraction of all attributes, which leaves one with the substance, which is 'divested of all difference'. This is still only a 'relatively necessary' thought, because (and here Leibniz's question occurs once again):

> if I want to go to the limits of all thought, then I must also recognise that it is possible that there might be nothing at all. The last question is always: why is there anything at all, why is there not nothing? I cannot answer this question with mere

abstractions from real being . . . . I must always first of all admit
some reality or other before I can come to that abstract being.

(ibid. p. 242)

The doubt about the reality of the world, with which philosophy
began, has so far always been what Heidegger will term 'ontic':
namely, doubt whether the particular reality in front of me is the true
kind of reality, whether it is really just my thoughts or really just
structured matter, for instance. This doubt, though, is grounded in a
prior 'ontological' question because it presupposes

> the *true* real . . . . If the doubt about the reality of the single being
> or reality meant doubting the reality of the real in a absolute
> way, then, for example, the supporter of Parmenides would
> remove his own presupposition, the presupposition of abstract
> being.
>
> (ibid.)

The being Schelling is concerned with does not exist so that

> there should be being which is rational (although according to
> our first progression [in negative philosophy] it can appear so),
> but rather, on the contrary, rational being and reason itself only
> are because that *Geist* is, of which we can only say that it is,
> which means as much as that it is without a ground/reason
> (*Grund*), or just is because it is, without any preceding necessity.
>
> (ibid. p. 247)

The argument is now directed towards a theology, which will prove
the reality of this *Geist*.

The historical significance of the specifically theological move
evident in the rejection of the ontological proof, which leads Schelling
to these arguments, should not be underestimated, as the following
constellation can suggest. Franz Rosenzweig discusses the ontological
proof in Kant and Hegel in the *The Star of Redemption*, as follows:[28]

> Kant is a conclusion, via his criticism of the proof by the sharp
> distinction of being and existence; Hegel however praises the
> proof, because, of course, it coincides with the basic concept of
> philosophical truth, with the thought of the identity of reason
> and reality, and thus must be valid of God just as much as of
> everything else; and precisely via the naivety of this praise he,
> without knowing it, deals the proof the fatal blow in the eyes of
> theology, philosopher that he is. In this way the path is clear

for the philosophical establishment of divine existence independently of the universe's being–thought and of its being; God must have existence before all identity of being and thinking; if there is to be any deduction here, then it must rather be that of being from existence than the deduction of existence from being which was always tried in the ontological proofs. It is the Schellingian late philosophy into whose path we move with such reflections.

(Rosenzweig 1988 pp. 19–20)

Rosenzweig's influence on Emmanuel Levinas is well known; Levinas, of course was, along with Heidegger, Derrida's major influence. If one takes the ontological proof of God as the classic example of the metaphysics of presence (which is the basic point of Schelling's critique), then it is evident that the rejection of that proof leads to two possibilities. The first is a different approach to theology, of the kind evident in the fact that Schelling tries to construct a philosophy of revelation, rather than a rational theology. This attempt still lives on in theology of the kind developed by Rosenzweig, Paul Tillich and others. The second possibility is that theology itself becomes undermined and the rejection of self-presence takes on the forms we have already looked at in Derrida and Heidegger.[29] Schelling's late work involves conceptual moves which point towards both these possibilities. It is, then, as well to consider the fundamental weakness of Schelling's theology here, before seeing the consequences of the strictly philosophical argument in relation to Hegel, so as to show that the failed theology does not invalidate the rest of Schelling's argument.

Schelling's aim is to drop the concept of God 'in order to begin with that which just exists, in which nothing more is thought than this existing – in order to see if I can get from it to the divinity' (II/3 p. 158). It is a question of 'philosophical empiricism' as to whether God can be proven, and this proof is 'continually progressing, continually growing' (Schelling 1977 p. 147), rather than being the result of an a priori concept. As Michael Theunissen and Alan White point out, however, what Schelling actually does is to invert the ontological proof: as with all inversions in metaphysical arguments, the result reflects, the other way round, the problem that was initially present in the counter-position. Theunissen shows that the intention of the positive philosophy is

a reversal of the received proof of God: it is not the existence of God that is to be proved, but the divinity of the 'merely existing'.

In the attempt to realise this intention the reversal reverses itself once more; positive philosophy falls back into the proof of the existence of God. It falls back because Schelling has to begin by attributing a divinity, that is supposed to be proved *per posterius* by the so-called 'consequence' of the actually existing world, to that which supposedly 'merely exists'.

(Theunissen 1976 p. 22)

This seems to me incontrovertible, and invalidates any chance of the later philosophy succeeding as theology.[30] Similarly, when Schelling tries to make the positive philosophy mirror the a priori necessity of development of the negative philosophy in the actual development of history, he ends up being open to many of the same criticisms he makes of Hegel. For our purposes we shall drop the notion of God, and leave it dropped, in order to consider how Schelling deals with the facticity of existence in relation to Hegel's way of overcoming the division of thought and being in the *Logic*.

What makes many people ill at ease with the argument presented by Schelling is the fact that it relies on a surrender of thinking. As he says, the positive philosophy 'can only begin from being which is *absolutely* outside thought ... absolutely transcendent being' (II/3 p. 127). If there were any sense in which this being were immanent, it would depend upon the development of the potential within thinking that is shown in the outline of the system. The point is that the potential of thinking itself must first *be* in a way that it cannot itself explain. Getting to the origin of the potential within thought would entail the ability to recognise the origin when it is reached, but this is the problem we have repeatedly encountered: how could it *recognise* something which is a priori *excluded* from knowledge, by reflection? Gasché seems unaware of this problem when he claims with regard to Hegel: 'With this self-inclusion of absolute reflection, which escapes any further reflection, not only is reflection overcome, for it is comprised, but also absolute reflection becomes the ultimate totality of all possible relations, the relation to self included' (Gasché 1986 p. 63). The question is how this could ever be *known*. The condition of such knowledge would be a *prius*, a beginning, which is relative to what ensues from it, which has a reflexive relationship to it, but this is where the problem lies that Schelling reveals. The positive philosophy cannot be a system in the sense that negative philosophy must, because it cannot be finally closed. Negative philosophy

is a science which is completely enclosed within itself, which has come to a permanent end, thus in *this* sense a *system*; positive

166

philosophy on the other hand cannot be called a system in the same sense, precisely because it is never absolutely closed.

(II/3 p. 133)

Schelling's mistake in the theology is to try to close it, as we just saw. His initial moves, though, are not prone to this problem: 'we must begin with/go out from what I have called that which *merely* exists, from being which is immediate, simply necessary, which is necessary because it precedes all potential, all possibility' (ibid. p. 160). Whilst negative philosophy arrives at this by abstraction from all determinate being, positive philosophy does so immediately.

The argument justifying this goes as follows. If being is the result of abstraction, it is arrived at from somewhere else – thought – and is therefore the result of something else, which would therefore itself be the necessary principle. To avoid this consequence one must 'drop the concept and retain only *pure* being, being without any What' (ibid. p. 161). Thought has to give way to the fact of existence: 'for thinking has precisely just to do with possibility, with potential; thinking therefore has no power where this is excluded' (ibid.). Whilst it is invalid to suggest within thought that there is something which precedes the first thought – being – it is not invalid to suggest that being outside thought precedes thought: 'for it is not because there is a thinking that there is a being, but because there is a being that there is a thinking' (ibid.).

Schelling himself sees the obvious Hegelian objection: 'One might object: a reality which precedes all possibility cannot be thought. One can admit this in a certain sense and say: precisely for that reason it is the beginning of all thinking – for the beginning of thinking is not yet itself thinking' (ibid. p. 162). If thinking had no beginning, then it would have always been and a self-enclosed infinite system would be possible. Schelling, though, maintains that thinking is 'posited outside itself' by the facticity of being. Hegel, he claims, only makes being the beginning of philosophy as 'a mere moment of thinking' (ibid. p. 163). If philosophy is concerned with pure thought, it can only be a reflection of itself, but the issue is the truth of thought's relationship to being, given that thought, as we saw in the critique of Descartes, is only a 'way of being'. Schelling sums up the fundamental alternative:

For either the concept would have to go first, and being would have to be the consequence of the concept, which would mean it was no longer absolute being; or the concept is the consequence of being, in which case we must begin with being without the concept.

(ibid. p. 164)

Let us now have a more detailed look at Hegel's own view of these relationships.

THE LOGIC OF REFLECTION

Here is Hegel on the 'concept' in his own particular sense, making very clear the difference from Schelling by the sequence of the terms:

> The concept shows itself . . . as the unity of *being* and *essence*. Essence is the *first negation* of being, which can thereby become *appearance*, the concept is the *second*, or the negation of this negation, thus being which has been restored, but as the infinite mediation and negativity of being in itself.
>
> (Hegel 1969 II p. 269)

The structure is the 'negation of the negation', in which each moment reveals its inadequacy and is *aufgehoben* in what follows. The crucial moments of the *Logic* are those moments when the transitions from one phase to the next are made, from being to essence, from essence to concept, and the transition beyond the *Logic* from the completed Absolute Idea to the philosophy of nature. As the passage cited shows, the crucial factor is the revelation that the apparently immediate is actually mediated, 'reflected in itself'. Dieter Henrich shows the problem with this conception in a seminal essay on 'Hegel's Logic of Reflection' (in Henrich 1971). Henrich thinks that the problem can be overcome in Hegelian terms; Manfred Frank shows how this problem had already been identified by Schelling, and how a Hegelian solution to it is impossible (Frank 1975).

The point of the first section of the *Logic*, the logic of being, Henrich suggests, was to show that 'the difference of a basis of determinations which is in itself, on the one hand, and the mutual relationship of those determinations to each other on the other hand is proved to be untenable' (Henrich 1971 p. 105). In other words, that which seems to be undifferentiated One, or the substance, and the different attributes, are really the same, albeit as yet in a manner which is not fully transparent. Putting it another way: what begins as 'simple immediacy' (Hegel 1969 I p. 68) is actually mediated. The problem Henrich shows lies in Hegel's notion of immediacy. Hegel rejects any kind of immediacy: the very attempt to say anything about it already moves

168

one beyond it. The statement of identity, 'A is A', itself involves a degree of mediation: there cannot be a statement 'A'. Being, which is 'as nothing', in an initially similar way to Schelling's 'absolute freedom', has to negate *itself* (if the negation were the result of another subject, the whole construction would disintegrate) to make possible any articulation at all. This was what Hölderlin meant by the *Urteil*, the 'judgement/original separation'.

Because it negates *itself*, being can, in Hegel's construction, unlike in Hölderlin's or Schelling's, *know* itself as negated, once its structure has been articulated. Henrich terms the self-negation 'autonomous negation', its law is within itself. The essential difference of this from negation of the negation in traditional logic is that in the latter it is the positive statement that is presupposed: 'A is not not A' presupposes 'A is A'. In Hegel 'positivity, if it emerges, can only come into effect as a result (not as a presupposition) of double negation' (Frank 1989a p. 453).[31] Hegel claims the statement 'A = A is initially nothing more than the expression of empty *tautology*' (Hegel 1969 II p. 41). In consequence there is, for Hegel, no founding proposition: the vital 'proposition' is the complete revelation of the identity of identity and difference at the end, the final negation of the negation. It is in the transition to the logic of essence from the logic of being that the problem with this conception becomes evident.

'Essence' (*Wesen*) is characterised in the *Encyclopaedia Logic* as 'being which mediates itself with itself via the negativity of itself' (Hegel 1959 p. 123). Because being has been shown to be one-sided, immediate, it is only 'negative', because it depends upon an other which cannot be itself. The Other is also, as part of this relationship, 'negative'. The aim, though, is to show that this Other is really being's 'Other of itself'. If this were not so, the relation would not be to itself and there would be a necessary other presupposition (on this, see Frank 1975 pp. 32–7). In the process being is to be revealed as only one aspect of the fundamental structure which makes possible the construction of a system, whose truth can only come at the end and which does not rely on a presupposition which is not part of the system itself. To achieve a presuppositionless system the following move must be shown to be legitimate. Hegel suggests that 'simple immediacy is itself an expression of reflection and relates to the difference from what is mediated' (Hegel 1969 I p. 68): the determinacy of the *category* of simple immediacy can only be arrived at by a relation to something else in 'reflection'. This is the argument we saw Brinkmann using when he suggested that 'being' is just the category

169

for 'absolute otherness in relation to thought': given the mutual dependence of the two sides, they must ultimately be identical. This identity, though, depends upon the 'category' being the real basis, not being, in that being has no way of articulating any identity without an other to which it is related.

Frank makes clear what Hegel must achieve if the system is to work: 'Hegel's logic of reflection can only cash in its programme if the internal relationship present in reflection can completely take over the role of and replace being's characteristic of absolute independence from any relationship' (Frank 1975 p. 37) – the difficulty is that being and nothing are not symmetrical.[32] Instead of the initial immediacy of being, which Hegel terms 'sameness only with itself', the aim is to reveal that this apparently positive presupposition is the 'product of the self-relation of negation' (ibid. p. 50), of 'reflection'. Hegel terms reflection the 'movement of nothing to nothing, thus negation which goes together with itself' (Hegel 1969 II p. 25). This leads him to the invalid move analysed by Henrich: he equates two different forms of 'immediacy'.

Why is this so significant? The answer is that the system's ability to be complete in itself depends on it. Without the ability to move from the one form of immediacy to the other, it becomes impossible to *aufheben*, in Hegel's threefold sense of negate, preserve and elevate, being into essence, immediacy into reflection, and so on. If this move is allowed, the *Logic* is able to function, because the need for a presupposition is overcome: the apparently most irreducible, being, is actually itself negative, dependent upon what follows it, essence, and concept, rather than vice versa.

The central issue is 'reflection': any attempt to talk of being has to confront the fact that we have repeatedly encountered: namely, that it can only be talked about negatively. For Hegel this means – hence the emphases – that the '*truth* of *being* is *essence*' (ibid. p. 13). It is the movement beyond immediacy that results in the truth, so that even immediacy is a form of reflection. This is because reflection entails a relationship between two moments, which means that each moment is 'negative', dependent on the other. At one level this argument is unproblematic, in that any attempt to say anything about being depends on reflection, upon 'judgement' in the sense of joining what is separate and thus dependent. Essence is the basis of knowing about being. Schelling would not disagree, as he shows in the outlines of the systems we have considered, where the possibility of knowledge entails a reflexive division. The problem is Hegel's identification of the two meanings of immediacy (*Unmittelbarkeit*), which Henrich terms 'U1' and 'U2'. Being is 'sameness only with itself', U1; essence is 'the relation of the negative to itself', U2. Henrich shows that Hegel's argument leads to the fact that 'essence presupposes *itself* as its other. For thereby more is said than that essence posits its other [being] and sublates (*aufhebe*) it' (Henrich 1971 p. 123). In this way U1 and U2 become identified. What was the other of reflection, being, now turns out to *depend* upon reflection, so that it *is* reflection, and can thus be sucked up into the forward move of the dialectic.

This argument, though, itself depends upon a *presupposition* of the identity of U1 and U2, which is what Hegel thinks he can avoid. Thus Henrich:

> Only if immediacy is fundamentally already grasped as self-relation can the demonstration that there is not an external relation between presupposition and reflection be the cause of assuming the same self-relation in presupposition and reflection.[33]
>
> (ibid. p. 128)

Manfred Frank has made the implications of this clear. The crucial point is that there is nothing within Hegel's construction which allows one to *show* the sameness of the two sides of the relationship. The fact is that U2 must logically depend upon U1, for the following reasons:

> Hegel claims immediacy which is unrelated and independent (!) of negation (U1) as a result of self-relation, but it — as independent of determination — already bears in its name the fact that it cannot be the result of the negation of reflection. On the contrary: *if* immediacy emerges as the other of reflection (U1) it must already for that reason be something other than the shadow of that self-cancellation of negation (U2), because it *is*, i.e. survives the non-being of its 'ground' [i.e. negation]. It cannot therefore be reduced to it.
>
> (Frank 1975 p. 57)

There is, then, a difference between being's necessary dependence on essence for it to be known and essence's dependence on being for it to be: this is the distinction between cognitive and real ground which we have already encountered. Hegel tries to merge the two. He does so by assuming that one side of a relation, essence, can show its identity with the other side. This, though, requires a third position, which would logically have to be that of essence, rather than of the immediacy of being. Hegel thinks this position is that of the concept, the next negation of the negation. The problem is that this position cannot itself depend upon a relationship to an other, because this would lead to a regress, where each negative (related) position tried to arrive at the position of independence of relation. The final insight into the whole process that Hegel sees in absolute knowledge thereby becomes impossible. The only possible position that would make the construction viable must *already* be immediate: 'because reflection is a relation with only two places and is grounded in its own structure, it must presuppose self-identity as a fact which is external to reflection' (ibid. p. 60). This self-identity is precisely how Hölderlin already understood being in *Judgement and Being*. Schelling insists:

> If we want anything at all which is outside thought, then we *must* begin with a being which is absolutely independent of all thinking, which precedes all thinking. Hegelian philosophy knows nothing of this being, it has no place for this concept.
>
> (II/3 p. 164)

He excludes this being, 'necessary existence', from essence in the following manner: 'It is incoherent to ask what sort of being (*Wesen*) *could* exist necessarily; for in that way I assume that an essence (*Wesen*), a What, a possibility precedes necessary existence' (ibid. pp. 166–7). The move to essence and concept is from being: 'existing is not here the consequence of the concept or of essence, but rather existence is here itself the concept and itself the essence' (ibid. p. 167).

NON-IDENTITY

Given Schelling's notion of transcendent being, what of the Kantian suspicion of positive notions of transcendence in philosophy, which was one root of Hegel's attempt at a self-bounded system? Schelling's answer encapsulates his later position. The problem with 'transcendence', Schelling maintains, is that it has also been thought of reflexively: 'it only *is* in relation to something that is transcended' (II/3 p. 169). This was the problem with the ontological proof, which moves invalidly — 'transcends' in the sense Kant will not permit — from the idea of the highest being to its existence. The point is, though, to exclude reflexivity at the beginning, in order to obviate the impossible demand of demonstrating the identity of the two sides of the relationship between thought and existence from within the relationship:

But if I *go out from* what precedes all concepts, then I have not overstepped anything, and instead, if one calls this being transcendent and I progress in it to the concept, then I have overstepped the transcendent and in *this* way have become immanent again . . . . Kant forbids transcendence to metaphysics, but he only forbids it to dogmatising reason, i.e. to reason which wishes to arrive by conclusions from itself at existence.

(ibid. pp. 169–70)

The next move in Schelling is again to theology, in which the 'crisis of the science of reason' (II/1 p. 565) moves reason beyond what thought can comprehend to the demand for the reality of God, but the philosophical failure to prove the divinity of existence does not invalidate the points made in favour of ontological difference.

Schelling arrives at 'being which precedes all thought' (II/3 p. 173), the 'pure *That*', by the 'overthrow of reason' (ibid. p. 162), in which reason 'is posited outside itself, absolutely ekstatic' (ibid. p. 163). He posits 'conceptless being' in order to 'again make it the content of reason' (ibid. p. 170), not to renounce reason. This is, then, a philosophy of 'non-identity' or 'alterity', of the kind which Adorno will later also develop against Hegel and which has been the theme of much recent philosophical debate (see A. Bowie 1993a). Gasché says of Derrida's relation to reflexivity that he has 'the insight into the solidarity between the terms of negativity, contradiction, sublation, dialectics, and homogeneity, a solidarity in the service of the evacuation of the heterological from the speculative unity of the totality of all oppositions' (Gasché 1986 p. 95). This is, as should now be apparent, Schelling's position against Hegel.

Schelling explicitly uses the notion of non-identity, when contrasting negative and positive philosophy:

Pure or infinite potential . . . is the content which is *identical* with thinking, and can therefore, because it does not go towards thinking (for it is identical with it), only go out from thinking. On the other hand being that just is is that which is not identical with thinking . . . but for that reason must first be brought towards thinking *because* it is originally outside thinking.

(II/3 p. 170)

He thereby denies, in the way we have seen, any possibility of grounding the relationship of thinking and being reflexively: there cannot be a return to a position where the relationship of the two is

173

known, because that would depend upon the primacy of thought and lead to the regress shown in Hegel. Schelling's arguments are still much less well known than Hegel's and the argument is not easy to grasp: let us, then, to conclude this chapter, very briefly go through some of the main points again as they are made in the Lectures, which include the most extensive explicit critique of Hegel.[34]

Schelling shows that Hegel's attempt to identify being and nothing at the beginning of the *Logic* depends upon the invalid attempt to arrive at the notion of pure being, which is a result of abstraction, in order to show the *logical* necessity of moving beyond it:

> The fact that he nevertheless attributes an immanent movement to pure being means no more, then, than that the *thought* which begins with pure being feels it is impossible for it to stop at this most abstract and most empty thing of all, which Hegel himself declares is pure being.
>
> (I/10 p. 131)

The real state of affairs is that the fact that there '*is* a more rich being which is more full of content' (ibid.) makes the philosopher move beyond the empty abstraction. As such, in Hegel:

> the beginning point behaves in relation to what follows it as a mere minus, an emptiness which is filled and is admittedly, as such, negated as emptiness, but in this there is as little to overcome as there is in filling an empty vessel; it all happens quite peacefully – there is no opposition between being and nothing, they do not do anything to each other.
>
> (ibid. p. 137)

The fact is that Hegel has to rely on 'intuition', Schelling's term for immediacy, even when he denies it: 'Hegel already presupposed intuition with the first step of his *Logic* and could not take a single step without doing so' (ibid. p. 138). The attempt to reveal immediacy as mediated leads to the inversion of the relationship of concept and being upon which Hegel's particular notion of the concept is based. But, Schelling insists: 'Concepts as such do in fact exist nowhere but in consciousness, they *are*, therefore, taken objectively, *after* nature, not *before* it' (ibid. p. 140). The attempt to work in pure thought, even in the way Hegel does, where pure thought inherently involves its Other, is open to the objection to the ontological proof. It might be the case that 'everything that is is in the Idea or in the logical concept, and that as a consequence the Idea is the truth of everything'. This does not mean, though, that one can *prove* that it really is, because 'what is logical . . . presents itself as the merely negative aspect of existence, as that *without* which nothing could exist, from which, however, it by no means follows that everything only exists *via* what is logical' (ibid. p. 143).

This difficulty becomes particularly apparent in the transition of the *Logic* to the philosophy of nature, where Schelling is at his most biting. Horstmann, in a useful essay that shows some of the ways in which Schelling did misread Hegel, claims that Schelling's argument about nature as the 'being-other of the Idea' is not a problem for Hegel:

> yet there *is* a systematic problem in the connection of the relationship of logical Idea and nature, which can be precisely formulated in the question why the logical Idea has nevertheless to prove itself as nature (and in another way than as *Geist*).
>
> (Horstmann 1986 p. 301)

It is clear, however, that Horstmann's problem is, even down to the choice of the word 'prove' (*bewähren*), exactly Schelling's problem with the relationship of Idea and nature, as one would expect, given Schelling's view of 'negative philosophy':

> But in the Idea there is no necessity *at all* for any kind of movement . . . . People have tried to back up this idea, in order to give some reason or other for the Idea to go further, by saying: the Idea admittedly exists at the end of the *Logic*, but it is not yet *proven*, it must therefore go out of itself in order to prove itself.
>
> (I/10 pp. 152–3)

Given the self-sufficiency of the Idea, however, there can be no *logical* reason for it to prove itself by the fall (*Abfall*) into nature: 'for whom should the Idea prove itself? For itself? . . . should it have to prove itself for a spectator? But where is the spectator?' (ibid. p. 153). If, as Hegel claims, it is a free decision of the Idea, then the Idea must be 'something really existing, a mere concept cannot decide' (ibid. p. 154), as the arguments of the *WA* and the *Initia* suggested. Once again the reflexive structure is unable to provide an adequate philosophical account of the relationship of thought and being. Schelling's implication is that Hegel is actually in a sense failing to get beyond Spinoza. To get beyond Spinoza entails renouncing a self-grounding system and facing the consequences for reason which this entails.

Walter Schulz cites Schelling's description of the God of Hegel's system, whose relation to nature is that He continually 'throws Himself into it' in:

an eternal, continual happening, but for that very reason [it is] not an authentic, i.e. real happening . . . . He is . . . the God of continual activity, of constant agitation, who never finds the Sabbath, He is the God who only ever does what He has always done, and can therefore not create anything new; His life is a circle of forms (*Gestalten*) in which He continually externalises Himself in order to return back to Himself, and always returns back to Himself only in order to externalise Himself again.

(ibid. p. 160)

Schulz comments: 'In these words Schelling indicates that an eternal happening is senseless and nihilistic, for in it nothing really happens, what comes out is only what already once was, there is no meaningful action into the future' (Schulz 1957 p. 104). The recent temptation to use Hegel's work to characterise the notion of the 'end of history' is evident in the contrast of Schelling and Hegel. The main influence for the idea was, of course, Kojève's interpretation of Hegel. The intellectual bankruptcy of the idea – even if it is an invalid way of using Hegel – must give pause for thought. How can one ponder the *end* of history without *already* knowing what history is? Whilst it is wrong to suggest history is totally unintelligible, that does not mean that its concept can be articulated in a putatively Hegelian manner as something which can be described from within itself in its totality. Schelling remains significant because the temptations of reflection recur in so many ways. The situation revealed in Schelling's critique is, then, indicative of a basic tension in modern philosophy that has most recently reappeared in the post-structuralist attention to 'alterity'.[35]

This philosophical tension is apparent in the defences of Hegel against Schelling, which we saw in Hartmann, White and Brinkmann. For them Hegel demonstrates the necessary identity of determinations of thought and of being and avoids the consequences of the assertion of 'being' in a transreflexive sense. The defences depended upon a critique of Schelling's reliance on 'immediacy'. For Schelling the necessity of this immediacy meant that Hegel's system became impossible to ground, because the position from which it could be legitimated was not available in the way Hegel claimed. The defences of Hegel do not, though, answer Henrich's and Frank's objections to the way Hegel deals with immediacy. Furthermore, Frank's dem- onstration that Schelling does not simply invoke pre-reflexive being, because it is the necessary positive ground of the self-cancellation of reflection, not a consequence of the failure to go through the exertion of the concept, seems to have escaped the attention of nearly all commentators who wish to defend Hegel against Schelling.

In my view it is not possible to find a reading of Hegel in these areas which can get round the problems Schelling shows. One must always come to terms with the fact that Hegel thinks the end articulates the truth of the beginning: to prove this requires precisely what Hegel has to exclude: namely, a presupposition which can be reflected at the end and which must therefore already contain its telos within it: 'What emerges at the end is also already a or the beginning' (Schelling 1977 p. 132). As Marx and others will suggest in the wake of Schelling, Hegel inverts the real relationship. Schelling claims:

> as Hegel himself only makes possible the free externalisation, the free action (Wirken) at the end of the development, he does not have it at the end as something active, but rather here as well as the final cause of the whole movement, as a cause not because of its own action but by the fact that everything tended towards it. The last is of course *also the highest final cause* but the whole sequence is only a continual sequence of final causes. If we go back, inorganic nature is cause of matter, organic nature cause of inorganic, the animal world of the plant world, man of the animal world. If now by the reversal the Absolute were to become the efficient cause, then man would appear as the efficient cause of the animal kingdom, etc. We do not know how far Hegel wishes to have this pursued.
>
> (ibid. pp. 132–3)

What comes to its truth at the end would have to be already familiar with itself at the beginning, otherwise there could be no way that such a *recognition* could take place. To see yourself as yourself in a mirror means that you must already be familiar with yourself before the reflection. This is a point which is almost invariably forgotten by philosophies of non-identity. Derrida's 'transcendental signified', for example, which can be understood as the truth of 'being', is the illusory *goal* which is always already lost once there is reflection. Schelling, though, is fully aware that being cannot be a result that is striven for: that is the whole point of his arguing that it must precede reflection. The real issue for philosophy after Schelling is what ensues from the undermining of absolute reflection.[36] In the Conclusion, I want briefly to suggest ways of considering the problems for reason in modernity which Schelling's philosophy reveals, in the light of Schelling's failure to find a convincing theological solution to those problems.

CONCLUSION

Schelling's insistence upon defending a conception of reason, despite his demonstration that we can neither prove from within reason why there is reason nor ground reason via its own operations, makes him in certain ways a more apt representative of the philosophy of modernity than Hegel. This fact alone invalidates many current views of the history of Western metaphysics. For Schelling, it is worth repeating, the vital philosophical realisation is of the failure of the attempt of reason to ground itself, the 'self-negation of reflection', the 'crisis of the science of reason'. He does not make an irrational appeal to mystical immediacy, which he explicitly rejects in his discussions of Böhme and Jacobi.[1] Since the demise of Hegelianism the defence of reason has involved the repetition in varying forms of attempts to overcome the problems Schelling articulates. The degree of enthusiasm from some quarters that has greeted the latest replay of some of these problems in post-structuralism is out of proportion to the actual philosophical achievements of Derrida, Lyotard and others, whatever their contributions may have been in other respects. As Habermas has reminded us, the relationship between conceptions of reason and modernity is much more complex than the adherents of post-modernity, or, for that matter, the authors of *Dialectic of Enlightenment* suggest. Quite why such enthusiasm has been generated in recent years for the condemnation of a historically very limited concept of reason will only become clear in the light of subsequent history. The crisis of reason is hardly a new philosophical topic, as I tried to suggest in relation to the Pantheism controversy. It is clear, however, that it is not in a hurry to go away, which is why Schelling can again demand our attention.

Schelling explores the implications of reason's attempt to ground itself in ways which do not succumb to the recent temptation to see reason as inherently narcissistic. For Schelling, as we saw, reason cannot be what represses radical 'alterity' in the name of the dominating subject.[2] From very early on in his career Schelling's understanding of the subject's relationship to the nature in which it is grounded led him to insights from which recent approaches to a new philosophy of nature still have much to learn. His later attempt to establish valid versions of 'negative' and 'positive' philosophy was intended to find a philosophical way of understanding the limits of reason. Schelling did so without moving towards the claim, so fashionable in recent years, to have unmasked reason as dependent upon a *determinable* other, such as power, desire, or whatever. The dimension that Hegel's system fails to confront, which the later Schelling is the first really to articulate for philosophy, is the dimension of ontology which cannot be dissolved into logic or semantics. In this dimension philosophy tries to come to terms with the fact that, as Hogrebe, echoing Heidegger's notion of 'being in the world', says of Schelling's ontology:

> in a certain sense we are always already outside the semantic dimension in *something or other that exists*, whence we always only come back to determinate things which exist . . . . This relationship to something or other which exists still comes through in every determinate predication, simply in the so-called existential quantifier . . . the predicative, rational echo of our non-predicative pre-rational relationship to something or other that exists.
>
> (Hogrebe 1989 pp. 125–6)

This 'something or other that exists' includes, of course, ourselves: otherwise the problems of reflection are just repeated, because we would remain imprisoned in the immanence of consciousness which Schelling, well before Nietzsche, Heidegger or Ryle, unmasked in his critique of Descartes.

In Schelling the 'ekstatic' relationship of reason to 'being which is not preceded by any concept' (Schelling 1977 p. 156) does not, then, lead to a philosophy which glorifies a primordial lost origin, as the standard worry about this kind of ontology suggests. This is particularly clear by the time of the late philosophy, where the origin is, even more than it was in the WA period, that against which one must strive in the name of reason, even though it can never be eradicated by being overcome by reason. As Schelling insists in the PO, the truth of being is a continual movement beyond itself. If this were not so we would remain within a system of necessity, that renders development incomprehensible in the way it was in the move from Hegel's *Logic* to nature:

> A being (*Wesen*) which had to remain in its primal being in which it is via itself could only be rigid and immobile, dead and unfree. *Even man must tear himself away from his being*, in order to begin a free being . . . . *Freeing oneself from oneself* is the task of all *Bildung*.
>
> (ibid. p. 170)

It is, though, crucially, only the 'form' (Schelling 1972 pp. 442, 447) of this primal being that can be 'broken', not 'this being itself'.[3] For Schelling we must both try to develop beyond the nature we are and find ways of coming to terms with the necessity that it imposes. In philosophy, as elsewhere, all we can do is reform the interpretations that we have of the world, for reasons which can never be finally transparent to us. This reforming is, however, no merely subjective projection, because the process is itself part of the manifest world in ways which we have no means of finally grasping. New interpretations can, though, still be validated, even if we have no Archimedean point from which to survey that validation. Here Schelling's notions of 'positive philosophy' and 'philosophical empiricism' already point to what Heidegger will term 'world-disclosure', the happening in which we as *subjects* – Schelling may subvert the subject, but he does not eradicate it – are always already located. Schelling's philosophy begins to reveal the inherent fallibility which any form of interpretation must confront: there is nothing which could ultimately mirror inter-pretation's own validity back to it, as Davidson, Rorty and others now remind us from within a different tradition.[4]

The attempt to approach Hogrebe's 'pre-predicative relationship', which is also central to Heidegger, brings us back to the problem of metaphor's role in philosophy that I raised at the beginning of this book. Much of Schelling's understanding of the development of the subject requires accepting, as in psychoanalysis, the imaginative access to that which cannot be represented as itself, which is opened up by metaphor. In metaphor the predicative aspect of language is always accompanied by a negation of the identity posited in the literal statement. If all metaphors could finally be made to have literal meaning, then we could, so to speak, return to Hegel, because the realm of signification would be determined by absolute reflection.[5] A 'negative philosophy' must ultimately cash in its metaphors, or presuppose that they can finally be cashed in, which means that what they reveal is always already inherently subsumable within the movement of the system. Schelling's philosophy, from the *STI* onwards, shows that this is a path which involves an invalid 'closure'. To understand why this is so, let us take a final look at the constellation outlined in the Introduction.

The period following the demise of Hegelianism has again become the object of philosophical attention, largely because, as Habermas pointed out, we are still dealing with many of the same problems. This also applies, as we saw, to certain aspects of the Pantheism controversy. Habermas describes the intellectual situation following Hegel as follows:[6]

> Feuerbach stresses the primacy of the objective . . . Marx sees spirit as rooted in material production . . . Kierkegaard opposes the facticity of one's own existence . . . to a chimerical Reason in history. All these arguments reclaim the finitude of spirit against the self-related-totalising thinking of the dialectic – Marx speaks of the 'process of decay of absolute spirit'. Admittedly all the Young Hegelians were themselves in danger of hypostasising the *prius* of Nature, Society and History into an in-itself and thus of falling back into a covert pre-critical thinking.
>
> (Habermas 1988 p. 47)

By their failure to reach the level of theorisation of Kant and Hegel, Habermas maintains, the Young Hegelians left open the door to Nietzsche's totalising critique of reason. The best of the late Schelling's philosophical arguments cannot, though, be considered in this way. As I have tried to show, he does reach the level of Hegel, albeit only in certain areas of philosophy. Clearly Schelling does not have Hegel's systematic breadth, but his approach to the crucial problem of the self-grounding of reason is superior both to Hegel's and to that of his contemporaries. Nor can Schelling be regarded as pre-critical, even though he can fall back into pre-critical thinking in aspects of his theology.[7] Schelling reveals the problem of reason in post-metaphysical thinking because he shows in a post-Kantian manner that philosophy cannot arrive at a conceptually determinate *prius*. Despite his losing touch with the immediate socio-historical and political realities of his time, the later Schelling is still philosophically important, precisely because of his avoidance of some of the traps into which Nietzsche and his precursors, from Schopenhauer to Feuerbach, fell, and into which Nietzsche's successors continue to fall.

Habermas's assessment of the Young Hegelians' critique of Hegelianism depends upon their relationship to alterity.[8] Alterity – the centre of Schelling's late philosophy – is the result of the failure to articulate a totality which is 'self-related' and which, by being 'self-related', can overcome the split of subject and object. In naming what subverts this totalising relationship of self-knowledge the young Hegelians, Habermas argues, make the same mistake as pre-Kantian thinkers, in that they claim immediate access to what can only be known reflexively. It would seem, then, that the basis of Habermas's criticism of the Young Hegelians' failure to prevent the wholesale rejection of reason in Nietzsche is that they come to terms with alterity by invoking a thing in itself, which they term Nature, or History.[9] To begin with, though, one should not just assume that Nietzsche's notion of the self-destruction of reason is itself post-Kantian.[10] With occasional exceptions Nietzsche himself relied precisely upon a thing in itself, be it the 'will to power', or Dionysus. In 'On truth and lie in the extra-moral sense' he claims, for instance, that the real being behind the appearances manifest in language is 'an X that is inaccessible and indefinable to us'. Nietzsche's main concern is that the thing in itself should not be surreptitiously subsumed into Reason by linking it to God, as he thinks Kant and Hegel do. Instead Nietzsche often makes rationality itself into a form of self-deception. It is vital to make the distinction between this move and what Schelling does.

If one accepts the theoretical moves via which Schelling undermines the basic model of reflection, then Nietzsche's notion of reason cannot be a serious alternative. However one looks at it, making reason into a self-*deception* entails the ability to *identify* the deception, which means Nietzsche's model is itself reflexive. One side of a relationship must see the other side as the determinate negation of itself if the notion of deception is to be intelligible.[11] If the claim about deception is to be stated, the real truth about reason must be known in some way. This would only be possible via access to a determinate (Hegelian, or pre-critical) knowledge of, or an absolute intuitive access to, *what* true being is, as opposed to the deception. This in turn requires access to something which must, as Schelling showed, already be familiar if it is to be re-presented. Nietzsche famously sees truth as a 'moving army of metaphors', but he sees metaphors as illusions, thereby making the truth embodied in language an illusion which people have forgotten is an illusion. What allows Nietzsche, though, to claim in language that the truth furnished by languages is an illusion? The claim entails a performative contradiction. It depends upon a conception in which the subject represents the object to itself merely in its own terms. These terms are supposed to be a self-deception, precisely because they do not take account of the fact that they are merely the subject's terms. To *show* that this is the case, though, requires a meta-perspective from which it can be established that the terms are only those of the subject, and so on, which is, of course, the problem of reflection all over again.

Once truth is no longer understood in terms of the subject's adequate representation of the object,[12] one is left with the alternative of either trying to understand how truth works *within* language, which means truth cannot even be conceived of outside of language, or trying to find a way beyond what can be said. This alternative leads us back again to what is one of the most vital issues in contemporary philosophy, that is manifest in debates of the most varied kinds, namely the tension between conceptions of language as the medium of propositional assertion and of language as the medium of world-disclosure – a tension which in certain ways corresponds to the difference between negative and positive philosophy. Many of the intractable differences between the analytical and 'European' approaches to philosophy are the result of this tension, as Rorty has suggested. This tension also appears within the tradition of the Frankfurt School, as what separates Adorno from Habermas. Adorno insists, in the tradition of the *STI*, that the 'mimetic' refusal of modern art to communicate in the manner of the rest of a society now completely dominated by instrumental reason is the only hope left for a strong philosophical conception of reason, whereas Habermas wishes to show a new path for reason in modernity based on communicative action orientated towards validity claims.

The fact is that the historical roots of this tension in modern philosophy are precisely the roots of Schelling's own philosophy, which helps explain why Schelling's work has gained a new actuality. Manfred Frank claims that it was 'the becoming non-transparent of the Absolute for reflection from which both the turn towards aestheticism and to the philosophy of language emerged in early Romanticism, in one and the same movement' (Frank 1992b p. 65). In both aesthetics and the philosophy of language the notion of representation is subverted because it is impossible to say *what* the Absolute, understood as that which would ground the relation between subject-representer and object-represented, or ground the correspondence between language and world, really is. In art this subversion is manifest in the manner we saw in the *STI*, where the endless possibility inherent in the interpretation of the work was the only way of *showing* the Absolute. The philosophy of language becomes central because of the subversion of the subject's attempt at self-presence, which forces it into

183

engagement with the order of language if it wishes to arrive at the truth. The Absolute is the goal of universal agreement, but it can now only be a goal. Philosophy cannot circumscribe the universal, because the means of attaining the universal is the individual, whose own real interpretative and communicative activity is the basis of this goal.[13] This is the state of affairs that Habermas confronts in his communicative theory of reason. The underlying question here is whether some of the arguments made by Schelling against Hegel's system might not also, when translated into the terms of contemporary debates about reason, apply to these more modest conceptions of reason.

Habermas, along with Heidegger, sees reflection as inherent in the Cartesian 'paradigm of subjectivity', in which an isolated subject tries to cross the gap between self and not-self. The paradigm of subjectivity is therefore that of reflexivity, which, seen from the subject's side, must necessarily fail to cross the gap between the subject and its Other, as was already evident in the best arguments of Schelling's identity philosophy. Habermas's alternative is to reject the very notion of the 'isolated subject', and see self-consciousness as always already formed in intersubjective communication. This in some ways Hegelian position has been questioned by Frank and Dieter Henrich, because it is inadequate to explain the nature of individual self-consciousness, which cannot be understood in terms of the subject's reflexive relationship to itself or of its self-reflection in the Other. We saw aspects of this argument in the last chapter when considering Schelling's critique of Descartes.[14] By revealing one undoubted problem inherent in the reflexive paradigm of self-consciousness Habermas thinks he can avoid the other aporias of reflexivity. They can be overcome, he argues, via the paradigm of communicative action orientated towards the postulate of the ideal speech situation. The ideal speech situation is a kind of Absolute which is internal to communication, because it negates the relative particular interests of the participants in communicative action, who acknowledge the higher telos of agreement inherent in the very fact of communication orientated towards agreed validity. This telos, it should be added, in order to escape the looming Hegelian trap, must be reliant upon the pre-reflexive familiarity, on the part of the participants in communication, with the truth inherent in language: otherwise they would not even recognise when agreement had been reached, or even, presumably, desire to reach agreement at all. Vital as Habermas's project is in the attempt to work out a new understanding of reason in the light of the demise of a metaphysically grounded notion of reason, it still involves the danger of resurrecting a Hegelian thought of precisely the kind that Schelling's arguments put into question.

The point at issue here is too important and complex for me to do any more than briefly suggest how Schelling's version of the crisis of reason can begin to raise questions about Habermas's attempt to develop a theory of communicative rationality and thus suggest a different approach to the history of post-Hegelian defences of reason. My aim is not to deny the necessity for such a theory, but to ask whether Habermas's approach to it does not exclude certain key considerations. The Hegelian moment in Habermas lies in the relationship of the theory of communicative action to the praxes of communicative action. The problem is evident in the way Habermas separates the world-disclosing capacity of language evident in metaphor, or in any kind of communicative articulation, such as music, which results in new understanding which cannot be defined in terms of existing rules, from the discourse of validity. Here is Habermas in a recent text on Wittgenstein:

> Contemporary debates show what insights we owe to the concentration on the world-constituting and eye-opening, and at the same time concealing (*vorenthaltende*) function of language and aesthetic experience. I see in this a specifically German contribution to the philosophy of the 20th century, which one can trace back via Nietzsche to Humboldt and Hamann. However much we stand in this tradition and feel ourselves indebted to it, for some of us equally specific experiences of this century have also left behind traces of scepticism. This scepticism is directed against an abdication of problem-solving philosophical thinking before the poetic power of language, literature and art.
>
> (Habermas 1991 p. 90)

He warns against losing sight of the 'interdependence' between the differing cognitive, ethical, and aesthetic spheres of modern rationality. Whilst it is surely right that the aesthetic can only be constituted in some kind of relation to the non-aesthetic, the fact that the disclosing power of language is potentially present in *any* form of communication makes this distinction only a relative one, which is what Habermas seems not to want to accept. Once one has admitted that one can solve problems with metaphors, as psychoanalysis demonstrates, for example, it seems at least likely that the distinction of problem-solving and disclosure must be relativised. The question of world-disclosure in language echoes issues central to the *WA*, is fundamental to hermeneutics, and now even appears in some aspects of analytical (or 'post-analytical') philosophy.[15] The recent interest in the issue of world-disclosure is based on the realisation that the linguistic turn was achieved at the expense of attention to our pre-propositional relationship to existence.

Schelling's much maligned attention to immediacy, to 'intuition', has now begun to look less suspicious than it did in the light of Hegel's demand that immediacy be shown really to be reflection, or in the light of the claim that the analysis of linguistic usage would be able exhaustively to describe truth conditions. Immediacy can anyway, as I have suggested, be seen as a step away from the idea of thought as representation. Here is Schelling on the question of immediacy in the Hegel-critique:

> If thinking is concerned with the determination of this matter ['being', the 'absolute subject'], then it does not think of this basis itself but of the determination of the concept which it imprints in it . . . it is therefore what in thinking is not really thought. A thought which is not a thinking thought (*Ein nicht denkendes Denken*) cannot be far from an intuiting thought.
>
> (I/10 p. 151)

Metaphor is part of the attempt to bring this 'intuiting thought' to the level of 'reflection' in language, which, as Schelling's argument for positive philosophy suggests against Hegel, cannot ever be finally achieved, because of the nature of the relationship between reflection and its ground. The contemporary manifestation of this realisation is the attention to the fact that rationality is inherently bound to the need for interpretation, which cannot be finally formalised, even on the basis of theorising the always already existing everyday praxis of communicative action. Habermas, as we saw, repeatedly argues that one should not conflate problem-solving and world-disclosure. He thereby repeats on a less speculative level the Hegelian move of suggesting that there is a higher truth which is arrived at by raising intuition to the level of the concept, which led Hegel to subordinate art and religion to philosophy (see A. Bowie 1990 chapter 5).

Hilary Putnam has questioned, in ways which point back to Schelling and the Romantic heritage, Habermas's way of arriving at a non-positivist conception of rationality:[16]

[Habermas's] attempts clearly represent a recognition of what I might call the *nihilism* that lies behind positivism; the unsupportable suggestion that there is nothing at all to the ideas of insight, intuition, wisdom, except in so far as intuition and wisdom issue in laws and mathematical results which can be publicly verified.... But the method seems to me the wrong one.

(Putnam 1983 p. 299)

It is wrong because even within the 'problem-solving' sciences validity is far more dependent on interpretation and intuition than Habermas's theory can allow. Putnam goes on to suggest that one cannot, as Habermas tries to,

achieve a correct conception of rationality by pasting together a positivistic account of rationality in the 'nomothetic' sciences and a vague account of rationality in the 'ideographic' sciences. A better approach would be to begin by recognizing that interpretation, in the very wide sense of the term, and value are involved in our notions of rationality in every area.

(ibid. p. 300)

Habermas is not insensitive to the issue of problem-solving and world-disclosure, but his dogmatic separation of the two cannot be sustained, as Putnam suggests.

The importance Habermas attaches to religious language makes it clear that he sees this issue as central to modern philosophy. He insists in *Post-Metaphysical Thinking*:

As long as religious language brings with it inspiring, indeed indispensable, semantic contents, which (for the time being?) withdraw themselves from the power of expression of philosophical language and still await translation into discourses of legitimation (*begründende Diskurse*), philosophy will, even in its post-metaphysical form, be able neither to replace nor to repress religion.

(Habermas 1988 p. 60)

At the same time Habermas's assertion relies on a theory which would be able to draw the line between discourses of legitimation and religious language, of the same kind as he demands between the criticisable claims to validity of philosophy and of literature. In his legitimate desire to distinguish between the post-Nietzschean farewell to any serious attempt at justification that is present in the worst aspects of post-structuralism, and philosophy orientated to the testing

187

of validity, Habermas slips back into a position which asserts, in an essentially Hegelian manner, more than his post-metaphysical perspective can allow.

Manfred Frank suggests, against Habermas:

> we would not even need to set off on the road of intersubjective agreement − neither in literature nor in philosophy − if this agreement were a priori (or intersubjectively) guaranteed. But it is not guaranteed; and the fact that it is not is a result of the irreducible plurality of individual world-disclosure, without which there would be no pressure of motivation in the direction of interindividual agreement. We must come to agreement with each other as individuals, but not although, but rather *because* we cannot build on a system of agreement which is agreed in advance. If this were not the case the conception of truth as intersubjective consensus would lose its meaning: it would no longer be a specifically post-metaphysical alternative to the classical−ontological [representational] theory of truth.
>
> (Frank 1992b p. 83)

One can, with a degree of hermeneutic sensitivity, translate this back into the structure of Schelling's Hegel-critique.

The crucial factor is the refusal to accept that the *theory* which attempts to resolve difference into identity, in consensus, can rely on a basis which the theory itself can circumscribe. Whilst this approach undermines the totalising claims of the theory, it need not obviate the attempt to confront the prior problem that the theory justifiably strives to understand and move beyond. This is the core of truth in what Schelling intends by making a difference between negative and positive philosophy.[17] This kind of difference developed in subsequent philosophy into the difference between the idea that we can give a definitive theory of truth via a theory of meaning, and the hermeneutic insistence that such a theory must always rely on the uncontrollable reality of the fact that we are always already engaged in interpretation and understanding, so that circumscribing what understanding is becomes impossible, as we need understanding to do so. This repeats the essential point against self-grounding reflection made by Schelling. The underlying problem can, however, recur within hermeneutics itself. Even Gadamer, when he says things like this:

> Every word . . . relates to a totality via which alone it is a word. Every word makes the whole of the language to which it belongs resonate, and makes the whole world view that it is based on

appear. Hence every word also allows, as the happening of its moment, what is unsaid to be there as well.

(Gadamer 1975 p. 434)

slips back into a linguistic version of the Hegelian paradigm: how could he ever know this without just presupposing it?[18] Habermas seems to want to combine the analytical and the hermeneutic approaches, but this leads him into difficulties that are suggestive for subsequent attempts to marry analytical and hermeneutic approaches to philosophy.

The only basis for a post-metaphysical conception of reason is the striving for truth, identity, that is revealed in the very fact of communication, as opposed to the Nietzschean idea that communication is the exercise of power over the Other.[19] This means that truth is at least potentially present in *any* kind of communicative act in relation to another person. We must, then, confront the fact that all explanatory approaches to the awareness of the truth presuppose what they would explain, the fact of world-disclosure, which is why truth cannot be explained away by something else such as power; but it is also why theories based on the assumption of the irreducibility of truth cannot ground themselves. The exploration of this irreducibility of the structure of truth is Heidegger's main contribution to modern philosophy, and I have tried to suggest ways in which Schelling leads in this direction.[20] In order, then, to make a theoretically defensible distinction between truth claims and world-disclosure, the theorist would have already to be able to presuppose a complete theoretical knowledge of the difference between them.[21] This cannot be done in terms of a theory based only, as a post-metaphysical theory of this kind must be, on the real pragmatic success of communication. The essential issue is the relationship of the attempt to give a theory that would do justice to the rationality in which we are always already located via the fact of communication, to the realisation that one of the crucial factors about the practice of reason is its ability to look beyond anything that can be theorised. Habermas admits that the semantic potential of both religious and aesthetic articulation poses challenges that cannot be answered by philosophical discourse, but then defuses this challenge by giving essentially Hegelian primacy to that discourse. He thereby forgets, as Frank suggests, that this lands him back in metaphysical assumptions, because it requires a circumscribing of the absolute difference of praxes whose differences can only be continually tested in the contingencies of real communication.

The response to the crisis of reason, then, requires a theoretical openness that a Hegelian approach to theory, despite all Hegel's other contributions, excludes. Schelling begins to lay the ground for such an open conception as follows:

> It could . . . indeed be true . . . that everything which Is is in the Idea or in the logical concept, and that in consequence the Idea is the truth of everything . . . thus it could be admitted that everything is in the logical Idea, and in *such* a way that it could not be outside it, because what is meaningless can certainly not exist anywhere at any time. But in this way what is logical . . . presents itself as the merely negative aspect of existence, as that *without* which nothing could exist, from which, however, it by no means follows that everything only exists *via* what is logical.
>
> (I/10 p. 143)

Schelling, then, who for a long time has been regarded as merely a curiosity of nineteenth century philosophy, articulates certain aspects of the crisis of reason more appropriately than his contemporaries and his successors in the nineteenth century, as well as suggesting problems in contemporary theories.

Sometimes it is necessary to go back in order to go forwards. However much, when considering Schelling, one has to become involved with masses of hermeneutic problems that result from his merely context-bound concerns, particular manner of philosophising and attempts to salvage theology, he yet reveals issues that some recent theory threatens to lose touch with altogether. We are not going to get a theory of the origins of language which could be validated; but crucial ways of understanding the nature of which we are a part, which have been more and more marginalised into the expressive realm of pre-propositional forms of art like music, make more sense in the light of the *WA*'s theory of predication. We are not going to arrive at a philosophy of nature that wholly overcomes the problems of regression to pre-Kantianism; but Schelling makes more unsentimental sense of the need not to repress the nature of which we are an aspect than almost any other modern philosopher. Such philosophy is not merely literary, nor is it simply dependent on analogy: whilst it gains its power from its metaphorical resources, it also, at the same time and in the same texts, doggedly pursues answers to conceptual problems. We will not get the kind of synthesis of the spheres of modern knowledge that German Idealism and Romanticism hoped for, but we should not reject the very idea of such a synthesis. A properly modern conception of reason must remain open to all the resources available: the success of some of the critiques of reason in post-structuralism was not least a result of the literary resources mobilised in those critiques, which have been increasingly neglected by philosophies which attempt to defend a fallibilistic modern conception of reason. By keeping itself open to all the resources available, a contemporary conception of reason can, whilst coming to terms with the facticity of reason, still reveal the vacuity of the idea that we have arrived in a post-modern world in which we have awoken from 'the sleep of reason'. Schelling's contribution to the history of modern reason may be labyrinthine, and he often loses his way himself, but certain of the paths he opened are still worth exploring.

NOTES

INTRODUCTION

1 The most accessible location of Schelling's main arguments in his later philosophy, where the critique of Hegel is developed, is the lectures *On the History of Modern Philosophy*, which I have translated for Cambridge University Press (Schelling 1994), and which I shall refer to from now on as the 'Lectures'.

2 Deciding whether to capitalise the word 'being' when it is discussed in relation to Heidegger is a problem. I have decided not to do so, but to use the German *Sein* when discussing Heidegger's own use of the word. When Schelling uses the word *Seyn* I shall just use 'being' and will try to make clear from the context what is meant. Where necessary, I shall specify the word he uses for 'being' if it is not *Seyn*. Though Schelling evidently thinks in terms of ontological difference, he often uses *Seyn* and *Seyendes* interchangeably.

3 Interpreting Davidson himself on metaphor is difficult. What counts for Davidson is 'what a metaphor calls to our attention, and much of what we are caused to notice is not propositional in character' (Davidson 1984 p. 263). There is 'no limit' (ibid.) to metaphor's capacity in this respect. Davidson maintains that it is usually when we take a sentence as false, or trivially and tautologically true – hence when its status as proposition seems inadequate to explain what it *does* – that we are likely to look at it as a metaphor. Davidson further insists, though, that actually *any* use of language has no 'clear end' in terms of what it can make us notice, thereby making things less clear than the initial distinction between literal truth (Rorty's 'meaning') and metaphor would suggest. Nelson Goodman suggests in this connection: 'The acknowledged difficulty and even impossibility of finding a literal paraphrase for most metaphors is offered by Davidson as evidence that there is nothing to be paraphrased – that a sentence says nothing metaphorically that it does not say literally, but rather functions differently, inviting comparisons and stimulating thought. But paraphrase of many literal sentences is also exceedingly difficult, and we may seriously question whether any sentence can be translated exactly into other words in the same or any other language' (Goodman 1984 p. 72).

NOTES

1 ABSOLUTE BEGINNINGS

1 As Frank also shows, the issues raised by Fichte and developed by Dieter Henrich and himself play a major role in the disagreement between Habermas, who thinks the theory of the subject can be dissolved into a theory of intersubjectivity, and Henrich and Frank, who deny this is possible. This disagreement is at the heart of the debate about post-metaphysical thinking (see Henrich 1987; Habermas 1988; Frank 1991).
2 Hegel's 1801 *Differenzschrift* is an attempt to get beyond the alternative of Fichte's 'subjective subject–object' and the Spinozist aspect of Schelling's 'objective subject–object'. We shall show the problem with Hegel's developed conception of the overcoming of the subject–object split in varying contexts later. Oddly, as we shall see, it will be this text of Hegel's that Rodolphe Gasché uses to suggest the failure of pre-Hegelian thinking, including Schelling, in order to discuss Derrida's critique of reflection.
3 See Chapter 4.
4 This consequence is what Hegel is talking about when he refers in the *Phenomenology of Spirit* to the Absolute in other philosophies than his own as the 'night in which all cows are black'. (On this, see the beginning of Chapter 4.)
5 One can regard world-disclosure as a kind of positive gift, as the later Heidegger does, or as the opening-up of a world of division, as it largely is here. Walter Schulz cites Rudolf Bultmann's remark that 'God is the uncertainty (*Ungesichertheit*) of the next moment which the non-believer experiences as having to exist/be there (*Daseinmüssen*), but which the believer experiences as being allowed to be there (*Daseindürfen*)' (Schulz 1957 p. 52).

2 THE HERMENEUTICS OF NATURE

1 See, e.g., Cunningham and Jardine 1990; Heuser-Kessler 1986. The attention has, though, largely been in terms of the history of science, not of philosophy.
2 There have, despite this, been recent suggestions that some of Schelling's theoretical claims may, seen in the light of present-day science, not be so invalid as had been thought. The indirect influence of *Naturphilosophie* clearly continued into the second half of the nineteenth century and beyond.
3 See, e.g., Putnam 1983, and the last section of this chapter.
4 This does not mean, as we will see in a moment, the same as a 'force'.
5 The objection which is often raised against using Schelling's ideas in relation to subsequent scientific developments – namely, that one is just relying on deductions from analogies – seems to me mistaken. It is based on an untenable realist conviction that we can describe the progress of science in terms of convergence towards a realm of absolute objects, thus as better and better representation that is really independent of language. The suspicion of analogies – which is evidently valid in the praxis of scientific investigation – must always take into account both the fact that we can never be finally sure that we are not using metaphor *and* the fact that metaphor itself can play a role in scientific re-description. The certainty of working in a manner free of metaphor would require the sort of external perspective that Schelling reveals as inherently inaccessible. In Chapter 4, I shall consider Schelling's way of understanding matter and mind in detail.
6 Which, of course, he undoubtedly does much of the time.

7 In the same text Heidegger will, however, also maintain in a manner absolutely alien to Schelling: 'Presumably, of all beings there are, the living being [animal] is the hardest to think because it, on the one hand, in a certain manner is most closely related to us and, on the other, at the same time separated via an abyss from our ex-sisting essence (*Wesen*). Against this it can appear that the essence of the divine is closer to us than the alienness (*das Befremdende*) of living beings, closer, that is in an essential distance which as distance is yet more familiar to our existent essence than the hardly imaginable abyssal bodily relationship with the animal' (Heidegger 1978 p. 323). The difference for Heidegger (this is in 1946) is made by language. Schelling says in 1809 that 'Fr. Baader rightly says it would be good if the depravity of mankind only went as far as becoming animal; unfortunately, though, mankind can only stand below or above the animal' (I/7 p. 373).

8 The echoes suggested here of the 'anthropic principle' in recent cosmology will also recur in Schelling's later work. On this, see Hogrebe 1989. As will be apparent from the description of the productivity, Schelling's basic model already suggests the world of the 'big bang' and other aspects of contemporary theoretical physics.

9 This point will be vital for Schelling's later philosophy.

10 I shall not consider the question of whether the same does not actually apply to many of the major discoveries in the natural science of the nineteenth or, indeed, this century, which now are no longer seen as valid in the terms in which they were formulated, or in any others, for that matter. The specific problem of a *Naturphilosophie* can be discussed without getting into such deep waters.

3 THE HISTORY OF CONSCIOUSNESS AND THE TRUTH OF ART

1 See, e.g., the last two chapters of Ramberg 1989, who uses Gadamer in order to understand Davidson better.

2 This may well, incidentally, be the origin of Marx's notion of 'second nature'. Marx was familiar with some of Schelling's early work.

3 C.I. Lewis was, of course, familiar with German Idealist philosophy.

4 Though Bertrand Russell's theory of types can deal with the version of this problem that occurs in logic, it does not provide an answer to what is at issue here.

5 I am, of course, aware that the problem is more complex than this: my concern here is just to suggest some of the implications of the question of self-reference.

6 As we saw in the Introduction, Goodman suggests that this may be the case for any use of language.

7 I shall return to this issue in the next chapter.

8 Heidegger spends a lot of *Kant and the Problem of Metaphysics* looking at the imagination, which further suggests his proximity to aspects of Romantic philosophy.

9 If we read the *STI* in this way we are, incidentally, much closer to Gadamer's conception of art in *Truth and Method* than Gadamer's version of Romantic aesthetics would allow.

NOTES

10 If this seems merely paradoxical, try pondering what it is that music says. Related issues will later emerge in the work of Wittgenstein.

4 IDENTITY PHILOSOPHY

1 E.g., by Gasché 1986 p. 58.
2 The standard claim that Schelling invalidly invokes immediacy is evidently not even applicable here, in that the moment of immediacy is arrived at via the *philosophical* realisation of the need for a ground of reflection. The same claim is made against the later philosophy and is, as we shall see, equally indefensible.
3 Fichte himself, one should add, began to claim something analogous in later work, after the break with Schelling.
4 The later Schelling will arrive at a position in certain ways even closer to Heidegger's, as will be evident in the next two chapters.
5 Evidently Schelling puts these issues in terms, like the Absolute, which seem simply to belong to an irredeemably 'metaphysical' perspective; the structure of the arguments, though, makes it clear that what is meant cannot be understood adequately if the vocabulary Schelling uses is taken in the same sense as it would be in texts which clearly do belong to 'Western metaphysics'.
6 Frank's essay 'Identity and Subjectivity' in Frank 1991 is indispensable for the understanding of Schelling's identity philosophy, and I rely on it heavily here.
7 Again, this might seem just to be a version of Platonism, in that the appearing world is not the true world. This is evidently so in one sense, but the other consequences of the argument can be understood in a thoroughly non-Platonic way, in that Schelling sees the Absolute not as the repository of determinate true essences behind the appearances, but as the ground of the temporality of the world.
8 See Frank 1984 and 1992a for a detailed refutation of Derrida's conception. I repeat aspects of Frank's arguments here in another context because one has yet to see an adequate response to them from either Derrida himself or from those who trust his conception of the history of metaphysics.
9 Gadamer in particular has rightly protested against the very idea of such a language, which primarily derives from the later Heidegger, because delimiting it involves precisely the claims the term is trying to get away from. How do we *know* when someone is speaking the 'language of metaphysics'? See Gadamer 1986.
10 What is meant by God need be no more than the totality at this stage of Schelling's philosophy. Later such an equation is fundamentally rejected, as leading to Spinozism.
11 Nietzsche himself realises this at one point: 'Simple differences in power could not feel themselves as such: there must be a something there which wishes to grow' (Nietzsche 1980 vol. 12 p. 140). See A. Bowie 1990 chapter 8.
12 See ibid. pp. 219–52 for an account of just how far Nietzsche depends (generally without acknowledgement) upon Idealist and Romantic philosophy.

195

13 Gasché's whole discussion of Schelling is based on Hegel's account of the *Naturphilosophie* in the *Differenzschrift*. This is misleading, first, because it does not deal with Schelling's mature identity philosophy, and, second, because the later Schelling, who is never even mentioned, does not fulfil the criteria Gasché uses for his critique of metaphysics. Gasché, despite his enlightening interpretation of Hegel's early method, ends up adding to the myths about German Idealism, and thereby overestimating Derrida's philosophical achievement.

14 Making allowances for the talk of totality in Schelling – evidently Derrida avoids such terms – the idea is basically the same. The main difference from Derrida is discussed below.

15 Rorty also points out that the word now does have a meaning, whether Derrida likes it or not.

16 Provided, of course, that one accepts the analytical distinction that Rorty tries to make. The very fact that this distinction is not so easy to make suggests that saying what metaphysics is may well be the real problem, as Derrida himself sometimes suggests.

17 Cf. Dews 1987 chapter 1. Dews tends, though, wholly to equate the identity philosophy with Derrida. It seems to me that Schelling has a crucial advantage over Derrida's position which will be evident below.

18 One can even suggest that there could not even be a disclosed world in the terms Derrida offers, in that he offers no criterion for how we are aware of the articulated differences that go to make up a *world*.

19 As Frank points out, Derrida was aware of this problem 'when he admitted in his reply to Searle's criticism: 'Iterability requires a minimal remaining (*restance*) (like an albeit limited, minimal idealisation) for identity to be repeatable and identifiable *in, through*, and even *with a view to* alteration. For the structure of iteration – another decisive trait – implies at the same time identity *and* difference'. But Derrida cannot account for this minimal 'remaining' of the meaning of the sign (and of the self-consciousness which is mediated by it) by means of his theory – it remains 'just an assumption whose necessity can be admitted only if one relinquishes his position'. (Frank 1992a pp. 231–2).

20 Donald Davidson, who in this respect actually comes close to Heidegger, sees the understanding of the concept of truth as a 'primitive' in that it cannot be defined by saying the truth about the truth.

21 Schelling at times does work with a representational model elsewhere (such as in the opening part of the *STI*), but the aspects of his thinking that are still significant do not rely on the notion of adequation or representation.

22 The very term 'non-reductive physicalism' seems to me a misnomer: if physicalism is not to be reductive, it cannot be physicalism at all.

23 As we have seen, the System itself does much to undermine this conception in the aspects which were considered in detail above.

5 FREEDOM, ONTOLOGY AND LANGUAGE

1 However, as I suggested in the Introduction, one needs to be very careful about interpreting the meaning of apparently traditional theological vocabulary, particularly in Schelling's later philosophy.

2 Peter Dews has suggested to me in conversation that this prefigures the basic structure of the *Dialectic of Enlightenment*.

3 In the so-far available texts Heidegger, like many of his post-structuralist successors, never, to my knowledge, seriously discusses the later Schelling of the positive philosophy; indeed his whole approach to Schelling seems based on the *FS*, which, whilst vital to Schelling's development, is anything but a coherently worked-out version of his ideas.

4 How far Heidegger's shift towards the more unified history of *Sein* at this time is for the political and psychological reasons adduced by Habermas (1987) cannot be adequately discussed here. Along with the growing desire to escape any conception of a subject that is responsible for its actions and words – language, as in all Heidegger's later philosophy, does the talking now – the following remarks, seen in the historical context of 1941, suggest Habermas may well have a point: 'The thinking-out into the essence of *Da-sein* within the attention to that which is alone worthy of thinking for essential thinking, namely *Sein* and its 'meaning' (*Sinn*) ... can only prepare the experience of this essence, in order that the historical (*geschichtlich*) person is prepared in case a transformation of the relation of *Sein* to him takes place' (Heidegger 1991 p. 63). The 'transformation of the relation of *Sein*' to the person Heidegger presumably still includes the rise of Nazism.

5 Schelling's conception of 'willing' as 'primal being', which is evidently vital for Schopenhauer, and for Heidegger's conception of Schelling, is not always sustained in the later philosophy, where the issue of being is more complex. Heidegger's interpretation of the idea of 'primal being' as willing is also problematic, as Dieter Thomä suggests (Thomä 1990 pp. 166–75), because it conceals the fact that 'willing''s relationship to the human subject may not be transparent to that subject. Thomä's account of the relationship of Schelling to Heidegger (and Hegel) is highly recommended.

6 Not, as Heidegger rightly points out, for good *or* evil.

7 The idea of this failure of reflection will be the core of Schelling's late philosophy.

8 Clearly the question of the nature of the ego is more complex than I have made it here, but the basic point does help to clarify Schelling's argument.

9 As the basic issues remain the same, I shall not distinguish between the various now published versions – all unfinished – of the *WA* from 1811 to 1815.

10 We saw much the same problem in the last chapter, in Derrida's account of Nietzsche. Heidegger, incidentally, sees this question rather as Schelling does, and sees Nietzsche's position as the ultimate metaphysical position. I shall look again at this issue in the Conclusion.

11 This conception would also square with the clarification of Heidegger suggested by Ernst Tugendhat, which sees *Sein* in Heidegger's sense as meaning 'being true', which cannot be said of objects.

12 We have already seen a version of this problem in the *STI*. Schelling's description of the *STI* in the Lectures gives a particularly enlightening version of it (I/10 pp. 93–8).

13 See, e.g., Hilary Putnam's refutation of functionalism (Putnam 1988).

14 Schelling, confusingly, sometimes uses the words interchangeably.

15 This does not, *pace* all thinkers of non-identity, mean that it *is* overcome, as I have already made clear against Heidegger.

16 Kant, as usual, forbids turning this reality into God.

17 The point of the later *Philosophy of Revelation* will be to prove that the manifest world is God's work, which can only be done after the fact of the manifest world, which until then is radically contingent.

18 The proximity here to Sartre's *L'être et le néant* is quite striking. Both share the notion of a groundless freedom. See Sartre 1943 pp. 56–81.

19 In this sense, *pace* Derrida, it is '*toujours déjà différé*'.

20 To prevent any possible confusion, it is worth mentioning that Schelling will later discuss these forces rather differently: B will become like Plato's *apeiron*, a wild expansive force, and A in its various guises will be what makes this force into what can be intelligible by taking on forms. B remains in one sense the same in that it does not have any determinate boundary, which can only result from a relation to an other.

21 This conception of rotation also points forward to notions of eternal recurrence that develop in line with the growing domination of scientific materialism later in the century. Hard-line materialism does not give any privilege to the development of consciousness: if the mechanical laws of nature point to eternal recurrence, then any sense of development in terms of consciousness can be subordinated to natural laws, rendering freedom merely illusory, in much the same way it is in a world ruled by mythological forces. Schelling, of course, rejects such a conception.

22 Even later in life Schopenhauer was always concerned to hear what Schelling had to say. In 1841, for example, he sent his assistant Julius Frauenstädt to hear Schelling's first Berlin lectures.

23 I shall return to these issues in a contemporary perspective in the Conclusion.

24 Habermas (1973) points out that the idea of the contracting force has its origins in the Sohar, the thirteenth-century Castilian kabbalistic text, and in Isaak Luria's idea, which Böhme also employed, of the *zimzum*, the contraction of God that opens the space for creation and revelation.

25 This is, it seems to me, one way of understanding what Derrida might mean by the 'general text'.

26 It might again sound as though this condition is simply presupposed, but the point is that one arrives at the realisation via the failure to articulate a reflexive position that would make the identification possible.

27 The problems of this structure for the description of the structure of self-consciousness have been explored in Frank 1990.

6 SCHELLING OR HEGEL?

1 Most obviously in the work of Derrida, particularly as interpreted by Gasché (1986). I shall consider this issue at certain points later in the chapter.

2 I deliberately trace the pattern of the main arguments in a mainly chronological fashion: the different ways Schelling approaches the basic issues are enlightening in themselves as engagements with a fundamental structure in modern philosophy, and they have not been described in detail in English before. Given the unlikelihood of translations appearing of many of these

texts, this seems the best strategy, even at the risk of taking the reader on a somewhat exhausting journey.

3 Though I do not, for reasons of space, discuss Schulz's book, it should be stressed that it was vital for the change in perspective in Germany from attention to Schelling's early philosophy to attention to the late philosophy.

4 Although these lectures do not criticise Hegel directly, it is clear from I/10 p. 161–4 that Schelling was already publicly criticising Hegel during the Erlangen period.

5 In the Schelling edition, *On the Nature of Philosophy as a Science* is I/9 pp. 209–46. As with much of the later work, it is only since the Second World War that the main body of the lectures has become available in print. I suggested in the Introduction, though, that such lectures gained a wide currency precisely in the form of notes taken by those who attended them.

6 The point is probably derived from Kant's insistence that 'being is not a real predicate', i.e. that it is not an object in the Kantian sense. On this issue, see Heidegger 1978 pp. 439–74.

7 Sartre's proximity to Schelling, presumably via the mediation of Heidegger, is again apparent here.

8 This is why the notion of *absolute* reflection is so important in understanding Hegel, as Gasché rightly insists.

9 The validity of this apparently illogical notion of freedom will become apparent in the course of the argument. Heidegger's remark cited above from 'On the Essence of Truth' suggests how.

10 Hence Gasché's insistence on reflection.

11 Tugendhat says much the same of Heidegger's notion of the 'clearing' (*Lichtung*), the non-reflexive condition of possibility of predication: 'It is not in the sense that thinking falls back into a pre-transcendental attitude of naivety that the transcendental question is overtaken. The world as clearing is only reached in the passage through the analysis of subjectivity, not in the simple turn to something which is directly given' (Tugendhat 1970 p. 276). Tugendhat, like Heidegger, nowhere, to my knowledge, seriously discusses the later Schelling.

12 This does not mean, of course, that there might not still be such a correspondence, only that it could never be demonstrated.

13 These remarks are from 1927; Heidegger sees Hegel in the same terms in the late 1950s, after his engagement with Schelling, and makes no mention of Schelling's critique of Hegel. See Heidegger 1978 pp. 421–38.

14 This is the basis of Heidegger's critique, from *Being and Time* onwards, of neo-Kantian and other attempts to make philosophy the handmaiden of the particular – ontic – natural sciences.

15 Schelling is not always consistent in his use of the word: the context must always be consulted to avoid misunderstandings.

16 Lacan, of course, arrived at his views via a blending of Heidegger and Hegel; the conception should now begin to be more reminiscent of Schelling.

17 Although as I shall show, there is a fundamental flaw in Schelling's theology, its influence has been and is considerable, and it offers resources beyond its major failing.

18 Marcuse understood Schelling's positive philosophy in this way in *Reason and Revolution* (Marcuse 1967). In doing so he followed the general trend of Hegel-influenced Marxists in this century, who accepted the importance of the

Naturphilosophie and sometimes the *WA* philosophy, but tended to stay well away from the later philosophy.

19 Once again Schelling here asks questions usually associated with Heidegger, for whom logic itself had to be understood, rather than functioning as the unquestionable basis of understanding.

20 A version of which forms the text of the Lectures *On the History of Modern Philosophy* (Schelling 1994).

21 Dieter Henrich claims: 'Ontological difference is admittedly negated (*aufgehoben*) in the ontotheological proof. But precisely for that reason it is the condition of its becoming a problem. Greek philosophy never posed the problem of what it means *that* something is' (Henrich 1967a p. 264).

22 It is, as I suggested, more than arguable that the Schelling of the identity philosophy and the *FS* cannot be either, as the remarks about Fichte's ego indicated.

23 The basic thought was already inherent in the notion of 'gravity' we saw in the *FS* and the *WA*.

24 Hegel, of course, has more than one kind of reflection.

25 As such Gasché is right when he says 'all polemics against [absolute reflection] would be without ground', from the point of view of reflection. He cites Gadamer: 'The Archimedean point from where Hegel's philosophy could be toppled can never be found through reflection' (Gasché 1986 p. 64). This is exactly Schelling's point.

26 This kind of questioning makes it clear that Schelling, despite the frequent accusations from Lukács and others, cannot be considered an irrationalist. His importance lies precisely in the refusal to countenance irrationalism whilst confronting the philosophical questions which give rise to it.

27 There are highly original reflections on Aristotle in the *Presentation of the Purely Rational Philosophy*.

28 One presumes that by 'being' Rosenzweig here means being at the beginning of Hegel's *Logic*.

29 Both Heidegger and Derrida have, of course, been read in theological terms: the key question is the understanding of non-dialectical alterity, which is the core of Schelling's conception.

30 For an alternative view, see Brown 1990.

31 Frank analyses the proximity of Hegel's autonomous negation to Derrida's *différance* in this essay. See also A. Bowie 1985.

32 This was the point of Kant's reflections on the transcendental ideal that were considered in the last chapter: 'nobody can think a negation determinately without having the opposed affirmation as its ground' (Kant 1968 p. B 603 A 575).

33 The relations must be internal to ensure there is no external presupposition.

34 Frank, in his Introduction to the *PO* (Schelling 1977 p. 68), suggests that the Munich lectures are 'strongly oriented towards a distancing from the Idealism of autonomous negation' but thereby fail to carry out the internal negation of Idealism that is the end point of the 'overthrow of reason' in the negative philosophy of the *PO*. Whilst this may call in question some of its formulations concerning the relationship of concept and being, it does not finally invalidate the points presented here, which are refined in the later but briefer versions of the critique (some of the formulations remain literally identical anyway).

35 This has often, though, led to a concern in post-structuralism with *post-histoire*, on the assumption, which is present, for example, in Derrida's *Positions*, that the only serious philosophical conceptions of history were Hegelian or Marxist of a basically metaphysical kind.
36 This is why it is odd that Gasché, having made so much, in defence of Hegel, of the issue of absolute reflection then goes on to write a book about alterity in Derrida, all the while ignoring the later Schelling. 'Absolute reflection' is essentially 'negative philosophy' in Schelling's sense.

CONCLUSION

1 Most explicitly in 1/10 pp. 165–92.
2 The argument for the narcissism of reason derives from Heidegger's critique of Nietzsche, as we shall see in a moment. It is shared at least in part by the *Dialectic of Enlightenment*, and by many post-structuralists, such as Lyotard.
3 Cf. Sartre, *L'être et le néant*: 'it is not given to "human reality" to annihilate, even provisionally, the mass of being which is placed in front of it. What it can modify is its relation to this being' (Sartre 1943 p. 59).
4 One should not underestimate, though, the extent to which the American pragmatist tradition relates to German Idealism and Romanticism: C.S. Peirce, for example, was familiar with and identified at times with aspects of both Schelling and Hegel.
5 Clearly one cannot even begin to consider Hegel without admiring his own use of metaphor: the point is, though, whether the final ability to articulate his system does not require the abolition (*Aufhebung*) of metaphor because it is based in intuition or immediacy.
6 All the thinkers cited were, note, heavily influenced by Schelling. I consider Adorno's attempt to argue the 'primacy of the objective', the idea of which Habermas here attributes to Feuerbach, in A. Bowie 1993a.
7 That this does not apply to the theological arguments *per se* is evident from the rejection of the ontological proof quoted in the previous chapter: 'I must drop precisely this concept, the concept *God*, in order to begin with that which just exists, in which nothing more is thought than just this existing – in order to see if I can get from it to the divinity. Thus I cannot really prove the existence of God (by, for instance, beginning with the concept *God*) but instead the concept of that which exists before all possibility and thus without doubt – is given to me' (II/3 p. 158).
8 I suggested the link of Levinas to Schelling via Heidegger and Rosenzweig in the last chapter.
9 I showed in Chapter 2 how Schelling, in the *Naturphilosophie*, was often able to avoid a pre-Kantian position: 'nature' in Schelling need not be understood as a determinate thing in itself, in that he does not determine what it is, but only how it manifests itself. This already involves ontological difference.
10 Heidegger dramatises Nietzsche's pre-Kantian aspect into the idea of the culmination of Western metaphysics: namely, the idea that the manifest world is the result of a force, the will to power, which is derived from a conception of what drives the subject. The objection to Nietzsche is simply the one I

suggested in Chapter 4: the notion of will or force is a reflexive notion, that needs an Other to be itself. At times Nietzsche himself was aware of this problem, as I suggest in A. Bowie 1990, though this did not lead him to do anything about it, beyond making ironic admissions of the paradoxicality of his argument.

11 This can be understood via the difference between lying, which involves knowing what one considers to be true, and saying what is false, and saying something untrue when one thinks that what one says is true. The standard new-Nietzschean objection here is that what Nietzsche is engaged in are just rhetorical strategies to move us away from any foundations for truth at all. Be that as it may, even to maintain that Nietzsche is not engaged in argument requires, of course, the ability to identify something as being rhetorical, rather than being a truth claim: otherwise the *point* of its being rhetorical is unintelligible. It all comes down to what happens once one gives up the notion of truth as representation: one cannot use Nietzsche's essentially metaphysical argument against theories of truth which do not rely on representation.

12 Nietzsche admittedly often rejects the model of representation, but comes up with other versions of it at crucial points in nearly all his texts.

13 As Frank (1989a) shows, it was Schleiermacher who first revealed these consequences for modern philosophy: Schleiermacher, as I suggested in the Introduction, was heavily influenced by Schelling. On Schleiermacher, see A. Bowie 1990 chapter 6.

14 On this, see Frank 1991 in particular.

15 The almost exclusive concentration on 'world-disclosure' at the expense of validity claims is clearly also what gives post-structuralism an immediate appeal for so many people, which is a reason for Habermas's often justified suspicion of it.

16 Note the echo of the Pantheism controversy in the reappearance of 'nihilism' in relation to modern science.

17 As I have suggested, the difference becomes too symmetrical when Schelling tries to make the latter mirror the former: what the division points to, though, seems to me vital.

18 On this, see my review of Weinsheimer 1991 (A. Bowie 1993b).

19 This does *not* mean that communication cannot be used as a means of imposing power – which it clearly can be and is – but the very fact that we can *understand* this possibility of illegitimate imposition means that communication cannot be primarily based on it.

20 It is a pity Heidegger did not draw the ethical consequences which are entailed in the conception of truth suggested here, but that, of course, would require a theory of a subject responsible for the truth of its communication.

21 Ernst Tugendhat argues against Heidegger by insisting upon the difference between the world-disclosure inherent in any kind of meaning and the notion of a claim to validity that can be responded to negatively or positively by its recipient (Tugendhat 1970). Habermas clearly adopts Tugendhat's position. The implications of this issue require a book to be dealt with appropriately, so I shall leave it for the time being at Frank's point that all offers of communication entail the assumption on the part of the producer of the ability to understand and interpret the offer on the part of the receiver. The

prior need for interpretation suggests one way of questioning the priority given by Tugendhat and Habermas to cognitive validity claims over other initiatives of meaning. Frank claims that 'propositional truth is grounded in truth qua comprehensibility' (Frank 1992b p. 73). As Putnam suggests, it is the inherent ability to interpret that is prior, not one particular kind of communication.

BIBLIOGRAPHY

References (e.g. I/10 p. 121), are to Friedrich Wilhelm Joseph Schelling's *Sämmtliche Werke*, ed. K.F.A. Schelling, I Abtheilung vols 1–10, II Abtheilung vols 1–4, Stuttgart: Cotta, 1856–61.

An easily accessible substantial selection of the complete works has been published, ed. Manfred Frank, as Friedrich Wilhelm Joseph von Schelling, *Ausgewählte Schriften*, 6 vols, Frankfurt: Suhrkamp, 1985.

References to the *Ages of the World* as WA are to *Die Weltalter*, ed. Manfred Schröter, Munich: Biederstein, 1946.

All translations are my own. Books published in Frankfurt are all Frankfurt am Main.

Adorno, T.W. (1973) *Philosophische Terminologie. Zur Einleitung* Band 1, Frankfurt: Suhrkamp.

Apel, Karl-Otto (1973) *Transformation der Philosophie* Band 1, Frankfurt: Suhrkamp.

Beiser, Frederick C. (1987) *The Fate of Reason: German Philosophy from Kant to Fichte*, Cambridge, Mass.: Harvard University Press.

Bell, David (1987) 'The art of judgement', *Mind* 96.

Bowie, Andrew (1985) 'Individuality and *différance*', *Oxford Literary Review* 7.

—— (1990) *Aesthetics and Subjectivity: From Kant to Nietzsche*, Manchester: Manchester University Press, reprinted 1993.

—— (1993a) ' "Non-identity": the German Romantics, Schelling, and Adorno', in T. Rajan, ed., *Intersections: Nineteenth-Century Philosophy and Contemporary Theory*, Albany, NY: State University of New York Press.

—— (1993b) 'The Revenge of hermeneutics' [review of Joel Weinsheimer, *Philosophical Hermeneutics and Literary Theory*], *Radical Philosophy*, 63.

—— (1994) 'Re-thinking the history of the subject: Schelling and Heidegger', in Proceedings of University of Essex Philosophy Department Conference on *Deconstructive Subjectivities* ed. Simon Critchley (forthcoming SUNY 1994).

Bowie, Malcolm (1978) *Freud, Proust, and Lacan: Theory as Fiction*, Cambridge: Cambridge University Press.

Brown, Robert (1977) *The Later Philosophy of Schelling: The Influence of Böhme on the Works of 1809–15*, Lewisburg: University of Pennsylvania Press.

—— (1990) 'Resources in Schelling for new directions in theology', *Idealistic Studies* 20:1.

Cunningham, Andrew and Jardine, Nicholas (1990) *Romanticism and the Sciences*, Cambridge: Cambridge University Press.

Davidson, Donald (1980) *Essays on Actions and Events*, Oxford: Clarendon Press.

—— (1984) *Inquiries into Truth and Interpretation*, Oxford: Oxford University Press.

—— 'The structure and content of truth', *The Journal of Philosophy* 87:6.

Derrida, Jacques (1972) *Marges de la philosophie*, Paris: Seuil.

Dews, Peter (1987) *Logics of Disintegration*, London: Verso.

Fichte, J.G. (1971) *Werke I*, Berlin: De Gruyter.

Frank, Manfred (1975) *Der unendliche Mangel an Sein*, Frankfurt: Suhrkamp.

—— (1984) *Was Ist Neo-Strukturalismus?*, Frankfurt: Suhrkamp.

—— (1985) *Eine Einführung in Schellings Philosophie*, Frankfurt: Suhrkamp.

—— (1989a) *Das Sagbare und das Unsagbare*, Frankfurt: Suhrkamp.

—— (1989b) *Einführung in die frühromantische Ästhetik*, Frankfurt: Suhrkamp.

—— (1990) *Zeitbewußsein*, Pfullingen: Neske.

—— (1991) *Selbstbewusstsein und Selbsterkenntnis*, Stuttgart: Reclam.

—— (1992a) 'Is self-consciousness a case of *présence à soi?*, in *Derrida: A Critical Reader*, ed. David Wood, Oxford: Blackwell.

—— (1992b) *Stil in der Philosophie*, Stuttgart: Reclam.

Gadamer, Hans-Georg (1975) *Wahrheit und Methode*, Tübingen: J.C.B. Mohr.

—— (1986) *Hermeneutik: Wahrheit und Methode 2 Ergänzungen, Register*, Tübingen: J.C.B. Mohr.

Gasché, Rodolphe (1986) *The Tain of the Mirror. Derrida and the Philosophy of Reflection*, Cambridge, Mass., and London: Harvard University Press.

Goodman, Nelson (1984) *Of Mind and Other Matters*, Cambridge, Mass., and London: Harvard University Press.

Habermas, Jürgen (1973) *Theorie und Praxis*, Frankfurt: Suhrkamp.

—— (1988) *Nachmetaphysisches Denken*, Frankfurt: Suhrkamp.

—— (1991) *Texte und Kontexte*, Frankfurt: Suhrkamp.

Hartmann, Klaus, ed. (1976) *Die ontologische Option*, Berlin: De Gruyter.

Hegel, G.W.F. (1959) *Enzyklopädie der philosophischen Wissenschaften*, ed. Friedhelm Nicolin and Otto Pöggeler, Hamburg: Meiner.

—— (1969) *Wissenschaft der Logik I and II (Werke 5 and 6)*, Frankfurt: Suhrkamp.

—— (1970) *Phänomenologie des Geistes*, Frankfurt: Suhrkamp.

Heidegger, Martin (1960) *Der Ursprung des Kunstwerkes*, Stuttgart: Reclam.

—— (1971) *Schellings Abhandlung über das Wesen der menschlichen Freiheit*, Tübingen: Niemeyer.

—— (1978) *Wegmarken*, Frankfurt: Klostermann.

—— (1979) *Sein und Zeit*, Tübingen: Niemeyer.

—— (1983) *Die Grundbegriffe der Metaphysik*, Frankfurt: Klostermann.

—— (1989) *Die Grundprobleme der Phänomenologie*, Frankfurt: Klostermann.

—— (1991) *Die Metaphysik des deutschen Idealismus (Schelling)*, Frankfurt: Klostermann.

Henrich, Dieter (1967a) *Der ontologische Gottesbeweis*, Tübingen: Niemeyer.

—— (1967b) *Fichtes ursprüngliche Einsicht*, Frankfurt: Suhrkamp.

—— (1971) *Hegel im Kontext*, Frankfurt: Suhrkamp.

—— (1982) *Selbstverhältnisse*, Stuttgart: Reclam.

—— (1987) *Konzepte*, Frankfurt: Suhrkamp.

Heuser-Kessler, Marie-Luise (1986) 'Die Produktivität der Natur' Schellings Naturphilosophie und das neue Paradigma der Selbstorganisation in den Naturwissenschaften, Berlin: De Gruyter.

Hogrebe, Wolfram (1989) Prädikation und Genesis. Metaphysik als Fundamentalheuristik im Ausgang von Schellings 'Die Weltalter', Frankfurt: Suhrkamp.

—— (1991) 'Schwermut. Der späte Schelling und die Kunst', unpublished lecture, given in Leonberg 17 October 1991.

Hölderlin, Friedrich (1970) Sämtliche Werke und Briefe Band 2, Munich: Hanser.

Horkheimer, Max, and Adorno, T.W. (1971) Dialektik der Aufklärung, Frankfurt: Fischer.

Horstmann, Rolf-Peter (1986) 'Logifizierte Natur oder naturalisierte Logik? Bemerkungen zu Schellings Hegel-Kritik', in Rolf-Peter Horstmann and Michael John Petry, eds, Hegels Philosophie der Natur, Stuttgart: Klett–Cotta.

Jaspers, Karl (1955) Schelling: Größe und Verhängnis, Munich: Piper.

Kant, Immanuel, Werkausgabe I–XII, ed. Wilhelm Weischedel, Frankfurt: Suhrkamp 1968–77
    Kritik der reinen Vernunft (1968) (vols III, IV)
    Kritik der Urteilskraft (1977a) (vol. X)
    Metaphysische Anfangsgründe der Naturwissenschaft (1977b) (vol. IX).

Kierkegaard, Søren (1968) Concluding Unscientific Postscript, Princeton, NJ: Princeton University Press.

Kuhn, Thomas (1976) The Essential Tension, Chicago: Chicago University Press.

Lacan, Jacques (1971) Écrits, Paris: Seuil.

Löw, Reinhardt (1990) 'Das philosophische Problem der "Natur an sich" ', Philosophisches Jahrbuch 97.

McTaggart, John M.E. (1910) A Commentary on Hegel's Logic, Cambridge: Cambridge University Press.

Marcuse, Herbert (1963) Reason and Revolution, London: Routledge.

Marquard, Odo (1987) Transzendentaler Idealismus. Romantische Naturphilosophie. Psychoanalyse, Cologne: Dinter.

Marx, Werner (1984) The Philosophy of F.W.J. Schelling: History, System, Freedom, Bloomington: Indiana University Press.

Nagel, Thomas (1986) The View from Nowhere, Oxford: Oxford University Press.

Neuhouser, Frederick (1989) Fichte's Theory of Subjectivity, Cambridge: Cambridge University Press.

Nietzsche, Friedrich (1980) Sämtliche Werke, vols 1–15, ed. Colli and Montinari, Munich, Berlin, and New York: dtv.

Novalis (1978) Novalis Band 2. Das philosophisch – theoretische Werk, ed. Hans-Joachim Mähl, Munich and Vienna: Hanser.

Penrose, Roger (1989) The Emperor's New Mind, Oxford: Oxford University Press.

Putnam, Hilary (1983) Realism and Reason: Philosophical Papers vol. 3, Cambridge: Cambridge University Press.

—— (1988) Representation and Reality, Cambridge, Mass., and London: MIT Press.

Ramberg, Bjørn T. (1989) Donald Davidson's Philosophy of Language, Oxford: Blackwell.

Ricoeur, Paul (1986) Die lebendige Metapher (revised German edition), Munich: Fink.

Rorty, Richard (1991a) *Objectivity, Relativism, and Truth (Philosophical Papers* vol. 1), Cambridge: Cambridge University Press.

—— (1991b) *Essays on Heidegger and Others (Philosophical Papers* vol. 2), Cambridge: Cambridge University Press.

Rosenzweig, Franz (1988) *Der Stern der Erlösung*, Frankfurt: Suhrkamp.

Sandkaulen-Bock, Birgit (1990) *Ausgang vom Unbedingten. Über den Anfang in der Philosophie Schellings*, Göttingen: Vandenhoeck & Ruprecht.

Sartre, Jean-Paul (1943) *L'être et le néant*, Paris: Seuil.

Schelling, F.W.J. (1969) *Initia Philosophiae Universae* (1820–1) *(Initia)*, ed. Horst Fuhrmans, Bonn: Bouvier.

—— (1972) *Grundlegung der positiven Philosophie* (1832–3) *(GPP)*, ed. Horst Fuhrmans, Turin: Bottega d'Erasmo.

—— (1977) *Philosophie der Offenbarung* (1841–2) *(PO)*, ed. Manfred Frank, Frankfurt: Suhrkamp.

—— (1989) *Einleitung in die Philosophie* (1830), ed. Walter E. Ehrhardt (Schellingiana 11), Stuttgart: Frommann-Holzboog.

—— (1990) *System der Weltalter* (1827–8), ed. S. Peetz, Frankfurt: Klostermann.

—— (1994) *On the History of Modern Philosophy*, translated with an introduction by Andrew Bowie, Cambridge: Cambridge University Press.

Scholem, Gershom (1970) *Judaica 3*, Frankfurt: Suhrkamp.

Schulz, Walter (1957) *Der Gott der neuzeitlichen Metaphysik*, Pfullingen: Neske.

—— ed. (1968) *Fichte–Schelling Briefwechsel*, Frankfurt: Suhrkamp.

—— (1975) *Die Vollendung des deutschen Idealismus in der Spätphilosophie Schellings*, Pfullingen: Neske.

Theunissen, Michael (1976) 'Die Aufhebung des Idealismus in der Spätphilosophie Schellings', *Philosophisches Jahrbuch 83*.

—— (1978) *Sein und Schein. Die kritische Funktion von Hegels Logik*, Frankfurt: Suhrkamp.

Thomä, Dieter (1990) *Die Zeit des Selbst und die Zeit danach. Zur Kritik der Textgeschichte Martin Heideggers 1910–1976*, Frankfurt: Suhrkamp.

Tilliette, Xavier (1970) *Schelling: une philosophie en devenir*, 2 vols, Paris: Vrin.

Weinsheimer, Joel (1991) *Philosophical Hermeneutics and Literary Theory*, New Haven, Conn., and London: Yale University Press.

White, Alan (1983a) *Absolute Knowledge: Hegel and the Problem of Metaphysics*, Columbus: Ohio University Press.

—— (1983b) *Schelling: Introduction to the System of Freedom*, New Haven, Conn., and London: Yale University Press.

Wood, David, ed. (1992) *Derrida: A Critical Reader*, Oxford: Blackwell.

Wüstehube, Axel (1989) *Das Denken aus dem Grund. Zur Bedeutung der Spätphilosophie Schellings für die Ontologie Ernst Blochs*, Würzburg: Königshausen & Neumann.

A LIST OF TRANSLATIONS OF SCHELLING'S WORKS

The list does not claim to be complete, but does contain all the readily available texts that I have been able to trace.

The Ages of the World (1967) translated with introduction and notes by F. de W. Bolman, jr., New York: Columbia University Press.

Bruno, or On the Natural and the Divine Principle of Things (1984) translated with an introduction by Michael G. Vater, Albany: State University of New York Press.

Ideas for a Philosophy of Nature: An Introduction to the Study of this Science (1988) translated by E. E. Harris and Peter Heath, introduction Robert Stern, Cambridge: Cambridge University Press.

Of Human Freedom (1936) a translation with critical introduction and notes by J. Gutmann, Chicago: Open Court.

On the History of Modern Philosophy (1994) translation and introduction by Andrew Bowie, Cambridge: Cambridge University Press.

On University Studies (1966) translated by E. S. Morgan, edited N. Guterman, Athens, Ohio: Ohio University Press.

The Philosophy of Art (1989) Minnesota: Minnesota University Press.

Schelling's Treatise on 'The Deities of Samothrace' (1977) translation and introduction by R. F. Brown, Missoula, Mont.: Scholars Press.

System of Transcendental Idealism (1978) translated by Peter Heath, introduction Michael Vater, Charlottesville: University Press of Virginia.

The Unconditional in Human Knowledge: Four Early Essays 1794–6 (1980) translation and commentary by Fritz Marti, Lewisburg: Bucknell University Press.

INDEX

Bold numerals indicate a whole section or chapter devoted to the author or topic in question.

119, 123; cognitive, and real 86, 171; and *différance* 70, 73–5; in Fichte 18; and God 95–8, 107, 125; in Hegel 56, 176, 186; Heidegger on 92– 3, 152; in Hölderlin 26; in Jacobi 21; in Kant 103–4; in Romantics and Heidegger 53; Rorty on 76–8; in Schelling and Heidegger 60–1; in Spinoza 16

Habermas, J. 3, 10, 57, 59, 74, 133, 178, 181–2, 183–9
Hartmann, K. 141, 159
Hegel, G. W. F. 1, 2, 42, 92, 108, 126, **127–77**, 179, 181; on Absolute 55–6, 82–6; and Habermas 74, 188–9; Heidegger on 92; and identity thinking 67, 69, 126
Heidegger, M. 7, 9, 39, 53, 57, 64, 87, 95, 114, 128, 164–5, 179, 180, 192, 193, 197; on freedom 131; and metaphysics3, 25, 70–1, 150–2; on Hegel 138–9; on Hegel and Schelling 92–3; on truth 60–1, 75, 189
Henrich, Dieter 84–5, 149–50, 168–171
Heuser-Kessler, M.-L. 34–5, 38
Hogrebe, W. 98, 99, 101, 104, 108, 179
Hölderlin, F. 26, 46, 51, 96, 109, 132
Holz, H. H. 7–8
Horkheimer, M. 10, 58, 178
Horstmann, R.-P. 175

identity philosophy 13, 33, **55–90**, 92, 110–11, 119, 124, 130, 144, 149, 156–7
immediacy 1, 63, 148, 168–72, 176, 178, 195; Gasché on 142; Hegel on 55, 132, 134, 161, 168–72, 174; and metaphor 186
intellectual intuition 18, 24, 26, 46, 56, 57, 83, 155, 161

Jacobi, F. H. **17–25**, 102, 132, 178
judgement 25–6, 32–3, 62, 99, 111

kabbala 116–17
Kant, I. 15–19, 23, 25, 52, 53, 64, 125, 172–3; on nature 31–6; on ontological proof 160–3; on transcendental ideal 103–4; and thing in itself 134–5
Kierkegaard, S. 3, 4, 181
Kojève, A. 176

Lacan, J. 47, 105, 118, 122, 140, 156
language 6–8, 22, 28, 50, 54, 73–5, 100–1, 114, **115–22**, 125, 182–4, 188–9
Leibniz, G. W. 33
Levinas, E. 165
Logic (Hegel's) 55, 85, 108, 129, 132, 138, 140, 143, 144, 159–62, 166, 174–5; Logic of reflection 168–72, 180
Löw, R. 34, 37, 42–3

McTaggart, J. 160
Marx, K. 3, 58, 148, 177, 181
Mendelssohn, M. 150
metaphor **5–10**, 50. 54, 70–1, 105, 113–14, 120, 156, 180, 185–6, 192, 193
metaphysics 1, 10, 17, 118, 126, 165, 189; Derrida on 68–9, 71; Habermas on 3, 10; Hegel and 87, 127, 142; Heidegger on 93, 152; and metaphor 6–7; and reflection 49
modernity 10, 140, 177, 178
mythology 113, 146

Nagel, T. 15
Naturphilosophie **30–44**, 94, 125, 146, 155
negative philosophy 13, 88–9, 129, 140, **141–7**, 152–5, 166–7, 179, 180, 183, 188
Neuhouser, F. 15, 18–19
new mythology 53–4
Nietzsche, F. 67–9, 99, 114, 126, 152, 179, 181–3, 189, 195, 201–2
nihilism 17, 42, 176, 187
Novalis (Hardenberg, Friedrich von) 49

ontological difference 63–4, 70, 89, 111, 121, 124–5, 138, 139, 147,

Made in the USA
Lexington, KY
03 June 2012